D1610594

JAMES JOYCE
AND THE
PROBLEM OF
PSYCHOANALYSIS

From its very beginning, psychoanalysis sought to incorporate the aesthetic into its domain, translating it as vagrant symptom or sublimated desire. Despite Joyce's deliberate attempt in his writing to *resist* this powerful hermeneutic, his work has been confronted by a long tradition of psychoanalytic readings. Luke Thurston argues that this very antagonism holds the key to how psychoanalytic thinking can still open up new avenues in Joycean criticism and literary theory. In particular, Thurston shows that Jacques Lacan's encounter with Joyce forms part of an effort to think *beyond* the 'application' of theory: instead of merely diagnosing Joyce's writing or claiming to have deciphered its riddles, Lacan seeks to understand how it can entail an *un*readable signature, a unique act of social transgression that defies translation into discourse. Thurston imaginatively builds on Lacan's notion of Joyce's irreducible literary act to illuminate Joyce's place in a wide-ranging literary genealogy that includes Shakespeare, Hogg, Stevenson and Wilde. This study should be essential reading for all students of Joyce, literary theory and psychoanalysis.

LUKE THURSTON is a Fellow of Robinson College, Cambridge. He is the editor of *Reinventing the Symptom: Essays on the Final Lacan* (2002) and the translator of several works on psychoanalysis, and has published widely on modernism and literary theory.

JAMES JOYCE
AND THE
PROBLEM OF
PSYCHOANALYSIS

LUKE THURSTON

Robinson College, Cambridge

CAMBRIDGE
UNIVERSITY PRESS

PUBLISHED BY THE PRESS SYNDICATE OF THE UNIVERSITY OF CAMBRIDGE
The Pitt Building, Trumpington Street, Cambridge, United Kingdom

CAMBRIDGE UNIVERSITY PRESS
The Edinburgh Building, Cambridge, CB2 2RU, UK
40 West 20th Street, New York, NY 10011–4211, USA
477 Williamstown Road, Port Melbourne, VIC 3207, Australia
Ruiz de Alarcón 13, 28014 Madrid, Spain
Dock House, The Waterfront, Cape Town 8001, South Africa

http://www.cambridge.org

First published 2004

Printed in the United Kingdom at the University Press, Cambridge

Typeface Adobe Garamond 11/12.5 pt.   *System* LATEX 2$_\varepsilon$ [TB]

A catalogue record for this book is available from the British Library

ISBN 0 521 83590 9

In our culture – undoubtedly in others as well – discourse was not originally a thing, a product, or a possession, but an action situated in a bipolar field of sacred and profane, lawful and unlawful, religious and blasphemous. It was a gesture charged with risks long before it became a possession caught in a circuit of property values.

Michel Foucault

'So I wasn't dreaming, after all,' she said to herself,
'unless – unless we're all part of the same dream.
Only I do hope it's *my* dream . . .'

Lewis Carroll, *Through the Looking-Glass*

Contents

For Paula and George

Acknowledgements

This book grew out of a doctoral thesis that I wrote at the University of Kent. I am grateful to Caroline Rooney for letting me know that the time had come to finish the thesis, and to Martin Stanton for responding so positively to it. My special thanks go to Jeri Johnson, whose teaching at Oxford first introduced me to many of the ideas I explored in the thesis (and subsequently in this book) and with whom I have discussed my work on countless occasions since.

I was able to write the book thanks to my good fortune in winning a Research Fellowship at Robinson College, Cambridge. I am immensely grateful to Robinson as a whole – from Fellows to staff and students – for providing me with such a good environment to work in; but my particular thanks must go to the two Wardens in charge of the College during my Fellowship, Jack Lewis and David Yates, who both gave me crucial support at the right time; to Liz Guild for all her help and interest in my work; to my colleagues in English, Judy Weiss, Simon Jarvis and Steve Padley, who all helped me in various ways; and to Morna Hooker for telling me the truth about God's real name.

I am grateful to Maud Ellmann, John Forrester and Mary Jacobus, with all of whom I have discussed parts of the book. The Cambridge *Finnegans Wake* group has allowed me to meet a variety of Joyceans, with whom I have had very fruitful (and occasionally alcocoherent) debates; I am especially grateful to Finn Fordham and Wim Van Mierlo for helping with the group's inauguration, and to all of the participants – in particular Sue Asbee, Sylvia Raffan and Sarah Josephs – for giving me many new ideas and helping me to improve old ones. I am immensely grateful to Mark Sutton for making his vast knowledge of Joyce freely available to me, and for all his shrewd advice. My thanks must also go to the Cambridge University Press readers, whose remarks proved very useful, and to my editor Ray Ryan for helping me choose the right title.

I must also thank David Pascoe of Glasgow University for reminding me of the importance of 'Ecce Puer'; and Suzanne Chamberlain and Robert Bertholf of the State University of New York, Buffalo, who were so helpful about the cover photograph.

But above all my thanks go to my family – especially my very own ideal insomniacs, to whom this book is dedicated.

A note on texts and translations

The publication of Lacan's work in English has for a long time been notoriously inadequate. The appearance in 2002 of Bruce Fink's translation of selected *Ecrits* has greatly improved things for the Anglophone reader – although still far too little of Lacan's substantial body of work is available. For readers of French, however, there are various unofficial versions of the unpublished seminars (including Seminar 23, *Le sinthome*), the best of which are produced by the Association freudienne internationale. For a valuable discussion of the history and challenges of translating Lacan, see D. Noam Warner's interview with Bruce Fink in the *Journal for Lacanian Studies* (1.1). An incomparable textual archive can be found on the Web at <http://gaogoa.free.fr>.

References to Shakespeare's works are to the Arden edition.

Abbreviations

Abbreviated references in the text and notes are to the following editions of works by Joyce. Initials are followed by a page number (for *Ulysses*, episode and line number; for *Finnegans Wake*, page and line number).

CW   *The Critical Writings of James Joyce*, ed. Ellsworth Mason and Richard Ellmann. London: Faber, 1959

D   *Dubliners*, ed. Robert Scholes. London: Cape, 1967

FW   *Finnegans Wake*. London: Faber, 1939

P   *A Portrait of the Artist as a Young Man*, ed. Chester Anderson. London: Cape, 1968

SL   *Selected Letters of James Joyce*, ed. Richard Ellmann. London: Faber, 1975

U   *Ulysses*, ed. Walter Gabler. London: The Bodley Head, 1986

Other works are abbreviated as follows:

E   Jacques Lacan, *Ecrits*. Paris: Seuil, 1966

E:S   Idem, *Ecrits: A Selection*, trans. B. Fink. New York: Norton, 2002

JJ   Richard Ellmann, *James Joyce*. Revised edition, Oxford and New York: Oxford University Press, 1982

SE   *The Standard Edition of the Complete Psychological Works of Sigmund Freud*, trans. J. Strachey et al. London: Hogarth, and the Institute of Psycho-Analysis, 1953–74 [volume and page number]

Prologue: Groundhog Day

I

'What if there *is* no tomorrow?' asks jaded weatherman Phil Connors (played by Bill Murray) in Harold Ramis's 1993 film *Groundhog Day*. 'There wasn't one today,' adds Phil – at which point, hardly surprisingly, the person on the other end of the telephone line hangs up. If such a 'philosophical' question seems flippant in a Hollywood comedy, in another context – a note written by Nietzsche in 1882 (by coincidence also the year of Joyce's birth) – we are bound to take it more seriously. Under the ominous heading *Das grösste Schwergewicht*, 'the heaviest burden', Nietzsche demands:

> What, if some day or night a demon were to steal after you into your loneliest loneliness and say to you: 'This life as you now live it and have lived it, you will have to live once more and innumerable times more; and there will be nothing new in it, but every pain and every joy and every thought and sigh and everything unutterably small or great in your life will have to return to you, all in the same succession and sequence – even this spider and this moonlight between the trees, and even this moment and I myself. The eternal hourglass of existence is turned upside down again and again, and you with it, speck of dust!'[1]

The revelation of eternal recurrence, we should note in passing, is presented by Nietzsche as a *hallucination*: the news – that there will be no more news, and worse still, that there never has been any – is brought by a demon, a Mephistopheles come to haunt poor Faustus. This Nietzschean apparition will return more than once in our explorations of 'James Overman', as Joyce once signed himself (*JJ* 162).

The postmodern purgatory of *Groundhog Day*, however, has none of the ominous grandeur that Nietzsche ascribes to Eternal Return, even if Phil Connors does have to endure long hours of teeth-gnashing existential tedium before he can accede to the 'joyful wisdom' that eventually allows him to form a couple with Andie MacDowell's Rita, as the film relaxes into the reassurance of a stock Hollywood ending. And it goes without

I

saying that the cinematic game devised by Ramis and co-writer Danny
Rubin is 'philosophical' only in a strictly *irresponsible* sense, just as all of
Phil's acts on Groundhog Day are only 'acts', his every deed or utterance
robbed of psychological depth and authenticity by being a mere citation,
an empty iteration. The film thus plays fast and loose – but therein is
precisely its philosophical subtlety – with a philosophical problem that,
as we have already glimpsed, was of the gravest significance for Nietzsche.
Writing in 1888 (shortly before his terminal mental collapse), the philosopher described eternal recurrence as the 'fundamental idea of Zarathustra' and as indeed 'the highest formula of affirmation that can possibly be
attained'.[2] In Maurice Blanchot's view, the affirmation of eternal recurrence
corresponds to a 'limit experience' where thought itself becomes untenable, as the impossible affirmation of affirmation 'itself' sends Nietzschean
thought spinning into fatal self-deconstructive turbulence.[3] By contrast, in
Groundhog Day's cartoon topology (designed by Escher, one could almost
imagine), Phil discovers that precisely *nothing* can be affirmed; whatever
he 'experiences' is immediately struck out, nullified, by the iterative non-
temporality in which he is trapped (and this might even, in some allegorical
reading of the film, point to an implicit critique of the media industry itself,
with its passive customers trapped in pointless cycles of consumption, and
so on).

Nevertheless – or perhaps we should write 'therefore' – *Groundhog Day*'s
philosophical trickery has a great deal to tell us about Joyce and the eternal
literary institution he founded. Indeed, the film's scenario is not entirely
light-hearted; in exploiting the comic possibilities of repetition, it has simultaneously to touch on questions of individual destitution, suicide and mental breakdown. (One scene has Phil virtually paraphrase *Ecce Homo* when
he declares in a roadside café, 'I am a god.') But above all, for the Joycean
critic, *Groundhog Day* offers a comic version of an eternal institutional
embarrassment that is routinely addressed in every preface to a new book
on Joyce: namely, the problem of its being, in Yogi Berra's immortal words,
'*déjà vu* all over again'. How, it is asked, can Joycean criticism ever overcome
or escape from its essentially *tautologous* predicament, its eternal repetition
of what Joyce wrote as the 'sehm asnuh' (*FW* 620.17)? Like Phil Connors,
each Joycean begins in a stifling confrontation with the same-as-new, aware
that in his search for semic novelty he 'moves in vicous cicles' (*FW* 134.16),
in cycles of historical repetition inscribed by Joyce with Vico's authority
(and note that such cycles are literally made 'vicious' only by adding an
'I', in a subtle textual manoeuvre that we shall link to Lacan's reading of
Joyce).

But there are other reasons, beyond the anxiety-ridden comedy of Phil's ever-recycling day, for us to think of *Groundhog Day* as emblematically Joycean. Joyce's superstitious attitude to dates was first noted by Ellmann in the opening words of his biography:

James Joyce liked to think about his birthday. In later years, fond of coincidences, he was pleased to discover that he shared his birth year, 1882, with Eamon De Valera, Wyndham Lewis and Frank Budgen, and his birthday and year with James Stephens. That February 2 was Candlemas helped to confirm its importance; that it was Groundhog Day added a comic touch; and Joyce made it even more his own by contriving, with great difficulty, to see the first copies of both *Ulysses* and *Finnegans Wake* on that white day. (*JJ* 23)

The curious coincidence, as Bloom might have put it, of the church feast of Candlemas and Groundhog Day, itself turns out to be rooted in a veritably 'Joycean' act of cultural and linguistic hybridisation. The eighteenth-century German and English settlers of Pennsylvania chose to celebrate Candlemas in a new way by linking it to a Native American tradition: that of venerating the ancestral *Wojak*, neatly troped into English as 'wood-chuck', also known as the groundhog – so that every year on 2 February this squirrel-like rodent, the embodiment of ancestral wisdom, would by its activity foretell the coming of spring, which was likewise prefigured by the symbolic lighting of candles in church.

Joyce's sense of the fatal significance of dates was not, however, as Ellmann seems to imply with the curious phrase 'on that white day', a wholly pleasurable matter, the bringing of light and renewal. Indeed, an earlier biographer of Joyce, Herbert Gorman, had written of the author's birth – in a passage that was almost certainly, scholars have argued, 'ghosted' by Joyce himself – in the very blackest of tones:

The times were heavy with thunder and startled by unexpected flashes of cruel lightning . . . 1882 was an année terrible in the annals of Irish history. On May fifth (when James Joyce was three months and three days old) there was the famous torchlight procession through the streets of the city, a procession celebrating the liberation of Parnell and Michael Davitt from Kilmainham Jail and loud with optimism for the future . . . And in the twilight of this day . . . Joe Brady and his Invincibles left the public house near the gates of the Lower Castle Yard, drove to the Phoenix Park and there slaughtered the Chief Secretary for Ireland, Lord Frederick Cavendish, and the permanent Under-Secretary Thomas Henry Burke . . . James Joyce, sleeping quietly in his crib, was mercifully unconscious of the fact that he had been born in a black period.[4]

Far from being born on a white day, Joyce thus entered the world, according to Gorman's text, in a black period. The ghostly imprimatur (Wakean postmark or 'ghostmark', *FW* 473.9) of Joyce's co-authorship here is legible in the ominous rumble of thunder that accompanies the birth; as an avid reader of the *Scienza Nuova*, Joyce knew that Viconian cosmology marked the beginning of a *ricorso*, a new historical cycle, with a thunderclap. If the repetitive patterns of Irish history were indeed vicious circles, as the young Joyce had felt so bitterly, in the retrospective imagination of the older man that viciousness already loomed like a baleful storm cloud over the 'année terrible' of his birth (and perhaps, it is hinted, gave Joyce his lifelong fear of thunder). Hence the sole glimmer of light allowed into Gorman's tableau, provided by the torchlit nationalist procession, is revealed with dark irony to be pure Luciferan duplicity, its loud optimism exposed as a sham by the subsequent 'fiendish' murders that will in turn be 'slid lucifericiously within' the *Wake* (*FW* 182.5). The revelation or revaluation of light-rays and the enlightenment they symbolise as Luciferan double-dealing, figured unthinkably in the diabolic coincidence of 'darkness visible', will return throughout our study as it explores the sinful and brilliant act of writing in Joyce.

But, crucially, we shall also find that what is revealed in and by Joycean writing is irreducible to any particular historical meaning or narrative content; indeed, the literary act for Joyce will be shown to mark precisely the *breaking out of meaning*. If this cultural rupture is often considered the sign of a quintessentially modernist aesthetic, we shall show that it is best understood as corresponding to a properly *theological* concept of revelation: the idea that, as Giorgio Agamben writes, 'all human speech and knowledge has at its root and foundation an openness that infinitely transcends it'.[5]

II

1882, then, the year when Joyce shared his birthday on Groundhog Day with De Valera (whose name will be disfigured in the *Wake* as the mark of an Irish 'devil era' (*FW* 473.7–8), also saw the publication of Nietzsche's *Die Fröhliche Wissenschaft*, where eternal recurrence was proclaimed anew to the world. With this philosophical event, writes Pierre Klossowski, something changed, albeit paradoxically, in the human relation to history:

Beginning with the experience of the *Eternal Return*, which announced a break with this *irreversible once and for all*, Nietzsche also developed a new version of fatality – that of the *Vicious Circle*, which suppresses every goal and meaning since the beginning and the end always merge with each other.[6]

A vicious circle indeed: as Klossowski's reading makes clear, an intellectual 'history' of Nietzschean thought risks succumbing here to the most obvious booby trap, as the conceptual transformation in question marks each of the terms ordinarily used as historical co-ordinates – 'beginning', 'experience', 'break', 'new version', etc. – as Wakean 'quashed quotatoes' (*FW* 183.22), their semantic valence and coherence, if not suppressed, at least indefinitely suspended, put in doubt. The proper consequence of Nietzsche's 'break-through' – Klossowski goes so far as to dub it 'the law of the Vicious Circle' – is the 'metamorphosis of the individual' (71): not, that is, the mere trans-formation of particular human beings but a break with the very concept of self-identity, the *Principium Individuationis* that Nietzsche had borrowed from Schopenhauer to designate modernity's mechanistic appropriation of and alienation from the primal chaos of nature.[7]

The year of Joyce's birth, then, saw a great Nietzschean revelation; and if that date did not turn out to signal the end of all human history, it was certainly to acquire great significance in Joyce's own self-made history. Yet Joyce's superstitions about dates and historical coincidences are not, I hope to show, merely symptoms of an eccentricity to be smiled over indulgently by biographers. Rather, they are imaginary side-effects of the central – and indeed eminently Nietzschean – ambition of Joycean art: namely, to re-invent the historical status of the 'I', to grasp and body forth in writing an instance of human *poesis*, the power to name and make a world through artistic 'factification' (*FW* 496.34), in a way forever ruled out or misrepresented, rendered uncanny or laughable, by official realist histories.

Our reference to *Groundhog Day* and to the comic embarrassment of beginning again thus loses its accidental or coincidental status – or rather, that status becomes as such truly Joycean. Joyce's writing presents (that is, *re*-presents) in its 'teems of times and happy returns' (*FW* 215.22–3) – from the constrictive repetitions of *Dubliners* to the cosmic 'vicociclome-ter' (*FW* 614.27) of *Finnegans Wake* – the fundamental ambiguity of a time lived 'outside' history. On the one hand, such a condition may be experienced or diagnosed as a temporal *paralysis*, the failure to remember or symbolise properly. Psychoanalysis, as we shall see, first sets out to cure that symptomatic paralysis by interpreting it, by providing it with a *semantic* solution. (Note the etymological resonance here: paralysis, analysis and solution are all rooted in the Greek *luein*, 'to loosen', a root more visible in the German *Lösung*.) On the other hand the instant of 'madness' imagined outside linear history will be identified by Joyce – and here he looks back to a Romantic tradition exemplified above all by the madness of Blake – with an escape into the literary 'thing itself', the radical affirmation of *poesis*: what Nietzsche calls 'a sacred yes-saying'.[8]

The 'unspeakable' Joyce of Part II is located between these two aspects or interpretations of a revelation that can be either paralysing or liberating. Notwithstanding the many differences between its effects in philosophy and in literature, when that momentous unveiling is inscribed by Nietzsche in the year of Joyce's birth we are given a seductive formula for this singular coincidence of philosophy and the aesthetic – at precisely the point of the modernist 'metamorphosis of the individual', to recall Klossowski's phrase. The ultimately affirmative impetus of such a metamorphosis in Joyce is, as we shall see, inseparable from his unflinching awareness of the fatal and inevitable incompatibility – or better, *war* – between it and the ego, that endless self-identifying declamation. For Blanchot, in a comparable sense, the impossibility of bearing the force of Nietzschean affirmation is encapsulated by the self-undoing (self-dissolving or self-analytic, *auto-luein*) instance of the personal pronoun:

He who kills himself is the great affirmer of the *present*. I want to kill myself in an 'absolute' instant, the only one which will not pass and will not be surpassed. Death, if it arrived at the time we choose, would be an apotheosis of the instant; the instant in it would be that very flash of brilliance which the mystics speak of, and surely because of this, suicide retains the power of an exceptional affirmation.[9]

An apotheosis of the instant: in Blanchot's vivid *reprise* of Nietzsche's eternal recurrence, the absolute time before history transcends the individual; the *Jetztpunkt* or immediate immersion in existence can never be re-presented before an appropriative 'I', made 'mine' or 'arrive at the time we choose'. Perhaps the suicidal ego falls into the trap of imagining some *other* temporality, where 'now' could somehow coalesce with pure self-affirmation, where I could occupy or identify with it in an act of *self*-apotheosis. But this 'fantasy of total affirmation', as Simon Critchley describes it,[10] is inherently self-defeating, self-unbinding: for what it struggles to represent in its transgressive act is precisely a moment at which the meaning-laden ego becomes irrelevant, finds itself consigned to aesthetic passivity, to being-acted-upon. We shall see how, in Joyce's moments of vocation (which Lacan links to the revelation inscribed as 'epiphany'), the fantasmatic affirmation is ascribed to the Other. When we consider what Derrida puns as *ouï-dire* – at once hearing the call of a voice and voicing the unrepresentable force of an affirmation[11] – we shall argue that for Joyce this problem entails entering into the Other's fantasy, taking up a position inside another's dream. And the crucial Joycean problem, as we shall see at the very end of our argument, is how to awaken from that dream.

But we should begin by asking how these questions of self-affirmation and self-dissolution bear on the problem of institutional embarrassment we touched on above – in other words, the overwhelming sense of *redundancy* in Joycean criticism? It is important here not to be distracted by what may be seen as the contemporary academic over-investment in Joyce. The real problem of Joyce for literary criticism now cannot be reduced to the impression of exhaustive or surplus interpretation derived, say, from a glance at the allegedly excessive levels of publishing associated with the writer's name. On the contrary, the challenge Joyce deliberately poses to the literary and academic institution bears precisely on the *integrity* of the 'now' in literary interpretation: a problem that, as we shall see, is bound up with the eccentric temporality of the human subject itself, as a self-theorising 'I' both caught up in and irreducible to language and history. And we shall argue that the 'sense of redundancy' in Joyce criticism is wholly bound up with this problem of 'now' (note how in 'seme asnuh' [*FW* 620.17] that word collapses into 'new') and that it lies at the very heart of the literary *thing*, the singular attraction and resistance that binds his work to criticism and to the wider institutions of culture.

But by the same token, of course, that 'thing' cannot be considered an exclusive property of Joyce, even if the author were held to be some supreme end or realisation of literature (a kind of 'James Overman'). In the first place, the 'same' problem – of unaccountable literary excess – obviously afflicts or enriches our critical response to the work of Joyce's favourite artistic precursor, Shakespeare. Frank Kermode writes of how 'redundancy is in the very nature of *Hamlet*':[12] Shakespeare's work already poses in itself the question of textual surplus that returns today, as it were symptomatically, in the embarrassment of institutional over-production. We shall see how Joyce treated this coincidence of literary and critical excess as a way to address questions, not simply of his 'own' work as institution and legacy, but of institution, testament, will, as they determine and disturb all interpretation.

III

'Anima enim facit novas compositiones, licet non faciat novas res.'[13]
St Bonaventure's edict forbidding creation *ex nihilo* to the mortal soul might serve as a legend to be carved above the gateway of the Joycean institution. There can only be new arrangements of the existing material; no new thing

can be introduced from the outside: such a vision of institutional closure
certainly corresponds to a popular image of Joycean scholarship, trapped in
its endless, self-perpetuating cycles. How can the invocation of psychoanalysis – even if Freud thought that, in the ideal case, analysis replaced passive
repetition with willed memory – possibly allow us to break the boundaries
of this self-enclosed institution? To answer this, we should begin by attend-
ing carefully to Bonaventure's words. In defining the *anima* (a term that, as
we shall see, has manifold significance in the encounter between Joyce and
psychoanalysis), the great Franciscan makes two statements whose apparent
complementarity masks a crucial difference: while the soul in itself 'makes
new compositions' – as one of its inherent properties – conversely *licet non*,
it is *not allowed* to 'make a new thing'. In other words, the description of the
soul is keyed to a specific prohibition, as if its very status as *anima* depended
on the obedience of a certain law. Joyce's work begins in a confrontation
with a ban on creation, and arguably it continues to grapple with that ban
in the evolving Joycean institution of today. Psychoanalysis, which itself
grew out of an interrogation of prohibitions and censorship, is the site of a
singular *poesis* – the transgressive 'factification' (*FW* 496.34) of precisely a
'new thing': a new problematic of sexual identity in terms of its *Unbehagen
in der Kultur*, its intractable conflict with social existence.[14] The 'Freudian
Thing', as Lacan dubbed it in 1955, entails the emergence – the *revelation* –
of something radically new: a singular point of resistance to the semantic
forms imposed by an authoritarian social discourse of identity (*E:S* 107–11).
And indeed Freudian theory itself partly constitutes an effort to restore
such a discourse, with its repeated attempts to convert the 'Copernican'
act of its discovery back into a suitably 'Ptolemaic' discourse[15] – above all,
that is, a discourse that would replace the integral meaning that had been
lost.

    The following study will not therefore attempt to apply psychoanalytic
ideas to Joyce's work, nor will it explore what Jean Kimball calls the 'textual dialogue' between psychoanalytic theory and Joycean creation.[16] A
brief discussion of my reasons for avoiding these two traditional ways of
coupling Joyce and psychoanalysis may shed some light on the aims and
presuppositions of my reading.

    It is well known that Lacan gave a seminar 'on Joyce' at the very end
of his career in 1975–6, under the title *Le sinthome*.[17] The first thing one
discovers, should one rashly attempt actually to *read* that seminar, however,
is that a phrase such as 'Lacan's seminar on Joyce' – with its implicit notion
of theory being exported from the clinical domain to a literary 'case' – is
altogether misleading. Indeed, at the conclusion of his address to the Fifth

International Joyce Symposium at the Sorbonne in 1975, Lacan himself made this clear when he declared with 'jocoserious' (*U* 17.309) hyperbole that 'L'orbe est sur Joyce'.[18] If the entire world were 'on' Joyce, it would be impossible to envisage that gargantuan figure as a single theoretical 'topic' to be treated in a seminar. As we shall see, in *Le sinthome* Lacan's aim was a more modest one: to try, in Jacques-Alain Miller's phrase, 'to take a leaf out of Joyce's book'[19] – in other words, to get involved in a *writing* practice that exceeded his theoretical discourse, touched on a problem irreducible to the psychoanalytic representation of the subject. When Lacan tries to take a leaf out of Joyce's book, we shall see that what he struggles with is an unworldly geometry, a topological 'writing' that testifies to nothing less than a *défaut dans l'univers*, a faulty or lacking universe.[20]

But as early as 1958, Lacan had brusquely dismissed the old tradition of 'applied psychoanalysis': 'Psychoanalysis', he wrote in his article *Jeunesse de Gide*, 'can only be applied, in the proper sense of the term, as treatment and thus to a subject who speaks and listens.'[21] It was not that Lacan had many doubts about the general interpretative possibilities that Freud's discovery entailed; rather, he was concerned that those possibilities should not be obliterated by a lazy disregard for the real *structural* differences between various kinds of linguistic event. In the popular 'Freudian' tendency to move freely between the talking cure and the literary text, taking both to be products of a single uniform 'unconscious', he saw nothing but muddled thinking.[22] Moreover, by the final decade of his work in the 1970s, the distinction between the speech of the analysand and the *écrit* – the latter term designating a singular problematic of writing exemplified above all by Joyce – had become in Lacan's eyes perhaps *the* central problem for psychoanalytic thought. In fact, as we shall see, one of the major instigations of Lacan's interest in Joyce was what he regarded as a deliberate artistic refusal of psychoanalysis. Thus, rather than seeking to find confirmation in Joyce's writing of the ideas pursued in his teaching, Lacan approached it in search of something *beyond* Freudian truth.

Now, what is often proposed as a more rigorous alternative to the 'applied psychoanalysis' model is the exploration of the so-called dialogue between Joyce's work and psychoanalytic theory: an attempt to trace in the author's research and intellectual development his engagement with theoretical motifs that then informed – or rather were deformed by – his writing. There is no denying that the examination of Joyce's art as a complex response to certain specific readings can be extremely useful, as was shown by Ellmann's *The Consciousness of Joyce* and by many critical studies since – a recent example being the work of Jean Kimball.[23]

Kimball's work provides a good illustration both of how fruitful this 'intertextual' approach to the link between Joyce and psychoanalysis can be and also, we shall argue, of its central weakness. Kimball begins by upbraiding earlier critics such as Mark Shechner and Sheldon Brivic for attempting to outline a notional 'psychoanalytic picture of Joyce's mind', offering instead her own perspective as resolutely 'textual'.[24] She thus avoids any attribution of psychological 'depth' to the author, unhappy with the very notion of dealing with 'Joyce's mind', let alone with its 'development' (a term she quotes from Brivic). But the trouble with this rigorous adherence to a non-psychological intertextuality – Kimball writes that her interest is 'in the way . . . texts talk to one another' – is that it completely fails to situate this 'dialogue' with psychoanalysis within Joyce's broader engagement with questions of subjectivity, his complex interpretation and subversion of traditional literary and philosophical ways of articulating the self.

In terms of our interest in the encounter between Joyce and Lacan, what is particularly striking here is how the alternative posed by Kimball – applied psychoanalysis or intertextuality – entirely misses out what Lacan isolates as the central problem in Joyce: that of the 'I', understood not simply as a character in the Freudian psyche but as an enigmatic problem of 'epiphany' or *apparition*. As we shall see, it is no accident that the latter term is usually associated not with the unconscious but with another Freudian motif, the *uncanny*: while the unconscious is governed by the endless repetition and deformation of discursive elements (as seen in 'the way texts talk to one another' enjoyed by Kimball), the uncanny or apparitional is precisely untimely, not subject to the temporal syntax of psychoanalytic – or indeed of any other – interpretation. The idea of the uncanny having at its kernel something radically untranslatable is of course massively resisted by Freudian theory, in which *Unheimlichkeit* is nothing but a privileged example of the return of the repressed, and as such an illustration of the normal-neurotic mechanism of the unconscious. But, as Slavoj Žižek's work has made clear, the anxiety triggered by the fantasmatic double has its roots in a problem of identity that is irreducible to the semiotic logic of the unconscious. The uncanny, writes Žižek, is rather a 'confirmation of how the Real persists in the very heart of the Imaginary': the formation not only of interpretable symptoms, but of the 'I' itself, is knotted together with the traumatic emergence of jouissance.[25]

Now, if we consider the 'I' a site of uncanny apparition, this would imply our taking seriously the old Shakespearean pun in which the personal pronoun doubles 'eye'. Joel Fineman has shown how this venerable literary pun in English indeed resonates with specific aspects of Lacan's teaching, and we shall see how Joyce rewrites this 'as Great Shapesphere puns it' (*FW* 295.4) alongside many other Shakespearean characters *and also Freudian ones*.[26] Indeed, one reason Joyce's reading of the 'freudful' (*FW* 411.35) culture of psychoanalysis is so antagonistic, we shall argue, is that he finds the interrogation of the 'I' supposedly launched there to be manifestly preceded – indeed, exceeded – in a range of literary texts, chiefly those by Shakespeare. But of course we should add that Freud himself willingly acknowledged on a number of occasions that his so-called discoveries were indeed nothing but scientific reformulations of things seen long before by artists.

We shall return to Kimball's account of Joyce's relation to psychoanalysis at the end of our argument. For now, let us simply note that the problem her work would erase – that of the 'I' and its untimely apparition both in and out of language – provides a good instance of the general problem of psychoanalysis, seen here in its relation to literary criticism. Just as the 'I' is both manifested in and irreducible to language, so psychoanalysis itself is both transmitted by a given set of texts and institutional practices and yet in the end remains *irreducible* to that discursive corpus. It is *this* problematic – the way that Freud's discovery opens on to the 'clearobscure' (*FW* 247.34) domain where an 'I' both becomes manifest and loses itself – that truly resonates with Joyce's work, and it is therefore impossible to restrict our exploration of it to an intertextuality defined by a list of books he probably read and raided.

So the problem of psychoanalysis in Joyce cannot be confined to an investigation of the writer's 'sources', much as critics have laboured to bring such an investigation to a definitive conclusion. Rather, it corresponds to something that emerges first of all in an encounter: one between an 'I' – as well as an eye – and a particular manifestation or unveiling. As we shall see, this encounter may occur either within or outside a text, but it is always an aesthetic experience involving an untranslatable, bodily singularity. Our first aim in reformulating the link between Joyce and psychoanalysis will thus be to consider the general problem of *shock* in the encounter between theory and the aesthetic: it is only by situating the disruptive force of that encounter that we can begin to grasp Lacan's notion that Joycean writing is unreadable, *pas à lire*.[27]

In Part I, 'On Traduction', we explore a series of shocking encounters that are, in Lacan's coinage, *extimate* – both interior and radically alien – to Joycean and psychoanalytic texts, and beyond them to the general relation between text and reader. These encounters are marked by a central aporia in the attempt to utter – to make the property of a coherent narrative 'I' or theoretical self – something that shows itself 'the seme asnuh' (*FW* 620.17): that is, as a new seme emerging *ex nihilo*, a *now* that is not yet representable, appears in breach of semantic legitimacy. If, as we shall see in our opening exploration of the story 'An Encounter', Joyce's work situates itself from the very beginning in this unspeakable scene, psychoanalytic theory struggles to translate its paradoxical extimacy into forms of consistent, authoritative representation. This theoretical struggle is clearly visible in Freud's own encounters with art – above all, as we shall see, with the representation of the father there. The attempt by Freud to restore the legibility and authority of artworks is at the same time, we shall argue, a fantasmatic restitution of the paternal law. We conclude Part I with an investigation of various efforts to utter the unspeakable through translation – both in the literal translation of psychoanalytic texts into English and in the ostensible transference of theory from psychoanalysis to literary criticism. As we shall see, something disappears in both these literal and metaphorical translations, and that 'thing' – or, as the *Wake* will write it, that 'Ding . . . in idself id est' (*FW* 611.21) – will be a major topic in Part II.

Our overall aim in Part II, 'Unspeakable Joyce', is to show how Lacan's encounter with Joyce amounts to a deliberate break with the traditional attempt by psychoanalysis to translate itself into and through the aesthetic. This, however, turns out to be a question not merely of an altered methodology, for what is at stake is the extravagant idea of Joyce's work itself being radically untranslatable, incommensurable with the logic of psychoanalytic interpretation – or, to put it more bluntly, *unreadable*. We go on to pursue the notion of 'radical foreclosure', which Lacan links to this breakdown of the unconscious or of psychoanalytic discourse, but in a way that Lacan himself did not: that is, by relating the question of the 'unreadable' in Joyce to its *literary* genealogy. We thus consider the fabled intertextuality of Joyce's work, finding the question of the limits of reading itself addressed in a range of his literary sources – or 'doubleviewed seeds' (*FW* 296.1) as we find them written in the *Wake* (reminding us of an ambiguity perhaps masked by such a term as 'intertextuality').

Our exploration of Joyce's confrontation with the literary thing, whether inscribed in religious discourse as the godlike acts of 'Great Shapesphere' or the diabolic apparitions of Hogg, Stevenson and Wilde, leads us in the end to re-examine some of the questions raised by Joyce in seemingly *theological* terms. The conclusion of our study is concerned with how these apparently theological aspects of reading Joyce can be related to what we explore in earlier chapters as the 'problem of psychoanalysis': its simultaneous hindrance to and renewal of our reading practices. The final question for our argument turns on whether psychoanalysis, its devastating critique of patriarchal tradition combining with a desperate struggle to reformulate phallic privilege, can still offer us new ways to think through the 'Father and the Son idea' that is half remembered at the beginning of *Ulysses*.

PART I

On traduction

Dans l'amour comme dans presque toutes les affaires humaines, l'entente cordiale est le résultat d'un malentendu. Ce malentendu, c'est le plaisir.

Charles Baudelaire[1]

The effacement of the thing itself is the sole foundation on which it is possible for something like a tradition to be constituted.

Giorgio Agamben[2]

CHAPTER I

An encounter

I

What takes place in an encounter? This question, with its immodest refusal to limit itself to any given cultural or historical site, might seem a flagrant symptom of all that is wrong with 'Theory', as it is called, in contemporary literary studies. If literary theory should, at least *in theory*, offer criticism a chance to reflect on its own interpretative practices – and above all to interrogate the history of those practices – what it *actually* does, so the argument goes, is to lead literary critics away from an authentic reading experience into a dark, tangled wood of pseudo-metaphysical speculation. The recent history of the literary academy can thus be viewed as a conflict between two starkly opposed forces: on one side, a properly adult criticism whose methods have remained rigorous (that is to say, fully subservient to the authority of historians), and on the other the siren voices of Theory, calling critics to ruin from across the sea. If the seductive allure of Theory has waned somewhat since its golden age in the early 1970s, it is none the less felt to be the duty of any responsible critic to guard against a return of the methodological muddle and sloppy thinking it ushered in.

The argument of this book is that we should reject the either/or implied by this polemical structure, its dichotomy between historical rigour and theoretical adventurousness, not only because such a dichotomy misrepresents the potential significance of still-current critical debates, but for a more direct reason: namely, that the principle site of our argument – the writings of James Joyce – entails in itself an urgent demand that we think through and beyond such a dualism, and escape from what Joyce sardonically portrays in *Ulysses* as a mythical choice between Scylla and Charybdis.

Our aim, then, is indeed to explore what takes place in an encounter, both the evolving textual encounter between literature and psychoanalysis – which will in turn involve considering ideas about 'an encounter' as such – and the 'real' one between James Joyce and Jacques Lacan. (We shall see why the inverted commas are necessary here.) In this, we shall confront unavoidable questions specific to Joycean criticism (how is Joyce's work illuminated in particular by this encounter with Lacanian thinking?); but shall seek to move beyond them to tackle broader topics of literary identity, artistic fabrication and the fate of the reader.

One of our central goals in this exploration will be to argue the case against the currently fashionable urge to exclude psychoanalysis from literary studies, to show that – despite all of the misunderstandings fostered by the transmission (or 'traduction', in the term we shall seek to introduce, without traducing it) between literature and psychoanalytic theory – the encounter of psychoanalytic thinking with the unspeakable enjoyment of aesthetic experience still harbours crucial lessons for our critical engagement with Joyce.

II

In his opening address to the 5th International Joyce Symposium in Paris on 16 June 1975, Lacan begins with a familiar theme of his: that of human destiny. The fabric of occurrences that we make into our history through speaking is essentially, Lacan states, an effect of the fact that 'we are spoken' by others – and in particular, he adds, by our families. Lacan introduces his 'homage' to Joyce with an anecdote he marks as a significant event in his own destiny: 'emerging from the sordid milieu' of a Catholic education, 'it happened that at the age of seventeen, due to the fact that I used to hang around at Adrienne Monnier's, I met Joyce. In the same way, I was present, at the age of twenty, at the first reading of the French translation which had come out of *Ulysses*.'[3]

Adrienne Monnier's was La Maison des Amis des Livres, at 7 rue de l'Odéon, a bookshop and lending library frequented by writers as celebrated as Gide, Valéry and Claudel. Together with her friend Sylvia Beach, the owner of the nearby English bookshop Shakespeare and Co., Monnier played an important role in the destiny of Joyce's work, helping to organise the publication and translation of *Ulysses*, as well as enthusiastically promoting its author's following among the Parisian intelligentsia. In what Joyce would later describe as the 'opening of my Paris career', on 7 December 1921 Monnier hosted an evening to launch *Ulysses*, two months before the book's publication on its author's fortieth birthday.[4] Valéry Larbaud, who was to play a central part in the efforts to translate Joyce's book into French, gave an introductory lecture, which was followed by some readings. (An American actor, the aptly named Jimmy Light, was coached by Joyce through readings from the 'Sirens' episode.)

The twenty-year-old Jacques Lacan was presumably among the people crammed into Monnier's bookshop; thus, as he declares to the symposium, 'j'ai rencontré Joyce'. Regarding the historical status of this encounter, we certainly have material evidence: Ellmann reproduces the card sent out by Monnier announcing the evening (and warning the public that they may be shocked by the *hardiesse d'expression* of some of the readings from Joyce) (*JJ* plate XXXIV). But what of the earlier encounter with Joyce mentioned by Lacan, supposed to have occurred when he was seventeen? According to Ellmann, during the year in question (April 1918 to the following April) Joyce was in Zurich, having moved there following the evacuation of Trieste by officials of an Austro-Hungarian Empire in the midst of the First World War; it was not until June 1920 that, persuaded by Ezra Pound, Joyce moved to Paris to begin the most famous period of his 'exile', finishing *Ulysses* there and writing most of *Finnegans Wake* as a celebrated 'paleoparisien' (*FW* 151.9).[5] It may, of course, seem highly plausible that Lacan's memory, reaching back almost sixty years, should have blurred the historical edges somewhat, perhaps muddling the dates of two events in his youth. For his part, though, Joyce was convinced as to the significance of dates: they were not the accidental properties of a subjective destiny, to be moved around behind 'screen memories' or manipulated by wishful fantasy; but were rather the very *text* of history, of our subjection to its 'vicous cicles' (*FW* 134.16) that are marked precisely by the lack of 'I', the absence of the ego's vicious circularity. For Lacan to begin his remarks in 1975 with talk of the *trame* (weave or texture) of destiny, seems to suggest a similar sense of the textual density of history: it was no mere accident or whim of retrospective arrangement that the encounter took place.

Here it is not a question of merely seeking to expose the fallibility of Lacan's memory, or of implying that his capacity for self-invention led him to treat historical facts too lightly. Although Lacan's teaching is often said to have been the fatal germ of a reckless ahistoricism, if we turn to his comments in a seminar of 1975 (the year in which he began *Le sinthome*) we find him to have been a staunch advocate of historical research in any interpretative project. In this seminar, given at Yale University, he responds to a question from historian Lucille Ritvo with disarming frankness:

Without a written document, you know, you're in a dream. What the historian demands is a text: a text or a bit of paper; at any rate, he must have somewhere in an archive something that certifies things, and whose lack makes history impossible ... That which cannot be certified in writing cannot be considered history.[6]

The uncertified anecdote (literally *anekdotos*, the 'unpublished')[7] cannot be written as history; it remains in the domain of the psychoanalytic subject – above all, that is, in the domain of *fantasy*. In this perspective, Lacan's first encounter with Joyce takes place 'in a dream': outside the legible text of history. We have to take Lacan's word for it (as does Rabaté, who does not worry about the dates and locations);[8] for all we know, it might be true – it is, of course, not impossible that in 1918 Joyce did somehow appear in a Paris bookshop, and that Ellmann's biographical research is simply faulty or incomplete. In other words, the space of subjective experience (like the dream 'in itself', experienced before the dreamer awakes) is not fully commensurable with that of historical evidence; it is a zone of supposition, of anecdote, of the uncertain. If we state that the encounter between Joyce and psychoanalysis may have taken place in a dream, however, this will not be to consign that encounter to fantasmatic obscurity. We shall see, rather, that by focusing our critical attention on what is irreducible to the narrative provided by certified historical documents, psychoanalysis allows us to think about Joycean writing as a particular mode of historical disfigurement, an attempt to grasp the disruptive force of a 'factification' (*FW* 496.34), a *poesis* excluded from the narrative of historical events.

Reading Joyce will be the best way for us to explore and interrogate the Lacanian opposition between the dream of undocumented existence and the textual scrap that precipitates history. First of all, let us simply take Lacan's demand for a written document seriously (or at least 'in jocoserious silence': *U* 17.369) by beginning our consideration of what takes place in an encounter with a 'bit of paper': a story from Joyce's *Dubliners* entitled, conveniently enough, 'An Encounter'.

III

Joyce's long and anguished struggle to secure the publication of *Dubliners* is well documented.[9] As early as May 1906, writing to the London publisher Grant Richards, he declares with bitter solemnity: 'I have come to the conclusion that I cannot write without offending people.' This ambiguous phrase – half complaint, half maxim – is followed by Joyce's splenetic list of the objections to his book from every imaginable quarter, including one item which, in an oft-noted cruel irony, probably drew Richards's attention to what he would otherwise have missed. 'The more subtle inquisitor', writes Joyce (thus clumsily or over-subtly implying a lack of subtlety on the part of his addressee) 'will denounce "An Encounter", the enormity of which the printer cannot see because he is, as I said, a plain blunt man.'[10] Once this unseen enormity has been unveiled, however, Joyce cannot make it disappear; even six years later, when, with a different publisher, *Dubliners* seemed at last to be on the verge of appearing, he found himself having to agree to the omission of only one story, 'An Encounter' (*JJ* 329–31).

So what actually takes place in 'An Encounter'? The question immediately twists round, in a conundrum that we shall see to be characteristically Joycean, to bear as much on the *event* of the text itself as on the content represented 'inside' it. For the literary event that was to make Joyce's name, to make him emerge from anonymity and become visible as a writer – namely the publication of *Dubliners* – seems to hinge on a textual scrap that is at first too small or insignificant to be noticed (by unsubtle printer and publisher alike) before it is transformed into a too visible 'enormity'. And the story we are told inside the text in turn hinges on something *appearing* in a possibly illegal or transgressive manner: on sight, insight and oversight. The problematic of literary apparition, as we might call it, which is adumbrated by Joyce in 'An Encounter', will in turn emerge as a major preoccupation – or perhaps we should say a symptom – of psychoanalysis in its dealings with literature.

To explore how this apparitional problematic can be in question at once inside Joyce's text and in its event *as* publication, we should consider how in one sense the story dramatises an encounter 'with itself': that is, an encounter – *our* encounter as readers – with Joycean artifice considered as literary 'thing', or fantasmatic act.[11] We might see the very difficulty of the text's publication, the sense that the sheer fact of its appearance is transgressive, doubled in its narrative account of a disturbing 'unfolding' or showing forth; and likewise the child narrator's encounter with the enigmatic domain of an adult's fantasy offers a kind of mirror, a Joycean cracked looking-glass, to reflect or refract the reader's encounter with this strange and troubling text. What is most disturbing about that encounter is, as we shall see, precisely that it unsettles our very notion of narrative event, of something 'taking place' in a site of consistent, faithful representation.

What first strikes us in this early text is the 'scrupulous meanness' of Joyce's style, how it carefully unfolds its central trope to cover every aspect of the narrative. The story thus begins with a version 'in miniature' of its key scene; the initial discussion of the Wild West has the boy narrator reflecting on his own ambiguous position in the playing out of a fantasy scenario imposed by another: 'The adventures related in the literature of the Wild West were remote from my nature but, at least, they opened doors of escape' (*D* 18–19). The idea of escaping from the actual, historical world into some other possible world clearly anticipates a cluster of motifs to be developed by Joyce in later works, notably in *Ulysses*, where Stephen Dedalus is shown to be partly detached from everyday Dublin by his obsession with alien cultures, with what is foreign and *immonde*, with otherworldly states of aesthetic ecstasy beyond the domestic nightmare of history.

Yet the narrator's grudging acceptance of Joe Dillon's cowboy games in 'An Encounter' already clearly points to a crucial feature of such a fantasy 'escape'; for all its tempting promise of freedom for anyone who chooses to shed the limitations of mundane existence by entering an alternative reality, the scenario is in the event compromised, skewed or distorted by an intractably individual desire, something impossible to transfer or collectivise. In other words, the alluring prospect seemingly offered by the Wild West adventures is a mere trick of perspective, whose real aim is to make room for a compulsive, meaningless repetition, always operating in favour of only one participant in the game: 'But, however well we fought, we never won siege or battle and all our bouts ended with Joe Dillon's war dance of victory' (*D* 18). Joe Dillon is the master of the narrative, and is able through its repetitive structure to impose upon the other children the unbridled self-enjoyment embodied in his dance with its 'autistic', proto-Wakean yell: 'Ya! yaka, yaka, yaka!' (ibid.).

But the story's narrator is prepared to put up with Joe Dillon's fantasmatic ritual (and the consistency of its formulaic repetition will perhaps even seem reassuring by the close of the story) until he eventually decides that this 'mimic warfare' lacks the excitement of 'real adventures' (*D* 19–20). Such a real adventure, he decides, 'must be sought abroad', away from the domain of easy identification and familiar routine. The key here is Joyce's insistence on the *proper name* as marker of secure identity, that which finally makes characters *legible*. In the very first line of the story we read the name of Joe Dillon, rooting the opening situation in the epistemological solidity of back garden and hall, where the neighbourhood embodies a shared, intuitive identity; where 'everyone was incredulous' (*D* 18) about a local rumour.

Joyce then sets up what appears to be a straightforward dramatic contrast between this familiar world and the subsequent 'real' adventure or encounter that gives the story its title; but it is worth pausing over his precise narrative strategy here. We recall that, in the opening pages, when the narrator introduces Joe Dillon and his brother Leo, we are given hardly any description of what these boys look like; precisely because we know their names and are being shown into a narrative space of familiar and consistent identity, there is no need for us to be given any superfluous details about the children's appearance. In other words, in so far as we can read these characters, we do not need to be shown them, to confront them as visible phenomena, as something in excess of interpretation. By contrast, when the boys later encounter the old man (and it is significant that critics cannot agree quite what to call this character, some choosing to borrow Mahony's phrase the 'queer old josser'), the narrative suddenly enters a distinctly specular and speculative mode, its confident voice giving way to a hesitant, increasingly anxious eye: 'I saw a man approaching from the far end of the field. I watched him lazily as I chewed one of those green stems . . . He seemed to be fairly old . . . We followed him with our eyes . . .' (*D* 24). Here the narrator's point of view is precisely no longer authorised, as it was in reporting the everyday world of games and school, no longer in full possession of the material it presents: in effect, the narrator is now unable to identify (let alone to identify with) the event in question. This accounts for the shift from brisk paratactic narration to a sudden paralysing intrusion of detail, where the narrative abruptly jolts to a halt, as in a shuddering cinematic freeze-frame. And Joyce is quite particular about what this freezing of narrative time entails: the eclipse of speech in a sudden manifestation or *epiphany*: 'The man, however, only smiled. I saw that he had great gaps in his mouth between his yellow teeth' (*D* 25). As the narrator himself makes clear, what results is a split between the content of a speech – something in principle possible to understand or translate – and the repulsive act of its utterance: 'In my heart I thought that what he said about boys and sweethearts was reasonable. But I disliked the words in his mouth' (ibid.). The obscene apparition of the speaking mouth eclipses the significance of whatever words it may have voiced, its message sliding, dissolving, into what *Finnegans Wake* will write as 'messes of mottage' (*FW* 183.21–2).

It is this crucial shift from a discursive, broadly realist account to a sudden vision of the *surface* of language – a palpitating surface, glimpsed as a speaking mouth permeated by enigmatic enjoyment – that effectively undermines the solidity of what takes place in the narrative and gives 'An Encounter' its properly Joycean enormity. The same problematic is touched on in 'The Sisters', the first text ever published by Joyce and which he kept as the opening story of *Dubliners*. There, a boy narrator confronts the enigmatic manifestation of a 'pleasant and vicious region' (*D* 9) in the adult speech that addresses him: 'But the grey face still followed me. It murmured, and I understood that it desired to confess something . . . It began to confess to me in a murmuring voice and I wondered why it smiled continually and why the lips were so moist with spittle' (*D* 9). As in 'An Encounter', the momentary vision detaches speech from a human subject, focusing on the disembodied matter where speaking organs and enigmatic utterance seem to blend. What is crucial is that the narrator feels himself specifically addressed, as if touched by that utterance: 'I understood that it desired to confess something.' With this fantasmatic reversal of subject positions between adult priest and child confessor, Joyce's narrative begins to unfold its first insight into how narrative itself functions. This is made more explicit in 'An Encounter':

He described to me how he would whip such a boy as if he were unfolding some elaborate mystery. He would love that, he said, better than anything in this world; and his voice, as he led me monotonously through the mystery, grew almost affectionate and seemed to plead with me that I should understand him. (*D* 28)

The obscure libidinal traces discerned by the narrator – 'almost affectionate', 'seemed to plead' – form an essential part of the narrative mystery unfolded in and by 'An Encounter'. The crucial perception is of something *more*, something in excess of the discourse uttered, a surplus that possibly indicates (and the element of doubt is precisely the point) the libidinal force or pressure of some hidden, fantasmatic object.

The child's encounter with the adult's speech here entails, as we shall see, exposure to a powerful and disturbing manifestation of the desire of the Other: a fantasy centring on *transmission*, where the unfolding of a mystery merges with a kind of libidinal 'recruitment' or seduction. Exploring this narrative fantasy will be one of the central guiding threads of our encounter with psychoanalysis and Joyce.

What 'seems', what comes under the sign of 'as if', is thus the key to 'An Encounter': the thing taking place is precisely not reducible to an event in the ordinary sense, of the kind that might occur in the world of the narrator's friend Mahony, who busies himself with boyish activities such as chasing cats. When the central 'enormity' takes place – which may consist of the old man going off to a corner of the field to masturbate[12] – it is Mahony who does not hesitate to verbalise it, to confront it with his active power to name the world:

'I say! Look what he's doing!'
As I neither answered nor raised my eyes Mahony exclaimed again:
'I say . . . He's a queer old josser!' (*D* 26)

But, crucially, the narrator does not look: for the purposes of the narrative, that is, the 'enormity' remains invisible. It is thus at once too little –
an element missing from the account we are given by the boy – and too
much, the force of its obscenity (the ob-scene literally designating the
offstage, the unrepresentable) too powerful for it to be included in the
narrative, translated and made legible for the narrator and for us. While
a straightforward realist such as Mahony can respond verbally to – even
identify, provide some kind of name for – what is shown, the narrator himself remains dumb, linguistically paralysed by the encounter. The doubled
'I say' that marks Mahony's response as an active speech-act, thus contrasts
with and underlines the narrator's silence. And the only response he does
manage bears revealingly on a certain crisis of the proper name; he proposes
the 'paltry stratagem' (*D* 28), as he later thinks it, of the boys' adopting
false names as some kind of protection against what is unfolding. Here
we see the emergence of the literary alibi in Joycean writing, the complex
forging of identity that recurs throughout his work. And we can see that at
least initially the adoption of a false signature has a clear purpose: to serve
as a defence against fantasy, a way for the subject to escape from the fatal
circuit of the Other's desire. We shall see how this problematic of the alibi
intersects with – but perhaps also undermines – psychoanalytic theories of
identity and fantasy.

But first we should return to the text of 'An Encounter' to explore in
more detail how Joyce situates the unfolding of fantasy within the narrative.
The narrator's encounter with what he aptly terms the old man's 'monologue' (*D* 26) occurs in two distinct phases, before and after the invisible
'enormity' takes place. If one of the disturbing aspects of the encounter
for the child is the lack of consistency he notes in the speaker, as the
'strangely liberal' outlook first voiced suddenly gives way to a sadistic meditation on whipping boys, the discourse itself, by contrast, has a strange
formal consistency, precisely as a fantasmatic yearning for some circular,
all-encompassing continuity:

He began to speak to us about girls, saying what nice soft hair they had and how
soft their hands were and how all girls were not so good as they seemed to be if
one only knew. There was nothing he liked, he said, so much as looking at a nice
young girl, at her nice white hands and her soft beautiful hair. He gave me the
impression that he was repeating something which he had learned by heart or that,

magnetised by some words of his own speech, his mind was slowly circling round and round in the same orbit. (*D* 26)

The rhythmic repetition is in fact a recitation, as the boy perceives: its discursive orbit is in no way spontaneous or unconstrained but rather 'magnetised', set on a predetermined course by the weight of some invisible object, word or image. And the same pattern occurs when the monologue resumes, in its second act 'after an interval' (*D* 27), but with a change of object, the soft young girl now replaced by a naughty boy who must be whipped: 'He began to speak on the subject of chastising boys. His mind, as if magnetised again by his speech, seemed to circle slowly round and round its new centre' (*D* 27). 'Its new centre': Joyce's narrative clearly spells out a certain discursive and psychical topography of fantasy (along much the same lines, we should note, as Freud was exploring in the period when Joyce was trying to publish *Dubliners*). The speaker's repetitive, insistent phrases point to an invisible centre, a fantasmatic black hole, at once restlessly motivating and always eluding his utterance. Yet his rapt pleasure seems to inhere in the very stuff of the words he uses: 'He repeated his phrases over and over again, varying them and surrounding them with his monotonous voice' (*D* 26). And this verbal jouissance is entirely circular, in the sense that it turns back on itself in masturbatory self-fulfilment: despite the narrator's sense of being obscurely urged to enter into, to participate in, what is being unfolded, his glimpse of 'a pair of bottle-green eyes peering at me from under a twitching forehead' (*D* 27) makes him turn away in revulsion. The old man's pleasure, like Joe Dillon's more innocent enjoyment of a fantasy Wild West where he always wins, is a private recess of self-gratification, a kind of libidinal autism.

IV

How, then, in the context of this perverse scenario in which adult fantasy is imposed upon a child, can we maintain that 'An Encounter' dramatises above all an encounter of the *reader* with Joyce's writing? It is here that the subversive implications of Joyce's art for our encounter with the literary object – for reading, responding critically, theorising – begin to become visible. The old man's perverse discourse in 'An Encounter', with its efforts to seduce the young narrator into signifying complicity, is a manifestly rhetorical performance, a recitation of something 'learned by heart'. And if we turn back to the history of English prosody, we shall find the definition of one rhetorical trope, by Puttenham in 1589, of particular relevance here:

'Then have ye a figure which the Latines call *Traductio*, and I the tranlacer: which is when ye turne and tranlace a word into many sundry shapes as the Tailor doth his garment, and after that sort do play with him in your dittie . . .'[13] As the etymological source of a cluster of European words for 'translation', *traductio* is especially relevant to our reading of 'An Encounter', a translation being primarily an attempt to make legible some opacity, to unfold hidden knowledge. In Giorgio Agamben's view, any transmission in language is both a disclosure and an effacement of language itself: 'The presuppositional structure of language is the very structure of tradition; we presuppose, pass on, and thereby – according to the double sense of the word *traditio* – betray the thing itself in language, so that language may speak about something.'[14] Lacan refers in an early writing to the same quasi-transcendental structure when he cites Mallarmé's image of language as the silent exchange of an effaced coin: 'Even if it communicates nothing, the discourse represents the existence of communication.'[15] But what Lacan's work will add here is that the Other – Agamben's presuppositional structure – is by its very actuality in concrete discourse, and not only because of its necessary imbrication in meaning, always-already defective, insufficient. In other words, discourse involves the subject in an irreducible enigma that arises, as Russell Grigg puts it, 'because the expectation of meaning that the signifier generates is radically disappointed'.[16] If *traditio* betrays the pure act of communication by always dealing in mere meaning, there is conversely never enough meaning to cover the enigmatic space opened by the Other (so that the subject, Lacan declares, is always left asking, 'Che vuoi?', wondering what the Other wants). And it is this very confrontation with signifying insufficiency that corresponds, for Lacan, to the instance of fantasmatic jouissance (*E:S* 305–6).

The event unfolded in 'An Encounter', then, involves the desire of the Other in this double sense – as both the anonymous transmission of language and its enigmatic, non-transmissible act. The old man's voice, repeating and varying his phrases – turning and trans-lacing or translating them, to use Puttenham's vocabulary – seems to Joyce's narrator overwhelmingly driven by an urge to transmit his message, to make legible his personal mystery ('. . . seemed to plead with me that I should understand him'); but this transitive aspect of the fantasy is countered by the masturbatory self-enclosure of its act, its circular and obscene enjoyment. The voice is figured as the embodied jouissance of the lack of its own signifying finality, the fact that it will never be able to say enough to 'express itself' fully. It is as if the *traductio*, the rhetorical orbit of repetition and variation, must spin for ever on its own axis due to an inherent impossibility of self-transmission, the words seemingly 'magnetised' by the dead weight of some untranslatable, untreatable or non-transferable singularity.

As we shall see, *traductio* as a rhetorical figure is only one of a range of senses emerging from the rich semantic history of the term 'traduction'. But Puttenham's trope, if we use it as a way to designate the discursive problem envisaged in 'An Encounter', provides us with a good starting-point for a broader examination of traduction (as, above all, a way of thinking about *theory*). We might begin by redefining *traductio*, with an eye to our Joycean and psychoanalytic concerns, as a rhetorical variation and repetition that consists in *making legible*, but at the same time, crucially, in *making pleasurable*; the old man's urge to unfold something for the child is bound up with the rapture of his speech, just as his voice seems to enfold and caress the repetitive phrases. Yet one might immediately object that 'An Encounter' shows precisely a failure to make anything legible or pleasurable, to explicate or translate for the other any message, let alone any seductive mystery. But this signifying inadequacy corresponds exactly to *traductio* itself; the trope, as we have redefined it psychoanalytically, entails an inherent antagonism between the drive to produce legibility (in the interests of the ego) and the 'autistic' self-enjoyment of the drive. There is always a split between the chain of signifiers and the concrete utterance embodying it, which itself remains outside the signifying chain: the object-voice, a raw pulsation of the real.

If 'An Encounter' dramatises this general condition of discourse – that is, the split between the diacritical signifier and the singular instance of the voice – the story can equally be read as a tale of the institution and sub-version of authority. At each of its interconnecting narrative levels – those of the boy's narration, the old man's discourse and in turn the responses of the two boys to that discourse – the text turns on the effort to make legible an enigma, to give a name to some opaque apparition and thus include it in discourse as social, collective milieu. As Mahony's verbal response to the 'enormity' makes clear with its doubled voicing of the active lin-guistic subject ('I say!'), this traduction is understood by Joyce's text as a struggle for semantic mastery, an eminently theoretical struggle. For the 'queer old josser', the rhetorical orbit of *traductio* goes along with an urge to seduce the listener with ideas, to make him part of a mysterious doctri-nal enjoyment; he introduces himself to the boys as a theorist, an exegete of truth, a hermeneutist. If the narrative game that he proposes to his listeners is in one sense just like Joe Dillon's Wild West adventures – com-pletely rigged in advance, its single aim being to procure the speaker's own enjoyment – it nevertheless differs from the repetitive cycle of childish escapism in one pivotal respect: the discourse is now supposed (by the Joycean narrator at least) to be the site of a certain authority. And while the narrator can comfortably dismiss Joe Dillon as a tiresome playmate and something of a charlatan, he is much more puzzled by the task of interpreting the old man's character. 'His attitude on this point struck me as strangely liberal in a man of his age' (*D* 25): the carefully phrased critique of the old man's speech emphasises the narrator's overriding concern to identify correctly, the mimic solemnity of the narrative voice embodying the boy's desire for a clearly defined locus of authority where the world can be properly represented, things rightly named. And when the monologue resumes, the old man 'seemed to have forgotten his recent liberalism' (*D* 27), as the narrator notes with a touch of strained irony: what is revealed does not make sense, it is something that precisely eludes the urge to make legible and properly identify the encounter. The semiotic force of the old man's discourse is in excess of the narrative itself; it marks the inability of discourse to make discursive its own (fantasmatic, toxic) enjoyment-in-discourse. What remains invisible to the boy – due to his refusal to follow Mahony's lead and confront or verbalise the 'enormity' – is precisely what cannot be integrated within a consistent, authoritative account.

In 'An Encounter', then, Joyce gives us an early indication of how his writing will pre-empt and challenge our theoretical response to his work: how, above all, it will undermine any response that would ape the story's narrator by striving to re-establish a fantasy of consistent, fully legible authority. The encounter staged in Joyce's text between theory and fantasy, between infant listener and adult seducer, is revealed as an oddly chiasmatic structure – the opposing terms are never firmly fixed, and tend to slide into one another. If the child's attempt to ward off the danger embodied in the adult discourse takes the form of theoretical questions (Is the man too liberal or too illiberal, and how should I therefore respond to him?), in turn the fantasmatic threat emanating from the old man is itself a matter of theory, of declarations about the proper nature and conduct of children. Here Joyce envisages the infantile root of theory as fully enmeshed with fantasy – where fantasy should be understood both as active linguistic transmission (thus, as a kind of traduction) and as passive exposure to the unsurpassable otherness of enjoyment-in-language (or *jouis-sens*, as Lacan puns).

The first theorist to grasp this sense of fantasy as the site of an undecidable, inappropriable doubling – of 'Dyoublong' as it will be written in the *Wake* (*FW* 13.4) – was of course Freud. We should begin by exploring some of Freud's crucial encounters with the aesthetic in order to approach the relation they stage between fantasmatic revelation and theoretical discourse. And we shall subsequently encounter in Joyce – on the side of the aesthetic, so to speak – an ambiguous enjoyment of the 'freudful mistake' (*FW* 411.35–6) or error-strewn discovery of psychoanalysis, an enjoyment to which Lacan will respond: *J'ouïs.*

CHAPTER 2

Freud's Mousetrap

We do not like the real Shakespeare. We like to have his language
pruned and his conceptions flattened into something that suits our
mouths and minds.

A. C. Bradley[1]

I

If psychoanalysis begins with a letter – one in which Freud tells his friend
Fliess, on 15 October 1897, of his discovery of the Oedipus complex – its
origin also marks its immediate entanglement with literature. For, in the
same letter, Freud speaks of finding the first 'response' to his discovery, the
first confirmation of the new knowledge, in a literary text – indeed, we
might say, in *the* literary text: Shakespeare's *Hamlet*. What Freud begins
as a casual afterthought ends up sketching a whole theory of the artwork's
Ursprung, one that will set the agenda for decades of so-called 'applied'
psychoanalysis:

> Fleetingly the thought passed through my head that the same thing might be at the
> bottom of *Hamlet* as well. I am not thinking of Shakespeare's conscious intention,
> but believe, rather, that a real event stimulated the poet to his representation, in
> that his unconscious understood the unconscious of his hero. How does Hamlet
> the hysteric justify his words 'Thus conscience doth make cowards of us all'? How
> does he explain his irresolution in avenging his father by the murder of his uncle –
> the same man who send his courtiers to their death without a scruple and who is
> positively precipitate in murdering Laertes? How better than through the torment
> he suffers from the obscure memory that he himself had contemplated the same
> deed against his father out of passion for his mother.[2]

So there is something 'at the bottom' of *Hamlet*: perhaps underneath the
stage, beneath the representational surface of the drama. There, Freud imagines another scene, closer to the truth (although it might simply be another
play, this time by Sophocles). This solution to the riddle of Shakespeare's

31

tragedy is incorporated, carefully reformulated, in the foundational text of psychoanalysis, *The Interpretation of Dreams* (1900). There, Freud writes that the central enigma of Shakespeare's play, which has baffled generations of critics, is that it 'offers no reasons or motives for [Hamlet's] hesitations'.[3] This double lack – of dramatic coherence and of critical mastery – will be abolished at once by Freud's interpretation, which is now supported by some broad historical brush-strokes. Because of the 'secular advance of repression in the emotional life of mankind', he writes, a change has taken place in the representational position of fantasy:

In [Sophocles'] *Oedipus*, the child's wishful phantasy that underlies it is brought into the open and realized as it would be in a dream. In *Hamlet* it remains repressed; and – just as in the case of a neurosis – we only learn of its existence from its inhibiting consequences. Strangely enough, the overwhelming effect produced by the more modern tragedy has turned out to be compatible with the fact that people have remained completely in the dark as to the hero's character. (*SE* 4:264)

In an oneiric Hellenic past, Freud imagines, fantasy could be directly enacted, given public representation. If modern representation has lost the capacity for such a bold *Realisierung*, Freud immediately marks this as a sign of repression; and in case there is any doubt here as to who represses (in other words, about the subject of this 'psychical' event), he adds: 'Here I have translated into conscious terms what was bound to remain unconscious in Hamlet's mind' (268).

   This last phrase – 'Ich habe dabei ins Bewußte übersetzt, was in der Seele des Helden unbewußt bleiben muß' – calls to mind the problematic of traduction we have begun to outline. In the first instance, we can see that Freud's *Übersetzung* here brings about a certain closure or isolation of representational uncertainty; the somewhat groundless speculations about the 'emotional life of mankind' can be left behind if we relocate the problem as one of translating the contents of 'Hamlet's mind'. Hamlet's character as paradigmatic riddle-solver (another 'Oedipal' feature, of course) is the key to Freud's involvement with *Hamlet* – not only to his enduring fascination with the play, but also, as we shall see, to his work's uncanny implication in it.

   To gain a clearer sense of this Freudian involvement with Shakespeare's play we need to follow his double reading closely. On the one hand, in Freud's view *Hamlet* bears with it, by a strange cultural transference, the *Oedipus* as its 'repressed' truth. The 'obscure memory' of the Greek tragedy somehow exerts an inhibiting influence on the Shakespearean drama or on our ability to interpret it, adding an illegible opacity to the text. At the same time (and in the same gesture, as it were), Hamlet the character is supplied in Freud's *Übersetzung* with an unconscious set of Oedipal fantasies of his own. Thus, what has left audiences and critics 'in the dark' over the centuries is the play's secret: that it conceals within it another play, entitled not *The Mousetrap*, but *Oedipus Rex*. 'The conflict in *Hamlet* is so effectively concealed that it was left to me to unearth it,' writes Freud in 1906,[4] the metaphor echoing his earlier comment that the play 'has its roots in the same soil' as the Sophoclean tragedy.[5] We shall see how these metaphors – of buried secrets, occult truths lying beneath the skin of representation – effectively root Freud's reading of *Hamlet* in the metaphorical economy of Shakespeare's text itself.

Before we begin a more detailed exploration of this – the way that Freud's reading remains embedded in the aesthetic soil where it digs – it is worth pausing briefly to consider Freud's own developing reflection on the relation between psychoanalysis and the criticism of artworks. In one sense, the hermeneutic labour involved in these endeavours seems to him uncannily similar: both analyst and critic set out to solve riddles, to bring new kinds of legibility to unravel the enigmas of human desire and creativity. Freud opens his 1907 paper on Jensen's novel *Gradiva* by remarking confidently that it is 'a settled fact that the essential riddles of dreaming have been solved by the efforts of the author of the present work';[6] and he implies that a similarly decisive *Lösung* ('solution'; also the 'dissolution' of a symptom) has been effected in the case of *Hamlet*: its secret 'unearthed', the symptomatic critical perplexity surrounding it should immediately evaporate. In this sense, Freud sees psychoanalysis and the interpretation of art as entirely compatible, their interpretative continuity signalled by a shared vocabulary. (Each faces its *Rätsel*, riddle or enigma, the opacity of which it strives to dissolve or solve through a 'pharmaceutical' *Lösung*.)

But, if this continuity between analyst and critic is restated in a paper Freud wrote in 1914, it is simultaneously – and dramatically – suspended. The article, entitled 'The Moses of Michelangelo', appeared in the journal *Imago* that year with the author's name replaced by three asterisks.[7] And beneath this veil of anonymity, Freud writes the following extraordinary passage:

Long before I had any opportunity of hearing about psycho-analysis, I learnt that a Russian art connoisseur, Ivan Lermonlieff, had caused a revolution in the art galleries of Europe by questioning the authorship of many pictures, showing how to distinguish copies from originals with certainty, and constructing hypothetical artists for those works whose former supposed authorship had been discredited. He achieved this by insisting that attention should be diverted from the general impression and main features of a picture, and by laying stress on the significance of minor details, of things like the drawing of the fingernails, of the lobe of an ear, of halos and such unconsidered trifles which the copyist neglects to imitate and yet which every artist executes in his own characteristic way . . . It seems to me that this method of inquiry is closely related to the technique of psycho-analysis. It, too, is accustomed to divine secret and concealed things from despised or unnoticed features, from the rubbish-heap, as it were, of our observations.[8]

The 'supposed authorship' of the critical or interpretative revolution in question is itself soon discredited: Freud was later, he continues, 'greatly interested to learn that the Russian pseudonym concealed the identity of an Italian physician called Morelli'. Just as he finds in an art criticism that focuses on 'unconsidered trifles' a mirror-image of the methods of psychoanalysis, so Freud's own decision to remain anonymous, his refusal to give his signature to the article, seems to be doubled by the pseudo-signature of this Russian or Italian, this 'hypothetical' man Freud has only heard about, who is supposed (ironically enough) to know 'how to distinguish copies from originals'. In a letter to Freud, Karl Abraham has doubts about the strategy of anonymity, wondering, *à la* Morelli, whether the style of the writing itself might betray the master's hand: 'Don't you think that one will recognise the lion's claw?'[9]

The question of authorship – ultimately always a question of the institutional organisation and control of knowledge – is one of the central stakes in the encounter between psychoanalysis and the aesthetic. A first approach to that question might be to wonder why Freud withholds his signature – effectively refusing to acknowledge this hypothetical 'layman's' work as an authorised psychoanalytic production – from the same text where he notes (in the quoted passage) how 'closely related' are the two interpretative techniques in question. The gesture with which Freud seeks – like one of the copyists exposed by Morelli – to pass off his work as another's, sets up a curiously self-undoing effect in a text that argues that the authentic trace of an author is to be read only in stylistic traits, the 'rubbish-heap' of significant details that subvert the closing authority of a signature. And if Freud's signature, the mark of 'the lion's claw' poorly concealed by the asterisks, has finally only one meaning – 'This is psychoanalysis, I authorise this' – Abraham's question could be rephrased as a question about the relation between psychoanalysis and aesthetics: what is it that allows us to distinguish 'copy' from 'original' here? Where can the line be drawn between authentic analysis and its identical twin?

In responding to such a question, Freud's writings on aesthetics have a significance that is primarily institutional. The dramatisation of a specific institutional crisis – relating to paternity and the law, to the question of signifying legitimacy – is what attracts Freud's attention to artworks, as is shown with singular clarity in his interpretations of *Hamlet* and the *Moses*. In exploring those interpretations, along with Lacan's attempts to reinvent them, we shall find ourselves already addressing the central questions posed by Joyce's work: questions of fatherhood and inheritance, creation and memory.

II

'Some of the grandest and most overwhelming creations of art are still unsolved riddles to our understanding,' writes Freud in 1914 (*SE* 13:209). The contributions to literary or art criticism made possible, in Freud's view, by the discoveries of psychoanalysis are invariably announced as definitive solutions to age-old enigmas, as if Freud's intervention were provoked not so much by the artwork itself as by the critical 'symptom', the interpretative difficulty. We shall find, however, that the key stake in this intervention will emerge as the possibility of maintaining a distance between a theoretical discourse and its aesthetic object, of criticism freeing itself from the 'obscure memory' of the artwork before it.

Hamlet, then, constituted a riddle because of a central gap in its structure and its hero's character: the lack of reasons or motives for Hamlet's famous hesitation to act. And that lack would be abolished at a stroke by Freud's Oedipal 'translation', thought up all at once on that night in 1897. We can begin to glimpse what this Freudian solution overlooks – how what it sees is caught up with a certain symptomatic blindness – by comparing it with another well-known idiosyncratic view of the play, that of T. S. Eliot. Writing in 1919, Eliot passed his notorious judgement that *Hamlet* was an artistic failure. The quality of 'artistic "inevitability"', as he put it, which

lies in . . . complete adequacy of the external to the emotion . . . is precisely what is deficient in *Hamlet*. Hamlet (the man) is dominated by an emotion which is inexpressible, because it is in *excess* of the facts as they appear. And the supposed identity of Hamlet with his author is genuine to this point: that Hamlet's bafflement at the absence of objective equivalent to his feelings is a prolongation of the bafflement of his creator in the face of his artistic problem.[10]

For Eliot, what is lacking is not some specific psychological content – 'repressed' from the drama, unknown to the critics – but a proper aesthetic fit between the textual surface and the emotional diegesis. The inexpressible affective trauma that disfigures the play is precisely what resists analysis, what leads to the 'bafflement' of character and artist – and of critic, we would add. For Eliot's reading reminds us of what Freud somehow fails to mention: that if *Hamlet* is a riddle, it is first of all so *in Hamlet's eyes*. 'S'blood, there is something in this more than natural, if philosophy could find it out', mutters the prince (II.ii.363–4): in other words, a crisis of interpretation is the play's very 'subject'. Thus the 'prolongation' of the riddle from author to character hypothesised by Eliot could be extended to the audience, left in the dark, not because of a particular, contingent dramatic flaw (the playwright's failure to include in the text the required details about Hamlet's complex motivations), but because of something itself opaque, 'inexpressible', in the situation that confronts Hamlet. And of course that situation, it is immediately apparent, is one of institutional crisis.

The death of Hamlet's father has precipitated, at the opening of the play, a severe social and political trauma. For Hamlet, the trauma even bears on representation itself, as is first shown in his struggle to symbolise an occurrence which for the play's audience must have been a shocking breach of institutional protocol: his mother's failure to respect the full term of widow's mourning. Gertrude's 'o'erhasty marriage' is, writes critic R. M. Frye, 'in sixteenth-century terms . . . utterly scandalous'.[11] Its effect, in Hamlet's first soliloquy, is the image of an ever-expanding and all-devouring feminine jouissance:

> Must I remember? Why she would hang on him
> As if increase of appetite had grown
> By what it fed on; and yet within a month –
> Let me not think on't – Frailty, thy name is woman.
>   (I.ii.143–6)

Mourning, as Lacan will put it in one of his 1959 seminars on *Hamlet*, is a response to a 'hole in existence'.[12] If the death of the royal father tears a hole in the socio-symbolic fabric of the state, this is made far worse by the queen's flouting of her mourning duties: a traumatic gap opens up between social existence – the 'government', whose coherence depends on conventional forms, consistent symbolic protocols – and the particularity of individual existence: here, the recalcitrant self-sufficiency of an irresponsible enjoyment.

We can perhaps already begin to make out here the principal open secret of *Hamlet*: how this most reflexive of plays presents in the predicament of its hero a simulacrum of our own predicament as the audience of the play – or even, at a deeper level, as participants in aesthetic experience as such. For Hamlet's initial discourse is at once a struggle to symbolise and to ward off something, something that imposes itself as both the disruption of language and an inescapable, fascinating spectacle. His own existence as prince and son seems to be threatened by the opening of this 'hole in existence' (to recall Lacan's phrase): thus his sense of the danger of even allowing himself to acknowledge it, to admit the 'hole' into his memory: 'Let me not think on't.'

In this sense, Hamlet's labour of interpretation is the precise equivalent of a critical traduction: it seeks to create a space of legibility by warding off the overwhelming force of what paradoxically exceeds and invades language. In such a space of traduction – it is hoped – things can be named, identities secured, reality re-established. The young narrator of Joyce's 'An Encounter', we recall, likewise struggles to render legible what threatens to disfigure the familiar space of his world, but feels a sense of shame at having to adopt the 'paltry stratagem' (*D* 28) of using a false name in order to protect his identity and save his reality.

Freud sees the riddle of *Hamlet* as above all a matter of *names*. As he puts it in 'Psychopathic Characters on the Stage', in Shakespeare's play 'the impulse that is struggling into consciousness . . . is never given a definite name' (309). By speaking that name, Freud hopes to undo the riddle and cure the symptom of cultural perplexity that is the play. If his first attempt at this is a formula so succinct as to sound almost banal – the epithet 'Hamlet the hysteric' appears as vacuous, as clichéd, as 'Frailty, thy name is woman' – Freud has to rework, rewrite, the act of naming in exactly the same way as Hamlet: that is, by writing another play into the play we are watching.

Hamlet discovers early in the play that mere repetitive signifiers – 'Words, words, words' (ii.ii.192) – will always fail to do justice to the experiential wealth 'beneath' them, to fit the rich complexity of the things they name (something that Eliot will express, in his terms, as the lack of 'artistic "inevitability" '). The conventional misogyny ('Frailty, thy name . . .') with which Hamlet gives up his search to express the scandal of his mother's behaviour is a last resort, uttered with a despairing irony, a sense of the gulf between trite platitude and unspeakable truth; likewise, he is unable to get away from empty formulas when called upon to name his dead father, to sum up the essential quality of his life: 'A was a man, take him for all in all' (i.ii.187).

If these rhetorical inadequacies point to the play's preoccupation with a discrepancy between the visible scene or surface of representation and some obscure depth beneath it, this finds its fullest realisation, of course, when the ghost of Hamlet's father appears. The ghost emerges as a traumatic disruption of the discursive space of the play (both metaphorically and 'in act', when it speaks from the 'cellarage' beneath the stage: the voice of royal authority emanating from the allegorical 'Hell' of the medieval mystery plays).[13] Hamlet has to encounter the ghost away from the court, outside the consistent socio-symbolic scene where its 'questionable shape', refusing to take part in discursive exchange, can only appear as a terrifying enigma. The ghost's initial warning to Hamlet indicates a radical incommensurability between its voice and what 'ears of flesh and blood' can hear:

> But that I am forbid
> To tell the secrets of my prison-house,
> I could a tale unfold whose lightest word
> Would harrow up thy soul . . .
>
> (I.v.13–16)

The ghost's secret is nothing less than an ear-poisoning: Shakespeare's metaphors turn the uncanny tale – of the 'lazar-like' corrosion of 'all my smooth body' – into a figure of the effect upon the play's signifying surface (as well as the 'body politic') of a corrosive secret, at once beyond it and secretly concealed within it.[14] The motif runs throughout the play in oppositions of the skin of representation and a subjacent wealth – treasure or ulcer – 'mining all within' (III.iv.150). Hamlet's immediate response is to dream of an absolute representation, freed from the mundane impurity of everyday discourse, in which he would be capable of writing down, *re-signing*, the ghost's word:

> I'll wipe away all trivial fond records,
> All saws of books, all forms, all pressures past,
> That youth and observation copied there,
> And thy commandment all alone shall live
> Within the book and volume of my brain,
> Unmix'd with baser matter.   (I.v.99–104)

The worn formulas of rhetorical convention – the only tools Hamlet could find in his vain efforts to symbolise his mother's jouissance or his father's finished life – are to be erased from his memory, to allow the pure inscription of the ghost's final 'Remember me!' But this desire for a pure representation suffers a bathetic reversal as soon as it passes into action:

> My tables. Meet it is I set it down
> That one may smile, and smile, and be a villain –
> At least I am sure it may be so in Denmark.   [*Writes*]
> So, uncle, there you are.   (I.v.106–10)

For all the emotional intensity of its author, the note scribbled down remains powerless to encapsulate what is essential, its arbitrary signifying elements entirely lacking any motivated connection with the thing itself (as is emphasised by the comic simplicity of the syntax and phrasing: 'one may smile . . . and be a villain').

With these reflexive questions about the possibility of representation 'unmix'd with baser matter', language that could somehow transcend its material basis in the bodily particularity of speech, *Hamlet* shows its uncanny power to address modernist (and specifically Joycean) problems *avant la lettre*. If we turn to the opening of the famous 'Mousetrap' scene (III.ii), we find Hamlet's 'directorial' remarks to the players especially revealing here. His instructions combine conventional (and thoroughly idealist) wisdom about theatre – 'to hold as 'twere the mirror up to nature' (III.ii.22) – with a specific injunction to avoid the 'pitiful ambition' (l. 44) of actors who disfigure the overall dramatic effect by some personal intervention or excessive stylistic gesture. Hamlet goes to some lengths to specify what he wants excluded from the performance: that is, laughter. His 'solution' to the riddle of the play is based on the fantasy of a full traduction: 'The Mousetrap' must be an efficient representation-machine; it can have no truck with any ambiguous enjoyment or 'poison in jest', any contingent or pathological remainder.

The mechanism of this signifying 'solution' is well illustrated during the performance of 'The Mousetrap' when Ophelia's question about the play's meaning is met by Hamlet's gleeful answer – 'The players cannot keep counsel: they'll tell all' (II.ii.137–8). Whereas the revelation of the ghost's secret at the beginning of the play had caused a dramatic dislocation of symbolic space, Hamlet has now arranged for that secret to be re-presented, unveiled, centre-stage – in the royal presence that in principle (but not in practice, as Hamlet knows) guarantees the consistency of the legal and political court. The players are therefore fulfilling their duty as royal subjects by openly confessing the secret in court – a confession that has the effect of driving its legal addressee, the king, offstage. The truth about the king has thus supposedly emerged in an open ('extant') play, entered into the public realm where things can be named: Hamlet's fantasy of full traduction comprises a vision of institutional plenitude and consistency that his 'Mousetrap' simultaneously exposes as a sham. The fantasy goes as far as Hamlet's triumphant conviction that he has unmasked the true name of Claudius, in contrast to the earlier barren attempt to 'set down' his character:

For thou dost know, O Damon dear,
This realm dismantled was
Of Jove himself, and now reigns here
A very, very – pajock.   (III.ii.275–8)

By Hamlet's prior arrangement, of course, Horatio observes the effects of the play on the court. His first comment – to object that 'pajock' does not fit in the verse because it doesn't rhyme (279) – is therefore precisely the point: something doesn't rhyme, just as 'something is rotten' in the state. In Hamlet's eyes, now that Claudius has been given his proper name, 'pajock' or patch-cock, 'a king of shreds and patches' (III.iv.103),[15] he is shown to be the very name of the institutional inconsistency, the flawed and unreliable representation, of the Danish court: its destitution. Claudius may be nothing but the patched-together semblance of a king, but nevertheless the supposed social and representational consistency embodied in kingship (and metonymically figured in Horatio's demand for conventional rhyming couplets) is preserved. 'The Mousetrap' is Hamlet's way of salvaging the father-king as a principle of signifying legitimacy, of institutional representation. Yet the Shakespearean text immediately exposes the fact that this restoration of full and law-abiding identity is an illusion. Hamlet's traduction of his earlier encounter with the ghost, his ecstatic sense of having exchanged terror and signifying paralysis for valid semiotic currency ('I'll take the ghost's word for a thousand pound', he tells Horatio: III.ii.260–1) is countersigned by a fantasmatic deification of his dead father, who is now declared to be no less than 'Jove himself' (257). The exposure of Claudius as a destitute father, one unworthy of the royal and paternal name, merely reconfirms Hamlet's *père-version*, to borrow Lacan's way of writing: his 'turning to the father' or reliance on a fantasy of signifying legitimacy.

It is worth pausing here over certain theological aspects of Shakespeare's play, which will prove highly relevant to our reading of Joyce. (As Jean-Michel Rabaté has remarked, more than any other modern writer Joyce 'has forced criticism to acknowledge its theological nature'.)[16] In his recent book *Hamlet in Purgatory*, Stephen Greenblatt has placed Hamlet's encounter with the ghost in the context of the fierce institutional conflicts of the English Reformation and the late sixteenth-century state. Greenblatt argues that Hamlet's worry about the ghost's identity – 'The spirit that I have seen / May be the devil' (II.ii.575–6) – is coherent with the radical ambiguity of its provenance. On the one hand, the ghost comes from somewhere that is clearly a Catholic purgatory in all but name. (Greenblatt shows how political repression would have ruled out a direct reference to the banned Catholic doctrine.) On the other, its call for vengeance is precisely incompatible with the purgation of sins – as Greenblatt comments, such a call 'could come only from the place in the afterlife where Seneca's ghosts reside: Hell'.[17]

In other words, one of the results of 'The Mousetrap' for Hamlet is the *redemption* of the ghost. (One thinks again of the imaginary thousand-pound pay-off). And here we need to supplement Greenblatt's meticulous historicist account by adding the critical elements derived from a psychoanalytic perspective: namely, fantasy and jouissance. (The notion of adding these elements is itself somewhat paradoxical, however, since they designate the instance of a certain *lack*, something bearing on, but irreducible to, the historical text.) For what is at stake in Hamlet's uncertainty about the ghost is precisely the authority of the father, and thus the question whether the call for vengeance is authentic, justified or tainted by sin, compromised by some hidden self-interest. The fear that the ghost might be a devil may indeed be theologically rational (as Greenblatt argues), but it is also Hamlet's apprehension of a fraudulent or flawed paternity – that is, one that fails to provide full legibility, that harbours some secret defect or jouissance that mars its power to represent, to give things their true names. Once again, we return to Hamlet's wish to exclude laughter and bodily excess from the performance of 'The Mousetrap'; the play must be a pure symbolic device, its representational authority uncompromised by the 'baser matter' of interest or enjoyment – if, that is, it is to cancel out any possible shortcoming in the father, to restore the sanctity of his name.

III

Is Freud's response to the riddle of *Hamlet*, then, nothing more than an exact repetition or re-staging of Hamlet's? We have seen that the 'solutions' proposed in turn by the Shakespearean prince and the psychoanalyst share a preoccupation with names, with finding the right signifier to unlock the mystery 'underlying' the play – which for each riddle-solver turns out to be a primal scene of parental trauma with inhibiting consequences for the surface of representation, the 'extant' drama. We saw how Freud's Oedipal reading of *Hamlet* shifted briskly from speculations about fantasy and its historical vicissitudes to a conventional character-based approach (confirming T. S. Eliot's worst fears). This shift allowed Freud to make 'Hamlet's mind' the crucial site of fantasy to be 'translated', rendered coherent and legible; and it is of course by inserting another play (one whose themes have not been 'repressed', but are still legible) that this traduction can be accomplished. Just like 'The Mousetrap', the *Oedipus* reveals the complete truth of an obscure, phantasmal scene, unmasks the fraudulent compromises of everyday life and lends a new diegetic consistency to action and motivation.

For all Freud's claim to have 'unearthed' *Hamlet*'s secret, and freed culture of its obsessive inability to understand the play, in the end his reading amounts to nothing more than an instance of something already powerfully dramatised by Shakespeare's play: traduction, or the urge to recuperate, render legible and comprehensible the excessive force of what disrupts, defies representation. We should be careful here, however, not to fall back on some easy universalism and figure this 'urge' in terms of a natural human instinct to understand (and thus another index of the play's timeless, universal appeal). It will be one of our tasks in engaging with Joyce and Lacan to show how the critical deployment of psychoanalysis can serve radically to estrange and bring into question our most 'natural' assumptions about reading.

To gain a clearer sense of what is involved in the uncanny mirroring we have glimpsed between Freudian thinking and Shakespeare's art, we need to turn to another of Freud's encounters with the aesthetic, one that shows more graphically the *unsettling of authority* that is central to the encounter. The best way to approach this – and a good example of what Freud might have called the 'over-determination' of these questions – is to quote Lacan quoting *Hamlet* in his 1959 seminar. In question is the 'distance' a subject takes before the object of fantasy; Lacan finds this well illustrated by a scene in Shakespeare's play:

. . . [Ophelia] has the good fortune to be the first person Hamlet runs into after his unsettling encounter with the ghost, and she reports his behaviour in terms that are worth noting.

> My lord, as I was sewing in my closet,
> Lord Hamlet, with his doublet all unbraced,
> No hat upon his head, his stockings fouled,
> Ungartered, and down-gyvèd to his ankle,
> Pale as his shirt, his knees knocking each other,
> And with a look so piteous in purport
> As if he had been loosèd out of hell
> To speak of horrors – he comes before me.
> . . . He took me by the wrist and held me hard.
> Then goes he to the length of all his arm,
> And with his other hand thus o'er his brow
> He falls to such perusal of my face
> As a would draw it. Long stayed he so.
>
> (II.i.77–91)[18]

Lacan reads Ophelia's account as a perfect *mise en scène* of the subject's relation to fantasy. Hamlet's posture is that of a spectator confronted by a dazzling, enigmatic object; the weave of his symbolic identifications having been 'unbraced' (like his doublet) by the ghost's harrowing, inhuman voice, his encounter with Ophelia becomes a search to position himself, to take up a place within a discursive, inter-subjective structure. It is no accident that this search is compared in Shakespeare's verse to an *artistic* activity – 'As a would draw it': it is an attempt to trace out a form, to introduce a minimal mark of representational difference that might serve to stave off the threat of obliteration.

Freud, in a letter to Edoardo Weiss of 1933, tells of a similar encounter:

Every day for three lonely weeks of September 1913, I stood in the church in front of the statue [the *Moses* by Michelangelo], studying it, measuring it and drawing it until there dawned on me that understanding which I expressed in my essay, though I only dared to do so anonymously.[19]

'The very interpretation of the figure is open to complete contradictions,' comments an art historian quoted approvingly by Freud; like *Hamlet*, Michelangelo's statue *Moses* is surrounded by a ceaseless buzz of critical activity, symptom of a complete lack of interpretative consensus. For Freud, the 'inscrutable' (*rätselvoll*, 'riddle-bearing') statue emits a gaze of blinding mastery:

How often have I mounted the steep steps from the unlovely Corso Cavour to the lonely piazza where the deserted church stands, and have essayed to support the angry scorn of the hero's glance![20]

Just as Hamlet has to leave the scene of the court to face the ghost, Freud has to walk away from the everyday world to take up his position in the fateful encounter with the *Moses*. 'No piece of statuary has ever made a stronger impression on me than this,' says Freud; with the insistence of the *Trieb* circling its object, he returns to confront the enigma, to try once again to measure or trace out its *rätselvoll*, encrypted significance.

What, then, is Freud's first interpretation of the statue's mysterious 'source of power' (located, like that of *Hamlet*, beyond what is immediately legible in the representational surface)? In a gesture characteristic of all his writings on art, and that goes beyond mere 'academic' convention, Freud identifies its aesthetic power with the mastery of an author. Having listed the bewildering range of critical opinions about the *Moses*, he asks whether the lack of consensus can be due to the 'master-hand' having 'traced . . . a vague or ambiguous script in the stone' (213); only the artist (together with a closed, consistent psychical space) can be the origin of the fascinating enigma. Freud never takes the step of positing, as cause of the symptomatic critical dissent, something untranslatable, irreducible to the explanatory narratives swirling around it; he simply adds one more narrative (but his is the *right* one, based on the 'cryptic' hermeneutic of a Morelli).

The *maintenance of authority* is therefore the theme of Freud's interpretation of Michelangelo's statue, just as it was of Hamlet's 'Mousetrap'. The master-hand of the artist is to be salvaged, as the principle of a firmly centred meaning, from the vociferous crowd of critics; likewise Freud's obsessive attention to the hand of the statue seeks to trace there the heroic safeguarding of authority against disruptive, centrifugal forces:

Nor will [Moses] throw away the Tables so that they will break on the stones, for it is on their especial account that he has controlled his anger; it was to preserve them that he kept his passion in check. In giving way to his rage and indignation, he had to neglect the Tables, and the hand which upheld them was withdrawn. They began to slide down and were in danger of being broken. This brought him to himself. (229)

The paraphrase Freud gives of the passionate lawgiver's psyche here is highly revealing: the safeguarding of authority at stake here goes beyond the vindication of Michelangelo's artistic intention, to touch on the very basis of Judaic law, of the Law itself: the authority of the father.

The figure of Moses, of course, held a lifelong fascination for Freud. He was to return to it in one of his last writings, the tortured *Moses and Monotheism*; and, while completing the latter text as an exile in London, Freud writes a note in his diary that provides a crucial clue to the significance of his earlier encounter with Michelangelo's *Moses*. 'I . . . work for an hour a day at my Moses,' he writes, 'der mich plagt wie ein ghost not laid [which torments me like a "ghost not laid"].'[21] This last phrase, written in English, is surely a ghostly echo of the famous English 'ghost not laid' that had haunted Freud since he first dreamt up the Oedipus complex: namely, the ghost of Hamlet. At any rate, if we compare Hamlet's encounter with his father's ghost and Freud's 'three lonely weeks' of visits to the *Moses* statue, we can trace some suggestive parallels.

In the first place, both encounters dramatise the destitution of paternal authority. The tangle of discordant interpretations around the Moses seems to Freud to risk jeopardising the authority of *der Meister*, exposing Michelangelo as guilty of working *undeutliche oder zweideutige*, without a distinct or unequivocal meaning.[22] And these doubts about the integrity of the artistic statement of course cast doubt upon the represented figure himself, the Judaic *Urvater*, whose status as lawgiver – as precisely the one who resolves doubt, makes things decisively clear – is thus undermined. Likewise, Hamlet is troubled by the ambiguity of what he has seen, of who it is that has addressed him: he admits the possibility that the apparition might have been the devil (II.ii.575–6). In both cases, there is something more than appears in what appears; and the task of both 'solutions' – Hamlet's play, Freud's drawings – is to restore the signifying legitimacy, the exhaustive veracity, of the paternal apparition.

Here, we can pause briefly over an aspect of Freud's essay on the *Moses* that critics often overlook, one that suggests an even closer parallel with *Hamlet*, one with eminently Joycean implications. For although Freud bases his interpretation of the *Moses*, *à la* Morelli, on a foregrounding of significant detail (the position of Moses' hand amid the tangle of the beard), he completely fails to mention the most obvious 'significant detail' to strike an observer of Michelangelo's statue: namely, of course, the horns on its head. Only a single one of the various critical quotations listed by Freud refers to this strange feature, alluding (in a telling phrase) to 'the Moses with the head of Pan' (212); nor does Freud feel it necessary to explain the source of this peculiarity of representation: namely, a Vulgate mistranslation of the Hebrew verb *qrn*, whereby the divine illumination of Moses' face, 'sending forth rays of light' (Exodus 34:29), became a Luciferan disfigurement, 'putting forth horns'.[23] The mistranslation had thus given rise to a tradition of portraying one of the primal Jewish patriarchs and law-bearers with a singularly 'devilish' characteristic (one that later Christian theologians would even try, with thinly veiled anti-Semitism, to justify).[24]

Now, by specifically failing to mention such a salient feature in the object of his discussion, Freud actually draws attention to it, highlighting it as in some sense especially significant (according to a paradoxical hermeneutic often invoked, of course, by Freud himself). Thus, Hamlet's fear that his father's ghost 'may be the Devil' might find a certain echo in Freud's preoccupation with the *Moses*, especially if we refer ahead to a paper published a decade later in which Freud writes of 'The Devil as a Father-Substitute'.[25]

If we return to our problem of traduction, we can clarify the link between paternity and interpretability and stop the argument from sliding into the banal psychologising that Freud himself often falls back upon. (The devil can be a father-substitute, he tells us wisely in 1923, due to emotional ambivalence.)[26] What Freud 'represses' by overlooking the horns on the head of Moses is not some hypothetical fear or hatred of his father, but a linguistic remainder, that which is left behind by the slippage or leakage of meaning between languages.[27] The traduction of the artwork seeks to make it legible precisely by excluding this signifying excess, by cutting through the distracting surface of the non-essential to treat 'the thing itself'. Thus Freud's 'solution' to the riddle of the *Moses* is to produce drawings that are 'emancipated . . . from the visual image of the statue' and an account representing 'an analysis of the motive forces behind it' (228). Like the *Oedipus* in the reading of *Hamlet*, these hypothetical sketches reveal the repressed truth of the artwork, its invisible origin; they offer a coherent narrative to account for the aesthetic enigma.

We might characterise the Freudian traduction of art, then, as a consistent theoretical effort to *redeem* the father, to rescue the symbolic function of paternity from its flawed embodiment. The reading of Michelangelo's statue shows with exemplary clarity how this is bound up, not with some speculative 'family romance' featuring Sigmund Freud and his father Jakob, but with the invocation of a law of signification. Freud's Moses is caught between his mission – to maintain God's law, to uphold its written surface in his hand – and the overwhelming affective (and in a crucial sense, as we shall see, performative) disturbance that dislodges the Tables, loosens the grip on them and threatens quite literally to break the law. Moses comes to himself – assumes his identity, his self-mastery – at this moment when disruptive passion almost undoes his grasp of the law: Freud imagines the statue's poise, a violent, twisting movement suddenly frozen, as encapsulating the essence of a restoration of Logos, the checking of 'infant' emotion (the unspeakable or unpresentable) by signifying law. The artwork thus, as it were, dramatises the maintenance of its own interpretability, the mythical struggle at the origin of Mosaic law emblematising the work's own struggle to wrench a comprehensible message from the obscure passion of its artistic genesis. In the same way, Freud's reading seeks to uphold the law of signification by literally cutting away the semiotic excess embodied by the statue's horns, the mark of a 'sinful' errancy that supervenes in the obscure transition between languages and between different forms of representation.

An all-too-Freudian approach to this interpretation of Freud's – one duly adopted by Ernest Jones in his biography – would re-inscribe the drama that Freud constructs 'behind' *Moses* as a version of another unconscious tragicomedy: namely, the struggle taking place around 1914 for authority in the psychoanalytic movement (principally, the conflict between Freud and Jung). One could even look for stylistic traits to support such a reading, perhaps finding a despairing 'unconscious' pun in 'the remnants of a terminated movement' that Freud observes in the statue's posture. In

Jones's opinion it is self-evident – nay, 'pretty obvious' – that Freud's recent troubles with his disciples have led him to identify with Moses the law-giver confronting the unruly crowd, a father caught between the onerous maintenance of the law and an unspeakable personal emotion.[28]

Such a reading by 'Professor' Jones (to give him his proper Joycean title) would dispel the enigma of Freud's obsessive fascination with Michelangelo's statue, restoring the psychological consistency of the master, and thus his authority; in short, it would restore the integrity of Freud's *name*. As an author (even one who sees fit to adopt the enigmatic mask of anonymity) Freud must be the site of 'motive forces' that can be accounted for, that make sense, that are law-abiding. Thus Jones, ever faithful to Freud, seeks to efface any trace of the aesthetic having disturbed or infiltrated the psycho-analytic narrative or encroached upon its proper – psychical or theoretical or political – terrain. In his account of Freud, Jones cuts away the semiotic excess that threatens to disfigure the narrative and jeopardise its legibility – just as Freud cut away the semiotic symptom of the *cornuta* from the head of Moses. Yet the signifying excess embodied by Freud's obsessive return to Michelangelo's artwork (as well as to *Hamlet*, a truly interminable Freudian analysis) is of course integral to the history of the discovery and develop-ment of psychoanalysis; for it corresponds to Freud's interpretative drive, the latter term designating an unmasterable erotic force, the jouissance that Lacan will explicitly contrast with pleasure. Jones's work amounts to an extended and thorough-going traduction of Freud (and here we might once again take the name *freudlich*): his biographical account systemati-cally deflects Freud's fantasmatic ecstasy in deciphering, in riddle-solving – transforming its symptomatic, 'aesthetic' opacity into a fully legible text: in a word, making it *Oedipal*.

IV

In his 1959 seminar on *Hamlet*, Lacan has fun holding up to ridicule inter-pretation of the Jonesian kind, with its appeal to the 'pretty obvious': such work, he declares with heavy irony, is best described as 'the psychoana-lytic wisdom of Polonius'. *C'est l'amour!* Lacan has a pantomimic Polonius shriek in response to Ophelia's account of Hamlet's odd behaviour; a comic version of the worst kind of 'applied psychoanalysis' (he is thinking of Ella Sharp's essay on *Hamlet*), which remains blind to the agency of the letter and prefers to deal with banal commonplaces – adolescent romance, rebel-lious disciples – rather than addressing the crucial Lacanian question of how to situate desire within an intricate weave of signification.[29]

Lacan's reading of *Hamlet* in Seminar 6 forms part of his effort to work out a theory of fantasy, or more precisely to isolate the relation between subject and object staged by fantasy. He therefore offers no anecdotal account of the artwork to restore its full legibility, but rather invokes aesthetic experience as testifying to some fundamental *opacity* – something *pas à lire*, beyond analysis – at the heart of our fantasmatic investments. As subjects, Lacan contends, we are always positioned in the fantasy relation, held in place by fascination there – and it is this that he finds illustrated by the scene of Hamlet gazing over his shoulder at Ophelia. Lacan seeks to encapsulate this fantasmatic positioning by writing a formula or 'matheme': $ \$ \lozenge a $. Between the divided speaking subject and the opaque, fantasmatic object a he inserts a lozenge to indicate what he describes as a relation of 'conjunction-disjunction', a tensely balanced pulling to and fro.[30] We shall return to this matheme and explore it as a speculative *topos* or figure of imaginative space that will provide a crucial resource in our readings of Joyce.

If for Lacan the Shakespearean text thus illustrates a relation of fantasy resistant to 'psychoanalytic wisdom' of the kind that would reduce what it represents to any 'pretty obvious' meaning, the 1959 seminar does not, however, take the next step: to ask whether the very relation between psychoanalysis and aesthetics might not be just such a relation of fantasy, of 'conjunction-disjunction'. For indeed, in our reading it is clear that Lacan's matheme of fantasy sheds a new light on Freud's perplexed manoeuvring around Michelangelo's statue: it stages his confrontation with an aesthetic trauma that seems to lie almost beyond the analytic gaze, at its outer limit. (Thus Freud's Hamlet-like hesitation about owning up to authorship: is this just inside – or just outside – psychoanalysis?) The aesthetic thing must be kept at precisely the right distance from psychoanalysis – near enough for the analytic subject to take up a position and elaborate a narrative, but not so near that distance collapses into uncanny doubling, loss of self-mastery. If Freud is, we might say, 'possessed' by the artwork – haunted by its enigmatic presence, enthralled by an enjoyment verging on something pathological – the fantasmatic theatre set out in his essay has a single, overriding aim: to convert this passive enthralment into active mastery, to *possess* the aesthetic thing by making it a legible, coherent object.

And here the notion of traduction is again useful, for it gives us another way of thinking the fantasmatic relation of 'conjunction-disjunction' between psychoanalysis and the aesthetic object. It is only by repeating the artwork's *traductio*, its semantic self-appropriation in the face of aesthetic madness or jouissance, that the analyst can pull off an impossible double gesture: at once joining it and maintaining a distance from it, identifying with and appropriating its traductive self-mastery or self-distancing.

If Freud, then, was able to establish his relation to *Hamlet* by doubling the play with *Oedipus* (and thus in a sense, as we have seen, himself 'unconsciously' doubling Hamlet), the essay on the *Moses* shows more vividly the reflexive logic of this Freudian narrative. The story of aesthetic (bodily, affective) disturbance and its control by the firm hand of the law narrates nothing so much as the semiotic upheaval provoked in psychoanalytic discourse by its fantasmatic confrontation with the aesthetic, how the 'Tables' on which it is inscribed begin to slip, then are returned to their proper place by the 'master-hand' Freud borrows from the artist in order to write his essay. Art thus both provokes the trauma jeopardising theory and guarantees its resolution in the theoretical recovery: it is theory's uncanny double.

The central paradox of 'Freudian aesthetics' (to use Lacan's phrase)[31] is that in order to assume a certain position before art – one that will mark a distance from the aesthetic, the warding-off of the affective turmoil it embodies – Freud's discourse has unconsciously or uncannily to mimic the traductive self-legislation of the artwork in question. Hence it is no surprise that the artworks that interest Freud always entail the reflexive mastery of the aesthetic, the portrayal of a law-bearing interpretative centre struggling to maintain its self-identity, its semantic consistency, in the face of some affective or semiotic disruption. For Freud to identify with the author of the work – taking up an identical position not 'psychologically', but in an uncanny traductive mimicry – is then also to subvert the very process seeking support in such an identification, which would establish a definitive, regulating distance between subject (or psychoanalysis) and traumatic enjoyment (or art). Our examination of the problematic of the double (in Chapter 5 below) will relate this question of the Freudian uncanny to Joycean writing.

v

Why then did we begin our reading of Freud's essay on 'The Moses of Michelangelo' by framing it with Lacan's quotation from *Hamlet*? We shall find an answer by turning to the seminar Lacan began a year after his seminars on *Hamlet*, namely Seminar 7, *The Ethics of Psychoanalysis*. There, Lacan first introduces to psychoanalytic theory an aesthetic motif that was bound to be especially appealing for literary and cultural critics, and which, by invoking it countless times in the subsequent decades, they were to turn into a veritable cliché of contemporary interpretation: namely, anamorphosis. But let us look closely at how in 1960 Lacan first introduces this by now all-too-familiar trope of theory:

[An anamorphosis] is any kind of construction that is made in such a way that by means of an optical transposition a certain form that wasn't visible at first sight transforms itself into a readable image. The pleasure is found in seeing its emergence from an indecipherable form.[32]

Lacan's first ever mention of anamorphosis is thus focused on the interpretative pleasure produced by deciphering, solving riddles or making things legible; and with this he certainly captures a crucial aspect of the psychoanalytic discourse on art, as we have seen it first taking shape in Freud. But anamorphosis was destined not merely to provide Lacan with a way of rethinking Freudian aesthetics; by 1964, when he takes the figure up again in Seminar 11, *The Four Fundamental Concepts of Psychoanalysis*, the full extent of Lacan's ambition for the trope has become apparent. Turning to Holbein's painting *The Ambassadors*, Lacan now outlines a project that is 'uncommonly audacious', as Malcolm Bowie puts it: namely, 'to write into the text of psychoanalysis the terms and conditions of its own impossibility'.[33] The psychoanalytic reference to aesthetics is no longer the purloining of interpretative self-mastery we identified as Freudian traduction but, it would seem, its very antithesis; for, in Lacan's eyes, Holbein's painting now shows us something precisely beyond analysis, impossible to transpose into a readable image. The 'paradox' of Lacanian theory here is often noted by critics: if the anamorphic stain is invoked as an index of the illegible, the intractable or untreatable, psychoanalysis must somehow have been able, in a topological torsion worthy of Escher, to include its own outside.

What critics have been less sensitive to in their eager adoption of an anamorphic 'real' lying both within and mysteriously beyond the text are the specifically clinical resonances of this psychoanalytic involution of something 'beyond theory'. For the outside of theory in question here is not some safe realm of praxis or of the rich singularity of the world, as unfortunately Lacan's use of the term 'the real' tends surreptitiously to imply. It corresponds, rather, to the problematic – in effect a constantly shifting challenge for psychoanalysis and its theory – of psychosis and thus, for Lacan, of foreclosure (and ultimately that of psychoanalytic nosology and topography in general). For psychoanalysis to write its 'own impossibility', in Bowie's phrase, into the theoretical text would thus correspond to the

internalisation of the untreatable; and Lacan's work moves with increasing emphasis towards a will to exclude psychoanalysis from the cycle of
traduction (of repetition, re-presentation, transfer, allegory) and even ultimately to identify the analyst with a certain 'psychotic' withdrawal from
socio-symbolic circulation. One of the ironies of 'applied psychoanalysis' –
a phrase that particularly annoyed Lacan – would thus be the extraordinary
popular currency it has given to anamorphosis as a tool of cultural criticism. It is as if the interpretative pleasure that Lacan first saw intriguingly
enacted by anamorphosis in his 1960 seminar had wholly engulfed and
subsumed his later attempt to gloss the trope as figuring the untranslatable,
the unworkable.

It is anamorphosis in this ambiguous sense, then, that provides an answer
to our question about how the Freudian traduction of art, as seen with
exemplary clarity in the essay on Michelangelo's *Moses*, can be understood
through an engagement with Lacan's reading of *Hamlet* – and in turn how
Lacan's turn to the aesthetic both forms part of the same psychoanalytic
tradition and is an effort to outdo or subvert that inheritance. Moreover, the
aim of the Freudian 'Mousetrap' – to posit an original Oedipal 'soil', both
sin and earth, out of which *Hamlet* grew – makes clear that the scenario of
filial traduction, of sons reworking the paternal will to consolidate or undo
it, goes back at least as far as Shakespeare's text.

One of the few critics to have linked a literary consideration of anamorphosis to Lacan's concept of foreclosure is Marjorie Garber.[34] In proposing that Hamlet is haunted by an 'anamorphic ghost', she connects the
prince's crisis of self-representation to the Lacanian – and eminently Shakespearean – theme of the failure of paternal metaphor: in other words,
the lack of signifying legitimacy that troubles Hamlet is equivalent to a
breakdown in the traduction or transmission of identification, of semantic assimilation, between generations.[35] It is of course unclear whether
this is because, as Freud may have thought, *Hamlet* exemplifies a specific pathology that might be ascribed to its author, or rather bears witness
to something inherently impossible or impassable within socio-symbolic
structure.

An anamorphic reading of *Hamlet* would therefore emphasise what the
play stages as an insistent crisis of meaning, a struggle to resolve and restore
to signifying consistency what has been left 'out of joint' (I.v.196) by
the withdrawal of paternal authority. The central ambiguity here would
bear directly on the potential significance of any psychoanalytic reading
of Shakespeare's play: does the 'crisis' enacted correspond to some specific
pathology (relating to the death of fathers and its Oedipal framework, as

Freud speculates) or rather to a general failure of language to signify or represent fully, consistently?

One aspect of the play where it stages its non-traduction, its presentation of the subject in language as failing to achieve a solution or adequate symbolisation, is clearly wherever it touches on sexual relations. If we return to the scenario on which, as we have seen, Lacan dwells at some length in Seminar 6 – that of Hamlet's fascinated perusal of Ophelia, as reported by her to Polonius in Act II scene i – we might use anamorphosis as a way to figure Hamlet as having 'lost the way of his desire', as Lacan puts it.[36] The subject in this tableau comes face to face with something indecipherable in the other sex, and is caught in a desperate effort to transfer this enigmatic blur to the realm of representation – 'He falls to such perusal of my face / As a would draw it' (II.i.90–1): Hamlet's agonised gaze corresponds to the search for the right position to bring about the anamorphic transformation, dissolve the enigma and encounter the object in its truth, as something properly named or identified. We might argue that Garber's conception of the ghost of Hamlet's father as anamorphic is still bound up with a certain 'Oedipal' desire to locate, like the guards in the play's opening scene, the fantasmatic 'thing' at once haunting, eluding and disfiguring representation. But, as Hamlet's first response to the ghost indicates, it is the entire realm of signification that is in jeopardy, under threat of being 'dismantled' ('I'll wipe away all trivial fond records': I.v.99); indeed, the play as a whole, its entire textual surface, is suffused with a sense of its non-traduction, its failure to embody the 'thing'. And at the very beginning of the play, before his ghostly encounter, Hamlet is already an eloquent theorist of the unspeakable, notably in the role of a son addressing his mother. When Gertrude questions her son about his excessive identification with mourning – 'Why seems it so particular with thee?' (I.ii.75) – she is met with the famous Socratic response that rejects the terms of the question – indeed, ultimately rejects language as such as a means to 'denote me truly': for, the son declares, 'I have that within which passes show' (85). Hamlet has, he feels, something irreducible to any objective correlative, an inner wealth immune to traduction, beyond troping or trapping.

The Shakespearean text immediately provides a clue to our psychoanalytic (and Joycean) interpretation here by having Claudius – as sham father and fraudulent king – describe Hamlet's posture as one of 'unmanly grief' (94). Here we can see how *Hamlet* itself actually sheds light on the interpretative strategies seemingly brought to it by Freudian theory and Joycean writing (although this is not to dismiss the irresolvable problem of the origin of ideas): that is, Hamlet's withdrawal into 'unmanly grief' – and, to a Lacanian ear, the diagnosis certainly rings true – marks the emergence of that which is precisely irreducible to traduction, that which is isolated by psychoanalysis as significant detail or symptom and yet which conversely defies being caught in the semiotic mousetrap of Freud's theory. Like Stephen with his parodic-naive biographical reading of Shakespeare in 'Scylla and Charybdis', Freud wishes to see the enigmatic subject of *Hamlet*, its 'I', bounded in the nutshell of a neat interpretative solution. Among the 'bad dreams' that prevent such a convenient *Lösung* from being realised is the rich excess here designated by Hamlet as 'that within which passes show': something 'particular', as Gertrude puts it, irreducible to the general exchange of signifiers. Now, for a subject to identify with an untranslatable particular, something impossible to reduce to a symbolic formula, is a distinctively feminine position, or so Lacan argues in his seminar *Encore*.[37] By adopting such a position – and Claudius' accusation comes to take on a dark irony as Shakespeare's tragedy unfolds – Hamlet is thus breaking the law. The father-king is attempting to reinforce the institutional coherence of the royal and legal court with this demand that the subject submit to self-disclosure, and accept the reduction or traduction of his fantasmatic interiority to arbitrary signifiers.

In *Ulysses*, Bloom wonders at one point whether Hamlet might have actually been a woman (and whether indeed that might be the play's secret, explaining such mysteries as 'Why Ophelia committed suicide': *U* 5.296–7). Joyce's subtle humour – tinged of course with darkness, suicide not being at all funny in Bloom's mind – reprises a very Shakespearean theme: that of exploring how positions in language, in particular those relating to the *limits* of language, are bound up with sexual identity. *Finnegans Wake* will spell things out more clearly when it poses as 'the first riddle of the universe' the question: 'when is a man not a man?' (*FW* 170.4–5) This question will return throughout our argument, notably in Part II, when we shall explore Joycean readings or raidings of Shakespeare (especially *Othello* and *Macbeth*), and of the 'Zweispaltung' (*FW* 296.8) doubled by and split between texts by Hogg, Stevenson and Wilde.

In one sense, then, it is already clear that when psychoanalysis, with its ceaseless return to Shakespearean texts, addresses questions of sexuality in language, it takes up the 'sehm asnuh' (*FW* 620.17), reprising some very old literary preoccupations. Indeed, as Lacan's teaching develops it becomes increasingly preoccupied with a Hamletesque sense of 'that within which passes show', with a jouissance that paradoxically both inhabits and exceeds linguistic forms. If that teaching, grounded in the talking cure, moved progressively towards a silent monstration that seeks somehow to present the unspeakable, one of the singular ironies of the reception of Lacan's work – above all in Anglophone literary criticism – has been the ceaseless flood of theoretical loquacity it has inspired. How has this verbose traduction taken place and what are its consequences for literary theory – and for Joycean criticism in particular?

CHAPTER 3

The pleasures of mistranslation

In German Hasidism, it is the word rather than the alphabetic sign whose hidden sense and unaltered preservation are of extreme importance. To mutilate a single word in the Torah, to set it in the wrong order, might be to imperil the tenuous links between fallen man and the Divine presence. Already the Talmud had said: 'the omission or the addition of one letter might mean the destruction of the whole world.' Certain *illuminati* went so far as to suppose that it was some error of transcription, however minute, made by the scribe to whom God had dictated holy writ, that brought on the darkness and turbulence of the world.

George Steiner, *After Babel*[1]

I

In 1975, the year when Lacan began his seminar on Joyce, there was at least one other significant transcription between French thought and Anglophone literary culture: the appearance in English translation of a brief work by Roland Barthes entitled *The Pleasure of the Text*. Barthes's book posed some tricky problems for the translator, the most troublesome of which, as Richard Howard comments in a prefatory note, being to find a single English term to render *jouissance*. The lack of a suitable English equivalent for this word – which in modern French encompasses a range of senses of enjoyment or possession, from rarefied appreciation to sexual orgasm – leads Howard to the rather gloomy conclusion that, in English, 'the nomenclature of active pleasure fails us'.[2]

The question of the limits of translation to be considered in this chapter will provide us with a way to focus more sharply on our notion of traduction and to discover its peculiar resonance for our engagement with Joycean writing. Examining the translations of influential post-structuralist texts by Barthes and Shoshana Felman, we shall consider the fate of

55

the word *jouissance* – or, more precisely, what becomes of the particular
linguistic problem that that word designates for Lacan – in the transition,
the risky transference, from French to English. We shall find in this both
an exemplary instance of theoretical traduction and an insight into how
the use of psychoanalytic concepts in literary criticism can illuminate our
reading of Joyce.

At first glance, perhaps, the fact that the *jouissance* in Barthes's text
cannot be translated into English might seem perversely appropriate. For
according to Barthes's own declaration, featured indeed on the back cover of
the French edition, 'le propre de la jouissance, c'est de ne pouvoir être dite'
('the distinguishing characteristic of *jouissance* is that it cannot be spoken');
so that if, in English, 'our words for our pleasures . . . come awkwardly when
they come at all', to quote again from Howard's preface, we might at least
find consolation in the notion that this cultural inarticulacy corresponds to
something, as it were, in itself 'inarticulate' – that is, something impossible
to chain up in discourse.

But the task of Barthes's translator Richard Miller remains: to render a
coherent English version of *Le plaisir du texte*. And unlike many a subsequent translator of French texts – notably those who will deliver English
versions of Lacan – Miller eschews the 'easy option' (a phrase we may have
to reconsider) of leaving the term *jouissance* untranslated, set off in spicy
italics from the drab surface of the English text. Instead, Miller has 'come
up with the readiest plausibility', Howard thinks, by translating *jouissance*
as 'bliss'.[3]

Translation will always entail interpretative choices that render certain
aspects or connotations of the source text and its language invisible, cut
them off or misrepresent them. But what is 'lost in translation', as the
revealing cliché has it, is of particular interest to us here as readers of Joyce.
The movement between languages to which Joyce gave such prominence as
both theme and source of his writing serves as a crucial portal of discovery, a
privileged point of symptomatic error giving on to a paradoxical *remainder*
in language: an element which – without being simply 'beyond language',
safely ensconced in some reassuring realm of self-identity – remains irreducible to traduction, to the semantic appropriation governing the predominant practice of translation and its history. The turbulence caused
by *jouissance* in the English text, with its apologetic preface, already seems
to point to such a remainder, to something non-traductible or asemic. If
jouissance were untranslatable, it would shatter the illusion of a referential
theory of meaning, evoking a point in language where the semantic network paradoxically exceeds itself, collapses to an illegible singularity. 'That
within which passes show', perhaps.

But to return to the English translation of Barthes – if the source is *jouissance*, for the receptor language to respond with 'bliss' seems nothing less than an attempt to hoodwink the Anglophone reader. What such a translation makes invisible is precisely the source of *jouissance*. For the translator of Barthes's text cannot avoid contending with another kind of 'translation' (although the assumed equivalence here remains to be examined): that is, the transference or exchange between the literary domain and psychoanalysis. To seek to understand Barthes's text (and perhaps also his 'pleasure of the text') is to attend to a subtle, edgy dialogue with psychoanalysis, the wary deployment of a body of ideas that struggles against any merely reductive application of those ideas. Nevertheless, the primary conceptual baggage of *Le plaisir du texte* looks like a direct import from Lacanian psychoanalysis: namely, the distinction between *plaisir* (pleasure) and *jouissance*. If Barthes, as he declares, would have these two terms constantly 'vacillate' in his discourse, nervous of any trace of theoretical closure or teleology, he cannot avoid, given that he chooses to use both terms and not simply one of them, also quoting the antinomy or antagonism that Lacan saw them as designating. *Jouissance* is, as Miller notes, 'the more ravaging term', and in Lacan's view it names something far from blissful; indeed, he locates it, like the Freudian death-drive, 'beyond the pleasure principle'.[4]

Barthes's discourse on textual pleasure thus circles around, and constantly risks collapsing into, something unspeakable called *jouissance*. (Note that the back cover of *The Pleasure of the Text* in its English edition specifically omits any mention of *jouissance* from its paraphrase of the original note by Barthes, adding instead that the book is a 'classic' and one of its author's 'canonical' works.) What is transcribed from psychoanalysis to the literary domain thus includes, paradoxically enough, a term that designates the unspeakable, that which is impossible to articulate – and presumably also therefore that which *eludes transcription*. Barthes considers only obliquely and allusively the question of critical methodology that is raised by this ostensible transcription or translation in his essay – apart from at a single point. There, it is directly addressed in a brief paragraph set entirely in parenthesis; this paragraph, together with Miller's translation of it, will repay our close examination:

(Le monument psychanalytique doit être traversé – non contourné, comme les voies admirables d'une très grande ville, voies à travers lesquelles on peut jouer, rêver, etc.: c'est une fiction.)

(The monument of psychoanalysis must be traversed – not bypassed – like the fine thoroughfares of a very large city, across which we can play, dream, etc.: a fiction.)[5]

It is certainly rare, in this gentle, playfully aphoristic text, for Barthes to strike such an imperative tone – '*doit* être traversé'. (Indeed, this may be why he chooses to set off the remark by enclosing it in brackets.) Miller's mistranslation here is as significant as – and indeed, we shall argue, is strictly consistent with – his traductive conversion of *jouissance* to 'bliss'.

The most striking semantic alteration in Miller's translation is its re-punctuation of the passage: by adding an extra dash, he confines the verb *contourné* to a parenthetical clause, thus separating it semantically from the main sentence. The effect of this, along with (in my view) a mistranslation of the term itself, is actually to *reverse* the sense of the text – or rather, to keep to Barthes's metaphor, to reverse its *sens*, its 'trajectory'. In the French text, a single dash followed by a series of commas indicates the emphatic opening of a non-restrictive clause leading to a colon that introduces the final point. As well as perhaps meaning 'bypassed', the word *contourné* can mean – according to the *Robert* dictionary – 'walk (or drive etc.) around'. So we might re-translate the passage as follows:

(The monument of psychoanalysis must be traversed – not strolled around like the fine thoroughfares of a very large city where we can play, dream, etc.: this is a fiction.)

In other words, Barthes is precisely *not* insisting that we enjoy the leafy avenues of a Freudian metropolis like idle cultural day-trippers, delighting in the pleasures offered by this 'fiction' (note how Miller cuts down *c'est une fiction*, which declares 'this (last thing mentioned)' to be a fiction, to the non-restrictive 'a fiction', which we can refer back more easily to the subject of the sentence, 'the monument of psychoanalysis'). Barthes's point, indeed, is to contrast this fiction – the fantasy of a leisurely stroll around psychoanalysis, without responsibility and where, crucially, time is suspended – with another approach, consisting in 'traversing' the psychoanalytic 'monument', going straight through it and moving on. This opposition between a direct, decisive traversal and a bit of pleasant *flânerie* is entirely undone by Miller's translation, the 'straightforward' *sens* reversed, diverted into aimless drifting ('play, dream, etc.'). In English, it seems, Barthes says the very opposite of what he says in French. We shall come back to consider some of the possible objections to this compressed reading of Barthes, and its implications for Anglophone literary theory.

First, let us try to clarify the sense for our argument of this apparently obscure sidetrack into questions of translation. We shall start by proposing a reading of Barthes that will seem too abrupt to do justice to his evasive, playful text: namely, that with his contrast between two ways for a cultural theorist to visit the psychoanalytic monument – direct traversal versus leisurely tourism – Barthes enacts or encapsulates the very opposition between *jouissance* and *plaisir* that proves so elusive for the translator. In other words, in this sketch of a possible relation between literary criticism and psychoanalysis, Barthes touches on the problem of representing a more radical opposition: between, on one side, an experience of pleasure defined as an instantly recognisable, fully translatable domain (we all have our favourite texts, scenes, etc.); and, on the other, a libidinal investment or involvement defined precisely as the disruption of that domain of easy legibility or identification. And, Barthes implies, it is pleasure – or more precisely: the fantasmatic *management* of pleasure – that characterises the misguided 'critic as tourist' approach to psychoanalysis.

In that case, what would the critical 'traversal' of psychoanalysis entail? Here, Barthes refrains from explicit comment, but perhaps *Le plaisir du texte* as a whole could be understood as an effort to bring about, to *perform*, a certain non-appropriative engagement with psychoanalysis: an attempt to explore its interpretative potential for criticism without at the same time effacing the specificity of its discursive site or praxis by folding it into some general scheme of legibility. And of course it is jouissance – defined by Lacan and Barthes as ultimately irreducible to discourse, unspeakable – that constitutes the singularity of psychoanalytic praxis. Jouissance, to be precise, is what defines the experience of psychoanalysis as ultimately untranslatable, impossible to appropriate or transfer to another scene of writing.

Miller's translation of the passage into English, then, expunges any trace of the opposition we have sketched, between an easy, pleasurable appropriation of psychoanalysis by the critic and another kind of approach, a criticism that might give weight to the disruptive, untameable linguistic force of jouissance. By having Barthes address us like a travel agent, blandly urging us not to 'bypass' psychoanalysis but to enjoy its 'fine thoroughfares', Miller effectively reverses the rhetorical impetus, reducing it to the standard poststructuralist view of psychoanalysis as simply yet another fictional resource to be freely exploited by theory. In other words, we conclude, Miller seeks to translate the *jouissance* of Barthes's text into bliss.

II

Before we consider more closely the implications of the theoretical traduction at work in the translation of Barthes, let us turn to another, perhaps clearer instance of the same process, in another highly influential exponent of the poststructuralist transaction between psychoanalysis and literary criticism: Shoshana Felman. Her work is especially germane to our exploration of translation, for it concerns (indeed, it seeks to *entail*) 'seduction in two languages', to quote one of Felman's subtitles. Poised between French and English, Parisian and American intellectual milieux, Felman transfers and translates from one to the other with seductive ease and in a manner that, as we shall see, both illuminates and curiously enacts the problematic of traduction.

La Folie et la chose littéraire was published by Felman in 1978, and then translated into English (with its author's assistance) as *Writing and Madness*, after a long delay, in 1985. It is immediately clear from these two titles that something has vanished from the original French version: namely, *la chose*, the 'thing'. 'To speak about madness', writes Felman in the introduction to the English edition, 'is to speak about the difference between languages: to import into one language the strangeness of another' (19). *La chose littéraire*, 'the literary thing', was, however, clearly too strange to be imported into English. What significance can we attribute to this *défaut de traduction* (as Felman translates a Freudian definition of repression)? There is, Felman writes in her concluding comments, a 'dynamic *resistance to interpretation* inherent in the literary thing' (254; emphasis original); perhaps then, by substituting for *la chose littéraire* the bland generality of 'writing', her English title would introduce a work harbouring less resistance to interpretation, less linguistic strangeness, less madness.

Or perhaps we could put things more directly and say that the title *Writing and Madness* simply designates a work with *less psychoanalysis* in it; but this calls for a brief elaboration of what is implied by Felman's use in 1978 of the term *la chose*. The key here is the notion of 'resistance to interpretation' (and, we could add, resistance to translation, noting how the English text, when it does not simply delete *la chose* in favour of 'literature', struggles to render it in cumbersome phrases such as 'the thing called literature' or, elsewhere, for the same phrase in the original French, 'the peculiar thing called literature': 16–17). Something about 'the literary thing' thus resists our reading, and encumbers or drags against our attempts to enmesh it in a discursive network or introduce it to an economy of signifying exchange or translation.

And the source of this resistance to discourse, so to speak, is clearly identifiable. In 1959 Lacan, in his seminar on *The Ethics of Psychoanalysis*, had presented his audience with 'An Introduction to the Thing', in which he had picked out a term used by Freud in his 1895 'Project for a Scientific Psychology', *das Ding*, to designate an element radically exterior to or foreclosed from the symbolic order, embodying a 'prehistoric Other that it is impossible to forget'.[6] At the level of desiring subjectivity and its circulating signifiers, Lacan asserts, 'the Thing is not nothing, but literally is not. It is characterised by its absence, its strangeness' (63). Lacan goes on to redefine the psychoanalytic notion of sublimation as the elevation of an object 'to the dignity of the Thing' (112), and gives a famous literary example of this in Sophocles' *Antigone*.

The notion of *la chose* as an element alien to discourse, essentially unspeakable, then, as introduced by Lacan, was already bound up with the literary (and, in this, seemed to echo a familiar post-Romantic aesthetic ideology, with literature held to embody the remnants of a language of full archaic spontaneity, of non-alienated immediacy, etc.). By taking up this literary-psychoanalytic *chose*, and by explicitly associating it with madness, Felman clearly seeks to transfer to literary criticism the Lacanian problematic of 'something beyond, something at the point of origin of the signifying chain', to quote again from Seminar 7 (214).

Now, as we saw in our reading of Barthes, this 'something' that disrupts interpretation or resists discursive appropriation is nothing less than psychoanalysis itself, in the sense that its practice comprises a singular, performative dimension irreducible to the generalising equivalence at work in all theory. Another name Lacan gives to this 'something', of course, is *jouissance*.

In the long period between the appearance in 1978 of *La Folie et la chose littéraire* and its translation in 1985, Felman published another work, one whose translation into English took place more rapidly and, for our purposes, more revealingly. If in the earlier work *la chose* had been partially 'repressed', emerging only in a distorted form (as a 'peculiar' thing) from the *défaut de traduction*, the translation of the later book shows more clearly, perhaps with less restraint, the overall logic of traduction. Again, though, the transformation of Felman's original French title speaks volumes; this time, the splendid *Le Scandale du corps parlant* becomes *The Literary Speech Act*, a rather desiccated academic formula, notably lacking both scandal and body.

While it is tempting to draw rapid conclusions from the translation of Felman's titles, which seems to carry out so manifestly the erasure or repression of a scandalous (French) thing or body from the scholarly groves of (Anglophone) theory, we should read further before we attempt to formulate more precisely what this traduction entails. It is nevertheless worth bearing in mind the quasi-Wildean principle put forward by Lacan in his 'Seminar on *The Purloined Letter*': namely, that the most obvious or most superficial may, from a psychoanalytic perspective, be the hardest to decipher.

The Literary Speech Act, then, for all the chastity of its English title, still centres on what Felman terms 'the scandal of the performative' as broached in the work of J. L. Austin. The Oxford philosopher is saucily accused of introducing a 'Donjuanism' to the study of language with his 1955 lectures *How to Do Things with Words*. So in what does Austin's feckless libidinal bravado consist? 'Ainsi, comme Don Juan,' writes Felman, 'Austin, lui aussi, introduit dans la pensée du langage la dimension de *jouissance*, bien distincte de celle de la connaissance.'[7] It is because Austin introduced to linguistics *jouissance*, that wayward 'thing' that makes so many translators unfaithful, that Felman likens him to Molière's scandalous seducer. And, talking of unfaithful translation, we should examine what Felman's English translator makes of this passage: 'Thus, like Don Juan, Austin too introduces into thinking about language the dimension of *pleasure*, quite distinct from that of knowledge.'[8] The major problem with translating *jouissance* in Felman's text as 'pleasure', even leaving aside the initial semantic problems we touched on in our reading of Barthes, is that the same English word is used to render the French *plaisir* when it occurs a few pages later in the same text. What is thus made to disappear is not merely a significant difference but a veritable antagonism, one whose formulation by psychoanalysis was apparently anticipated by Baudelaire, in an epigram quoted by Felman (and which serves above as our epigraph to Part I): 'Dans l'amour comme dans presque toutes les affaires humaines, l'entente cordiale est le résultat d'un malentendu. Ce malentendu, c'est le plaisir.'

Pleasure involves misunderstanding, mistranslation. To translate both *jouissance* and *plaisir* indiscriminately as 'pleasure' is to make the point, we might say, performatively: to 'do with words' the *malentendu*, rather than simply representing or expressing it. And this misunderstanding produces an *entente cordiale* between the French text and its English translation: in other words it rids their relation of any trace of that linguistic strangeness or madness Felman praises in her 1978 work; traduction can be seen here as a performative, an *act*, that of rendering legible, appropriable, appropriate, proper. The paradox – and this will be central in our further exploration of traduction – is that what distinguishes this particular 'speech-act' is the erasure of the act as such, or at least of what Felman sees as its constitutive dimension.

Let us look more closely at Felman's suggestive portrait of Austin as Don Juan. In what precise sense is the philosopher supposed by her to have introduced to linguistic theory an unprecedented, ungovernable jouissance? Felman certainly waxes lyrical about Austin's constant reliance on the marriage ceremony as a privileged example of the performative, with its 'I do' emblematising the pure speech act (152–3; 108–9). But this playful reference to the institutional regulation of sexuality can hardly be thought to amount to a philosophical scandal, the introduction of a bodily dimension in excess of any conceivable epistemology. Could we perhaps, then, define the performative itself precisely as a linguistic *act*, in terms that would link it to jouissance, to what Felman calls its 'constitutive dimension'? Here, we need to attend carefully to Austin's discourse: 'the act of marrying', he comments drolly, 'like, say, the act of betting, is at least *preferably* . . . to be described as *saying certain words*, rather than as performing a different, inward and spiritual, action of which these words are merely the outward and audible sign'.[9]

The crucial point here is that for Austin the speech act has no psychical correlative; it does not emanate from some 'inward and spiritual' action that would constitute its truth, the original of which it would be a mere re-presentation: in other words, the illocutionary force of the speech act is irreducible to an intention, an 'I'.

The speech act, as described by Austin, thus emerges as a veritable *coincidentia oppositorum*. If on the one hand it is entirely citational, a question of iterating the correct verbal formula at the required moment regardless of any inner state or spiritual condition, on the other it is utterly singular, the unique moment of my ceremonial declaration being impossible to repeat or quote. The speech act is both completely devoid of semantic depth, a pure semblance or rhetorical sham (an 'act' in one sense of the word in English), and at the same time possessed of a singular *weight* as contractual or legal 'deed', a weight that other signifiers entirely lack. And it is this peculiar double status that recalls the *dimension de jouissance*, which Felman links to the speech act and would set in opposition to any epistemology: for jouissance, like the performative, is both 'thing-like' and lacking any psychological depth, at once pure signifying surface and 'beyond words'. 'As Lacan put it,' comments Monique David-Ménard, 'no one can say "*je jouis*"':[10] the ego cannot inhabit or cohabit with jouissance, cannot appropriate or actively possess it; in other words, the subject's relation to jouissance is always passive or passionate, one not of possessing but of being possessed. Moreover, as we have seen, jouissance has the peculiar quality of evoking 'something beyond' language in the ordinary sense, of indicating a point of singularity or materiality that always resists 'translation' into a verbal equivalent.

The dimension of jouissance is thus clearly distinct from that of knowledge, first in that the 'I' does not govern it and next in that it does not refer to any identifiable object. Likewise, the performative speech act, where the 'I' dwindles to a mere catechistic response or quotation and where language 'is not *about* something; *it is that something itself*',[11] cannot be included within the sphere of epistemological judgements, of the *constative*, to use Austin's term. Another way to put this might be to place the performative alongside jouissance as a parallel instance of a special kind of non-translatability: not the property of a meaningless smudge, but that of a certain *autotelic* or self-grounding, self-enclosed moment in language (but therefore also in a sense 'outside' language, beyond its diacritical constituency). Such an instance would by the same token be illegible, impossible to identify or identify with; and it is here that we return to the crucial question of translation. For what is the pleasure of the text, as seen in the seductive and productive mistranslations at work in Barthes and Felman, but a resounding confirmation of Baudelaire's epigram: in other words, precisely a *malentendu* or traduction that would efface the dimension of jouissance by re-situating it within the sphere of knowledge, of the epistemic 'I' and its discrete object? To translate *jouissance* as pleasure (or as 'bliss' for that matter) is in effect to reinstate the appropriative and semantic 'I', to restore the *entente cordiale* governing the transaction between the subject and the otherness it confronts in the 'thing' – indeed, to give that recalcitrant thing back to the subject in the guise of an integral 'object'.

What we see taking place in the translations of these singularly influential theoretical texts, then, is more than a simple falsification of original meaning. Rather, the semiotic transformation or traduction involved entails precisely an injection of the semantic, the rendering meaningful of an original moment ungoverned by the 'I', by semantic appropriation. Traduction here is a matter of *turning jouissance into pleasure*; and this would entail the act of turning away from a certain 'irreversible' moment – something impossible to 'turn' or trope – an entry into a domain of authorial control and, above all, of *eternal legibility*, where the blissful exfoliation of meaning would be sheltered from alteration or temporal decay in a 'monument', to recall one of Barthes's metaphors.

In this study we have borrowed an anachronistic term, *traduction*, to designate this movement by which a subject or a theory transforms and appropriates – in effect, incorporates – something radically alien to it, beyond its language, something illegible or intractable. Indeed, 'traduction' reveals itself to be a singular *Knotenpunkt* or 'nodal point' (to use a Freudian expression): it unites a fertile cluster of linguistic chains, all of which expand

and complicate the semiotic richness of the term. In the first place, traduction is an obsolete term for 'transference' and 'translation' (we shall return to this crucial pairing in psychoanalysis); but it can also have meanings as diverse as 'transmission to offspring' and 'defaming, calumny', the latter sense deriving from those conquered or disgraced being 'traduced' by their captors, led along as a spectacle, exposed to public shame. And crucially, along this last linguistic chain, Milton uses the word to mean 'to falsify, misrepresent, pervert' (talking of a 'licentious Glosse which traduc't the Law').[12] Traduction, as we shall see, at once translates and misrepresents, transfers and traduces, what it appropriates. More specifically, it renders semantic what it thus simultaneously purges of a disruptive otherness: an insoluble or non-analysable, intractable or untreatable jouissance.

III

Having thus begun to outline the nature of traduction and its effects, we should situate it more clearly in relation to other works of criticism that have addressed the question of translation – most significantly, George Steiner's *After Babel* (1975) and Fritz Senn's *Joyce's Dislocutions* (1984). We shall subsequently engage in detailed readings of Joyce in order to explore the central ambiguity of the relation between psychoanalytic interpretation and the literary field. But let us open a first Joycean 'portal of discovery' on the question of traduction by transposing an observation from *After Babel*. There, Steiner writes:

An error, a misreading initiates the modern history of our subject [i.e. the field of translation and interpretation]. Romance languages derive their terms for 'translation' from *traducere* because Leonardo Bruni misinterpreted a sentence in the *Noctes* of Aulus Gellius in which the Latin actually signifies 'to introduce, to lead into'. The point is trivial but symbolic. Often, in the records of translation, a fortunate misreading is the source of new life.[13]

Thus, in a curious metalinguistic twist, the very word for – and therefore inevitably the concept of – translation is originally based on a *mis*translation; its implicit metaphor of faithful transmission is, as it were, belied by its own mistaken conception. And best of all, from a Joycean perspective, this *felix culpa* or fortunate error was perpetrated (at least if we are to trust Steiner's account) by a named individual, a veritable 'foenix culprit' (*FW* 23.16): one Leonardo Bruni. Having thus been identified as primal *mis*translator, Bruni emerges as a figure of archetypal significance for Joyce. Although Joyce may not actually have known of his work, Bruni's name will be caught up, through the unaccountable accidents of language, in the intricate textual knots of Joycean artifice.

Leonardo Bruni (1370–1444) is one of the seminal figures of early Renaissance humanism and the author of, among many other texts, *De interpretatione recta* (1424) (a title translated, with a certain irony in the light of Steiner's comments, as 'On the Correct Way to Translate'). This treatise bore on questions relating to one of the principal scholarly tasks that Bruni set himself: the translation of ancient Greek texts into Latin in order to make them accessible to a European scholarly community still largely ignorant of Greek.[14] 'The whole essence of translation', declares Bruni there, 'is to transfer correctly what is written in one language into another language' (218). Such a resoundingly 'modern' view was in sharp contrast to the 'literalist' conception that had previously governed translation, and indeed marks a significant advance towards modern notions of meaning, intention and authorship. Joyce, whether or not he knew of Leonardo Bruni, would certainly have relished the idea that the scholar who had first 'introduced' translation to the modern era as in principle the faultless exchange of semantic plenitude ('alteration is the translator's sin', as Bruni puts it (207)) in fact did so on the basis of a *mis*reading, a straying from original sense.

The name of Bruni, however, would have meant something altogether different to Joyce – and here we touch on one of the salient features of Joycean writing, often rediscovered with a mixture of consternation and delight by critics: its implication in and exploitation of a network of unlikely semiotic coincidences.[15] For, as Ellmann reports, it was Alessandro Francini, a friend of Joyce's and his colleague at the Berlitz schools in Pola and Trieste, who, 'to distinguish himself from the multitude of other Francinis, had added his wife's name Bruni to his own' (*JJ* 186). And it was this self-styled Bruni who much later (in 1922) was to give a lecture entitled *Joyce intimo spogliato in piazza* ('Joyce stripped naked in the piazza': clearly a kind of traducement or exposure to public mockery). Portraying Joyce 'in Chaplinesque caricature' (as Ellmann puts it: *JJ* 218), Bruni spoke of his old friend as 'a composite of incompatibles' (recalling, perhaps unwittingly, the *coincidentia oppositorum* that had so struck the young Joyce when he discovered it in Giordano Bruno – but we shall come to him shortly). More immediately, in 1905, Bruni and Joyce entered into a kind of linguistic exchange, with lessons given in Tuscan Italian on one side and in Dublin English on the other. (Needless to say, though, Joyce 'traduced' Bruni by failing to fulfil his side of the bargain.) They even, adds Ellmann, thought at one point of working together on a translation.

The adoption and adaptation, transplantation and translation of names form a central preoccupation, almost a signature, of Joyce's art. The 'proper' name (where the quotation marks indicate how Joyce's writing raises proto-deconstructive questions around the iteration and reproducibility of names, as has of course been acknowledged and elaborated by Jacques Derrida)[16] entails semiotic possibilities that are ceaselessly exploited, exposed, trans-muted and displaced in Joycean writing. Indeed, when in *Ulysses* Bloom's name appears amid the 'nonsensical howlers of misprints' in a newspa-per report as 'L. Boom' (*U* 16.1260), the disfigured name might serve as an ironic index of the semiotic explosion or over-production potentially triggered by automatic – or rather, telegraphic – accidents of language.

One such accident, hinging on a single letter, takes us from Bruni – the name, as we have seen, shared by a man who introduced translation to Euro-pean culture through a mistranslation of *traducere* and another who intro-duced Joyce to Italian and then 'traduced' or exposed him in the piazza – to Bruno. Giordano Bruno (1548–1600) has long been recognised as one of the seminal influences on the intellectual development of the young Joyce; indeed, ever since Beckett's pioneering essay in *Our Exagmination* critics have looked to Bruno as a major inspiration and conceptual root of all Joycean writing (and perhaps of *Finnegans Wake* above all). According to his brother Stanislaus, Joyce thought at one point of becoming an actor and even considered adopting Bruno's name – translated, of course, as Gordon Brown – as a stage-name.[17] And when the young Joyce dubbed Bruno 'the heresiarch martyr of Nola' he used terms that would resound throughout his subsequent writings.

What is the sense, though, of entangling our argument in this Joycean web of semiotic coincidence? And how does this cluster of punning names relate to the notion of traduction we have introduced? There is, of course, on an immediate level precisely no 'sense' to the linguistic accidents of Joycean history – although Joyce's own vocation as artist, and in turn his legacy to criticism, would consist in struggling to convert or translate those nonsensical accidents into material for literary artifice, *poesis*. Thus, in our struggle to make sense of the Joycean significance of Bruni and Bruno, we return again to the question of translation.

If, as we have indicated, Leonardo Bruni could be said to have invented translation in its modern sense, Giordano Bruno was best known in Elizabethan England as the proponent of a fertile (and politically danger-ous) intermingling of European tongues; it was Bruno who had claimed, as John Florio notes in the preface to a translation of Montaigne, that 'from translation all Science had its off-spring'.[18] But closer examination shows very different philosophies underpinning the work of these two translators, a difference that on the one hand clearly relates to the evolution of Renaissance thinking (Bruni's death, we recall, comes more than a century before Bruno's birth), but on the other provides us with another way to explore our notion of traduction.

For Bruni, the task of the translator lay in complete submission to the original: to state that 'alteration is the translator's sin' was to make explicit the religious implications of this ascetic fidelity, this self-effacement before a truth defined as belonging to the other, located in another language. By contrast Bruno, in *De la causa, principio e uno* (1585), sets out a metaphysic that effectively converts Bruni's 'sin' into a universal metaphysical principle: 'Every production, of whatever kind, is an alteration, while the substance always remains the same, since there is only one substance, as there is but one divine, immortal being. Pythagoras, who did not fear death but saw it as a transformation, reached this conclusion.'[19]

Hilary Gatti argues that Bruno's thinking, exposed to English literary culture through lectures in Oxford and publications in London during the 1580s, came to inform some of the central Elizabethan texts, among them perhaps *Dr Faustus* and *Hamlet*.[20] In the anguish of his last soliloquy, Faustus clutches at a Brunonian (and indeed a proto-Joycean) notion:

> Ah *Pythagoras Metemsycosis*; were that true,
> This soule should flie from me, and I be chang'd
> Unto some brutish beast.[21]

It is the deadly fixity of the soul, at least as described by the fatalistic theologians of the Reformation, that binds Faustus to his doom, preventing his subjectivity from shrugging off its contractual obligations and escaping into pure animal enjoyment. The Brunonian-Pythagorean concept of metempsychosis – the 'transmigration of souls', as Bloom is to gloss it (*U* 4.342) – will of course become a central trope in Joyce's work, where it will designate aspects of both the diegesis and the writing process itself.

A first conclusion, then, might be to place Bruno, with his metaphysic of fecund transformation and metempsychosis, in stark opposition to the ascetic Bruni. Indeed, Bruno's vision of the universe, going beyond the discoveries of Copernicus to envisage an infinite multiplicity of atoms (only theoretically totalised by an omnipresent divinity), opened on to an experience of sheer philosophical ecstasy: in contemplating the limitless energy of creation, he wrote, the mind was filled with 'a voluptuous torrent of joy and delight'.[22] It is clear that the young Joyce, who relished a description he found of Bruno as 'the god-intoxicated man', found this combination of intellect and libido irresistible; what he described as Bruno's 'vindication of the freedom of intuition' was for him a crucial model of how intellectual and aesthetic passion could triumph over social repression (*CW* 133–4).

Moreover, as we have noted, Bruno is often recognised by critics as the site of a characteristic Joycean identification, one especially prominent in *Finnegans Wake*. As Thornton Wilder comments, 'There are hundreds of allusions to Bruno in *Finnegans Wake* and in general Joyce identifies Bruno with himself as Shem – speculative, rebellious against authority, and – in his own eyes – persecuted.'[23] In the opposing figures of Bruni and Bruno – the first committed to the flawless delivery of ancient truth, the second to unleashing voluptuous torrents of aesthetic delight – we might therefore trace a primal version of Shaun and Shem, those Wakean embodiments of (on one side) the honest, public-spirited postal principle and (on the other) its criminal disruption. But the Joycean point, of course, is that these seemingly antithetical postures mask a tangled, hybrid semiotic root, with the opposition constantly collapsing, reversing or folding into new shapes. And Bruni, we should recall, begins his invocation of translation as a royal road to cultural renewal with, precisely, a *mis*translation: in other words, only by altering original meaning (and thus, in his own terms, by lapsing, committing a sin) is he able to open the way to the 'true' meaning.

IV

No doubt unwittingly, Jacques Lacan sends us back to Leonardo Bruni via a reference to James Joyce. Lacan's teaching is increasingly preoccupied during its final phase in the 1970s with a new problematic of writing, of the *écrit*, for which the name of Joyce comes to serve as emblem. The act of publishing a text in 1973 causes Lacan to invoke that name as the source of a kind of writing that he understands as *illegible* in a special sense:

Après tout, l'écrit comme pas-à-lire, c'est Joyce qui l'introduit, je ferais mieux de dire: l'intraduit, car à faire du mot traite au-delà des langues, il ne se traduit qu'à peine, d'être partout également peu à lire.

After all, the written as the not-to-be-read is introduced by Joyce – I'd do better to say intraduced (both introduced and not translated), because to deal with the word is to negotiate beyond languages, Joyce can hardly be translated at all, so that he is equally little-to-be-read everywhere.[24]

Lacan's paronomasia, shifting from 'introduit' to 'intraduit', recalls Bruni's *felix culpa*, the 'fortunate misreading' described by Steiner. Now, however, the semantic drift is reversed: where Bruni's error turned 'introduce' into 'translate', Lacan's *jeu de mots* turns on the first syllable, *in-*, punning on the negative prefix, to produce 'intraduce' or '*fail* to translate'. What Joyce introduces would thus be the very antithesis of the semantic opening metaphorically instated by Bruni's 'portal of discovery': a blockage or paralysis of reading. And, perhaps appropriately enough, here Lacan himself *ne se traduit qu'à peine*, can hardly be translated at all. The bluff self-evidence usually carried by the conjunction *car* is here deceptive: instead of the concise gloss of *intraduit* we might expect Lacan to offer here, we read the enigmatic phrase *à faire du mot traite au-delà des langues*, which McCabe renders valiantly as 'to deal with the word is to negotiate beyond languages'. Which word? And what precisely would *à faire du mot*, 'doing with the word' entail? Lacan's elliptical style seems bent on illustrating his point: that a certain kind of writing is *pas à lire*.

In one clear sense, at least, Joyce's writing treats or tropes 'across languages', without being constrained by linguistic border-controls; one need think only of the opening of his very first published text, 'The Sisters', with its child narrator entranced by the sound of the Greekish words 'paralysis', 'gnomon' and 'simony'. But why should this translingual mobility correlate with something untranslatable, with a closure of the linguistic border? Once again, it seems that the movement between languages is governed not by Bruni's principle of faultless semantic transmission, but by the collision of irreducible semiotic particles, perhaps in accord with Bruno's vision of an atomised, decentred universe.

Lacan had already made some forthright remarks about the possibility of reading and translating Joyce earlier in the same year, 1973. In his seminar *Encore*, he voices his agreement with Philippe Sollers's claim that 'Joyce's work is not readable' and adds that, at any rate, 'it is certainly not translatable into Chinese'.[25] What is clear from Lacan's bold rhetoric here is that the invocation of Joyce has a distinct theoretical impetus: Joyce *must* be untranslatable, at this moment in Lacan's work, in order to fit in with a new emphasis in the Lacanian conception of language.

These questions of translation and legibility return us to the notion of traduction. This term designates a particular semantic trope or appropriation, and as such contrasts with the understanding of translation in both Steiner and Senn (whose 'dislocution' serves, Senn writes, as an 'illustrative synonym for translation'):[26] that is, as a paradigm of language-use as such. '"Translation"', writes Steiner with scare-quotes, '. . . is a special case of the arc of communication which every successful speech-act closes within a given language.'[27] In contrast to this, traduction designates a specific operation by which jouissance, a moment of semiotic excess or insistent linguistic turbulence – the disruption, precisely, of Steiner's 'arc of communication' – is excluded or absorbed (although, as we shall see, it does not disappear). We saw a neat illustration of this in the translation of Barthes's *Le plaisir du texte*, where a rebarbative and alien *jouissance* was rendered legible, even comfortable, as 'bliss'.

The traduction of Barthes's text went further than the mistranslation of individual words, however. By misrepresenting the relation briefly sketched by Barthes between criticism and psychoanalysis, the English translation served to consolidate one of the predominant fantasies of 'poststructuralism': that is, its packaging of psychoanalysis as one of a range of options on the theoretical menu, another narrative or 'fiction' to be adopted or adapted as the critic pleases. If Barthes urges his reader not to linger in this ahistorical fantasy but to traverse the psychoanalytic monument – to seek to understand the distinct power and limitations of the Freudian legacy, its critical *quidditas* – his translator succeeds in turning the sense, or rather the *sens*, around.

To return to Lacan's invocation of Joyce in 1973, then, we should consider it in the light of this critical traduction (sometimes known as the 'application') of psychoanalysis. Indeed, Lacan did not need to be shown the perils of 'applied psychoanalysis' by poststructuralist critics eager to expropriate his conceptual tools; a long tradition of psychoanalytic 'exports', attempts to analyse everything from Leonardo to fairytales, reached back to Freud and his first colleagues. A statement made by Lacan during one of his 1975 lectures in America is a pithy condensation of his resolute opposition to that whole tradition: 'To explain art with the unconscious seems to me to be highly suspect; but it is what analysts do. It seems to me more serious to explain art with the symptom.'[28]

The notion of an intraductible Joyce – one whose writings, being *pas à lire*, would not lend themselves to facile theoretical appropriation, and would even undermine the representational architecture of any such theorising – clearly fits in with Lacan's attack on any easy transaction between the literary and the psychoanalytic. But in what sense can explaining art 'with the symptom' really differ from the classical Freudian approach?

PART II

Unspeakable Joyce

La poésie ne s'impose plus. elle s'expose.

Paul Celan

CHAPTER 4

How am I to sign myself?

JACK Personally, darling, to speak quite candidly, I don't much care about the name of Ernest . . . I don't think the name suits me at all.

GWENDOLEN It suits you perfectly. It is a divine name. It has music of its own. It produces vibrations.

Oscar Wilde, *The Importance of Being Earnest*

I know of no more heartrending reading than Shakespeare: what must a man have suffered to need to be a buffoon to this extent! – Is Hamlet *understood*? It is not doubt, it is *certainty* which makes mad . . .

Nietzsche, *Ecce Homo* (emphasis original)

PATRICK W. SHAKESPEARE

Writing in 1826, Charles Lamb had objected to the correlation, supposedly brought to light by Romantic poetry, between artistic creation and madness. The 'ground of the mistake' involved here, Lamb thought, was a failure to draw a clear enough line between sleep and wakefulness; hence 'men, finding in the raptures of the higher poetry a condition of exaltation, to which they have no parallel in their own experience, besides the spurious resemblance of it in dreams and fevers, impute a state of dreaminess and fever to the poet'. The notion – today, of course, a full-grown cliché – that genius is close to madness takes no account, Lamb insisted, of the active force of the conscious imagination, a creative activity that 'implies shaping and consistency'. If, as Lamb puts it, 'the true poet dreams, being awake' – in other words, is able to uphold signifying legitimacy even in the obscure and perilous sphere of fantasy, to master his theme and not be 'possessed by his subject' – the ultimate instance of such artistic control, the very linchpin of Lamb's argument, is, inevitably, Shakespeare. The entire force of Lamb's essay, indeed, can be seen condensed in a single line invoking the name of that True Genius: 'It is impossible', he writes, 'for the mind to conceive of a mad Shakespeare.'[1]

Lamb has a special place in Joyce's textual universe. When still a new boy at Belvedere, young Joyce had read *The Adventures of Ulysses* (1808), Lamb's retelling of Homer's *Odyssey* for child readers (*JJ* 46). If the 'true genius' for Lamb was someone who could keep his head in any crisis, and dominate a recalcitrant world through the shaping force of imagination, who better to illustrate this truth than *polumetis Odusseus*, Homer's 'man of many schemes'?

Above all, by translating the *Odyssey* into a bedtime read for children, Lamb made Homer *legible*; and together with his sister Mary, of course, he had done the same for Shakespeare. In this sense, as retailer of tales, deliverer and perhaps falsifier of letters, Lamb fitted one of the 'jocoserious' roles Joyce would develop in *Finnegans Wake*: that of 'Shaun the Post'. But perhaps Lamb was Shaun-like in another respect, too: that is, as someone who has to accommodate madness. In 1796, Mary Lamb had murdered their mother in a fit of insanity; her brother had subsequently taken constant care of her, helping her through periodic relapses, and all the while collaborating with her in the business of rewriting literary messages.

The 'shaping and consistency' implied by the imagination for Lamb in his 1826 essay can thus be seen to apply both to life and to art, to managing the psyche as much as to re-presenting Homer and Shakespeare. Something of this ambiguity is in play in *Finnegans Wake*, where 'Mirrylamb, she was shuffering all the diseasinesses of the unherd of' (*FW* 223.1) – the distorted name suggesting a mirror, perhaps a cracked looking-glass to be passed through – and where Shaun or Jaun confesses, 'I used to follow Mary Liddlelambe's flitsy tales, espicially with the scentaminted sauce. Sifted science will do your arts good' (*FW* 440.18–20). If Mary Lamb is thus amalgamated with Alice Liddell, both are travellers to a Wonderland or '*Fanciesland*' (*FW* 440.21), an upside-down world through the looking glass where fantasies of childhood merge with philosophical riddles or fits of madness. And the Lambs' tales to be digested are served with lashings of sentimental sauce, and probably also with 'quashed quotatoes' (*FW* 183.22); the simplified versions or traductions of Homer and Shakespeare are plainly 'sifted science', censored signs or filtered knowledge. But, as Jaun insists, they nevertheless 'will do your arts good'; the Lambs provide both heart-warming sentimental sauce *and* the vital source of a creative rewriting, 'instructual primers' (*FW* 440.24) that both falsify the original and give primary instruction about it to future artists like Joyce.

In a Shaun-Lamb, then, the traduction of literature joins with the suppression of madness, perhaps revealing its underlying logic as *institutional* practice. The name of Shakespeare serves to guarantee the ultimate sanity of the literary universe, and the sanitised bard delivered up by the Lambs in turn confirms this. The impossible concept of Shakespearean madness thus emerges as a threat to the very institution of English Literature, with its dense cluster of socio-political investments. And for that very reason, of course, such a concept was bound to appeal especially to Joyce, whose work proclaims itself not merely as an addition to the literary institution founded on the Sanity of True Genius – namely Shakespeare – but at the same time as its dismantling, the unveiling and exploration of its institutional status.

The relationship or 'rivalry' between Joyce and Shakespeare is an established sector of the literary-industrial complex, one first definitively mapped out by Vincent Cheng's marvellous 1984 study.[2] Here, once again, the spectre of critical redundancy seems to double an 'original' crisis in which the aspiring artist confronted an overwhelming paternal legacy, the 'will' insisting throughout Shakespeare, his name a synecdoche both for human desire and testamentary immortality. It is crucial, however, to distinguish between the 'psychology' at work here – in what we might call the Nora Barnacle reading, which features the spectacular clash of literary titans – and another kind of textual interaction, with no such easily legible scene of conflict. In this less easily represented 'scene', when Joyce looks back to Shakespeare he does so not in order to outdo his rival in some infantile phallic competition, but rather to engage with perhaps the first moment that English literary language assumes its crucial self-reflexivity and becomes suddenly capable of turning around upon and opening up to reflective consciousness the uncanny force of *poesis*, of linguistic creation and its production of the human subject. The result of Shakespeare's 'monstrous birth' (Iago, as we shall see, is an unavoidable figure here) is indeed an absolute rivalry – but not merely the rivalry of imaginary foes. It is rather a question of incompatible, fundamentally antagonistic *worlds* of language. As we shall see, it is by staging this opposition of radically different versions of being-in-language that Shakespearean tragedy first articulates and makes thinkable a mass of questions relating to what Lacan will call the *parlêtre*: the speaking subject whose innermost being is alienated *par lettre*. And the same questions recur, in inflected but still recognisably Shakespearean forms, in some of the theoretical discourses that most concern us here, those of Austin, Freud and Lacan.[3]

If, then, the notion of a mad Shakespeare appealed to Joyce just as it had appalled Charles Lamb, this was not merely because of a desire to bring 'his bardic memory low' (*FW* 172.28), to besmirch the literary institution by exposing its prime embodiment as flawed or in some sense

monstrous, less than human. 'Saying that a great genius is mad', Joyce
declared in a lecture on Blake in 1912, 'is like saying that he had rheumatism
or suffered from diabetes. Madness, in fact, is a medical term that can
claim no more notice from the objective critic than he grants the charge
of heresy raised by the theologian, or the charge of immorality raised by
the police' (*CW* 220). In other words, although 'madness' may be a name
applied to literary acts of social transgression (as Joyce strongly hints with
his pungent analogies, heresy and immorality), such moralistic judgements
have no place in 'objective' criticism. Literature, that is to say, occupies
a distinct epistemic world, detached – even if only minutely – from the
everyday world of vicars and policemen, and therefore not subject to the
same repressive value-judgements.

Would this therefore imply that art is ultimately autonomous, self-
legislative, as Walter Pater had argued in essays that were read attentively
by the young Joyce? The rather *fin-de-siècle* atmosphere of the debates associated with Pater and aestheticism belies the enduring importance of the
questions they raised: questions of artistic originality, tradition and reinvention that remained central to Joyce's literary self-conception. And the
inevitable Joycean pun on Pater's name is a crucial one: the questions of
beginning and of fictional self-legislation that are raised by Pater's ideas
are posed by Joyce as problems inseparable from paternity, that ambiguous
'legal fiction' pondered by Stephen (*U* 9.844).

Perhaps in one sense, then, Joyce's relation to Shakespeare involves
père-version, to cite the pun by which Lacan combines 'father version' and
'turning to the father'. What the subject seeks in turning to the father,
according to psychoanalysis, is a certain consistent institution or legality of
signification; paternity would thus be a legal fiction in an active sense, that
of instating a law-governed framework to render legible the vagaries of the
subject's aesthetic or bodily experience (and notably, in a psychoanalytic
perspective, its fantasy). As Lacanian analyst Serge André puts it, the Name
of the Father 'renders the fantasy liveable for the subject' by allowing a
certain minimal legibility or semiotic equivalence to bear on its enigmatic
object.[4] The subject's fantasy is literally given *shape* by the father, in so far
as without the primal signifying alienation installed by the *nom du père*
there can be no possible relation of desire, no escape from the formless,
pre-human domain of instinct.

The key here, as ever with Joyce, is to be found *inside* our reading of the
text. We must turn ineluctably to the famous discussion of Shakespeare in
the 'Scylla and Charybdis' episode of *Ulysses*. There, it is immediately apparent that Joyce centres everything on questions of acting or performative

language, and in particular on the status of *names*: the Shakespearean question 'What's in a name?' echoes as a leitmotif throughout the episode, as Stephen contemplates the peculiar verbal status of naming as speech-act (or as he thinks, 'Act speech': *U* 9.978). The performative dimension of language is thus both in question and in act throughout Stephen's self-conscious Shakespearean performance; above all, that dimension is *seductive*. 'And in the porches of their ears I pour' (9.465): in Stephen's imagination he casts himself as Claudius or Iago, a perverse inseminator of oral and aural poison, or 'poison in jest', where Hamlet's joke is also a venomous *geste*, a toxic speech-act. And Shakespeare's name, with its connotations of phallic bravado (amplified of course by the various puns on 'Will'), becomes a name for this seductive and transgressive rhetorical performance, this verbal insistence.

In a crucial Joycean reversal, then, Shakespeare – invoked by Lamb as the keystone of institutional sanity – becomes for Stephen the site of an 'unremitting intellect' identified with 'the hornmad Iago ceaselessly willing that the moor in him shall suffer' (*U* 9.1023–4). As we shall see, it is this last gloss on Shakespeare's name, where 'Will in overplus' (*U* 9.924) becomes an act of seductive transgression and of the inmixing of identities, that will allow us to grasp Joyce's investment in 'William Shakespeare and company' (*U* 9.729) without falling back on the tired old formula of Oedipal identification and rivalry. Joyce characteristically mocks that formula in the 'Cyclops' episode of *Ulysses*, by including in a comical list of ancient Irish heroes one 'Patrick W. Shakespeare' (*U* 12.190–1). The allusion is to the eminent Irish historian Patrick Weston Joyce, whose works included *The Origin and History of Irish Names of Places* and *English as We Speak it in Ireland*. By merging Shakespeare's name with that of an authority on naming and the English language in Ireland, Joyce could emphasise the *institutional* status of the name, its privileged position either as colonial imposition or as testament (both kinds of 'will'). And of course this imaginary Irish bard (Patrick Weston might be the name of a more 'western' Shakespeare) shares Joyce's own name, is 'another poet of the same name' (*U* 9.866), another entry on the dubious list of possible Shakespeares (or Joyces).

It is here, then, at the point where Joyce specifically plays at substituting his name for Shakespeare's, that criticism finds it hardest to respond without being immediately caught in the snares of Joycean mockery. For is it not obvious that the old drama of artistic rivalry, of the 'anxiety of influence' with its quasi-Oedipal scenario, is being performed yet again in *Ulysses*, in rehearsal perhaps for the fraternal strife of *Finnegans Wake*? At this point, however, Lacan's thought can rescue us from the obvious by indicating what such a reading misses; that is, if we concentrate solely on the imaginary domain – where the egos of Joyce and Shakespeare meet in a spectacular and eminently visible clash of literary mastery – we fail to account for naming itself as an act that ruptures the barrier between the symbolic and the real, an instance of transgressive *poesis* that is always in excess of the meaning-laden ego (and Joyce is careful not to miss reciting the names that Shakespeare gives to this semiotic excess: 'Will in overplus', 'the moor [i.e. more] in him').

It is therefore first of all because Shakespeare's work sets forth, drama-tises, brings within reach those aspects of 'acting speech' or moving and performing language that go *beyond* its imaginary surface that Joyce under-takes a complex *père-version* of that work, a turning to its forms of legibility and a torsion or metamorphosis of its will or legacy. What we might call the moment of Shakespearean 'overplus', where language surpasses its repre-sentability and becomes its own interrogation, is what makes Joyce's writing return endlessly to the same famous texts and their enigmatic signature. Only at a secondary moment does that intertextuality assume the guise of rival identities – although, if Shem and Shaun are Wakean names for the opposition thus set up between irresponsible verbal jouissance and traduc-tive legibility, this oppositional economy, with its 'firstly' and 'secondly', would itself fall on the side of semantic delivery, of Shaun the Post (in other words, the very architecture of the rivalrous scenario would be the product of one of its rival terms). To think 'on the side of' Shem would thus be to think outside the imaginary: an untenable thought, one impossible for a subject to 'have', although Joyce was constantly drawn to the notion of writing against identity, experiencing a language whose subject would be not an ego but a 'Nego', the first Joycean 'Naysayer' to be given a name in his writing.[5]

Here we return to the question of the literary 'thing' raised in the Prologue above. We recall that the Nietzschean attempt to affirm the immediacy of being in the 'apotheosis of the instant' (in Blanchot's phrase) necessarily implied the shrugging-off of fixed egoic identity, the metempsychotic rup-ture of the 'I'. What is revealed is untranslatable: it cannot be appropriated or identified by an individual at a given time (declared to be 'now'), so that the attempt to utter this 'thing' is inherently self-deconstructive, or, as Pierre Klossowski put it, subject to 'the law of the Vicious Circle'. For Joyce, as we shall see, the Shakespearean 'Will in overplus' already entails this intransigent linguistic thing that dooms literary criticism to an eternal recurrence of misreading and misappropriation.

To begin our exploration of Joyce's literary response to the questions of language first raised in Shakespeare's work – questions of naming, verbal creation and representation, the performative instance of subjective desire and its relation to institution – we need to turn to Ulysses again: not, however, this time to Joyce's novel, but instead to the shrewd politician we meet in *Troilus and Cressida*. The latter play sets out with exemplary clarity a crucial Shakespearean debate on the relation of individual ego to social institution, a debate that grows more complex in the course of the playwright's career – and a debate in which Joycean writing and its critical institution is still, we shall argue, thoroughly entangled. In an initial setting forth of the argument, Ulysses explains to the recalcitrant Achilles – in a prophetic paraphrase of Hegel and Lacan – that man's desire is the desire of the Other:

> no man is the lord of any thing,
> Though in and of him there be much consisting,
> Till he communicate his parts to others;
> Nor doth he of himself know them for aught,
> Till he behold them formed in th' applause
> Where th' are extended: who like an arch reverb'rate
> The voice again, or like a gate of steel,
> Fronting the sun, receives and renders back
> His figure and his heat.   (III.iii.115–23)

True autonomy or absolute self-legislation is impossible, Ulysses insists: there can be no private law or language, springing up *ex nihilo*, outside the world of social existence. The question of originality versus inherited tradition is again at stake in the famous speech where Ulysses supports the primacy of 'degree' in political institutions; but what is crucial here is how Shakespeare's language gives the ostensibly conservative argument a subtle paradoxical twist:

> The heavens themselves, the planets, and this centre
> Observe degree, priority, and place,
> Insisture, course, proportion, season, form,
> Office, and custom, in all line of order.   (I.iii.84–7)

'Insisture' is a curious word, glossed by the *Oxford English Dictionary* as 'the apparent stopping when a planet appears to become stationary at either end of its course': it is in fact a Shakespearean coinage, indeed a veritable *hapax legomenon* (there is no other recorded usage). If, as scholars suggest, Shakespeare derived it from Cicero's *institutiones*, his modification – or fortunate, proto-Joycean misspelling – of the word brings it close to the English 'insistence', thus implicitly robbing it of objective solidity, so to speak, giving it a subjective colour (note that the *OED* talks of '*apparent* stopping'). Thus, just as Ulysses is invoking the regularity of the cosmos as the supreme objective proof of the need for humans to submit to established institutions, Shakespeare puts into his mouth an original pun, newly minted to give the very idea of 'institution' a new twist, making it sound indeed like a matter of insisting, of a subject's *will*.

'He has hidden his own name, a fair name, William, in the plays, a super here, a clown there' (*U* 9.921–2): Stephen's cryptonymy offers a reading of Shakespeare radically inflected by the personal, by the singular instance of identity and desire. If the plays are one long signature, the name itself becomes an enormous pun, a polysemic node binding together insisture and testament, self-institution and self-perpetuation. Stephen's examples hint at such name-play: at one point Will is a 'super', both an 'overplus', or excessive self-insistence and a police inspector or law-bearing superego; at another, he – or it – is a clown, an anarchic subversion of law, an irrepressible comedic force.

Insisture thus seems both to embody and to name a strange coincidence; invoked as testimony to the solid regularity of the universe and man's instituted hierarchy within it, the word itself is utterly irregular, a singular poetic invention. And if we turn from Shakespeare's Ulysses to Shakespeare in *Ulysses*, we could say that Joyce redefines insisture as the performative instance of the name in the literary institution, its alchemical conversion of the particular instant to the timeless universal.

Thus, when in another famous debate later in *Troilus and Cressida*, Hector protests that 'value dwells not in particular will' (II.ii.53) – in other words, the ego cannot rely on its own irrational impulses to overrule the codes established by social institutions – we cannot read 'particular will' without thinking of the debate in 'Scylla and Charybdis', in particular of Buck Mulligan's facetious 'Which Will?' (*U* 9.794). Indeed, in the original text the pun on Shakespeare's name already sounds a note of mocking ambiguity: while Hector is clearly 'right' to argue against the naive voluntarism put forward by Troilus ('What's aught but as 'tis valued?': 52), we are craftily reminded that he is doing so in a play that *is* signed by a particular Will, so that in this text 'value' does indeed dwell in the institutional status of an individual author, his self-insisture or legacy.

It is clear, then, that Joyce's readings and raidings of Shakespeare turn on the name and its *poesis*, on name-making and inscribing the name into the world created: insisture, 'As Great Shapesphere puns it' (*FW* 295.4), is always a name-play that both shapes the universe and distorts it with particular will, with an illegitimate signature. But here we should try to clarify things: in what sense is creation always a distortion, and why is the authorial signature necessarily illegitimate? A first answer is provided by Lacan's notion of the *act*: that is, as precisely a point of rupture with the discursive bond of social existence. The truly original creative act for Lacan is an event outside discourse: it cannot be rehearsed or repeated, accounted for or translated. As such, the creative act is *illegal,* defying Hector's law according to which 'value dwells not in particular will', since it introduces something unprecedented, impossible to alienate from its momentary emergence and to make part of an established semantic reality – without, that is, calling on the institutional traduction that would imbue it with an ostensible truth or 'proper' meaning, diagnose it and cure it of its singular pathology.

The creative act in language, conceived in Lacanian terms, is therefore something of a paradox: radically non-discursive, outside the differential temporality of actual historical language, it is ultimately outside language itself. This clearly relates it to one of Lacan's most important, and most often misunderstood, concepts: that of foreclosure.

Foreclosure is for Lacan the portal of discovery leading into psychosis and the dimension of the real. As Bruce Fink writes, 'it is only that which is *not foreclosed* from the symbolic order that can be said to exist':[6] the root of psychotic experience therefore lies in something that lacks the status of historical reality, something impossibly singular and hence extrinsic to social discourse. In entangling his work with Joycean writing, Lacan sought to extend the concept of foreclosure by outlining a new, 'radical' version of it. If Joyce is fundamentally *pas à lire,* as Lacan saw it, this is because his art, in its very *quidditas*, entails a foreclosure of meaning. Such a foreclosure is more topologically radical than the foreclosure of the *nom du père* that Lacan had earlier situated at the root of a delusional system such as Schreber's:[7] in Joyce the 'I' itself, the primal inscription of subjectivity, is overwhelmed by jouissance and initially prevented from weaving its fabric of imaginary material (in the delusional but still 'meaningful' manner of a Schreber). The secret of the *sinthome*, in Lacan's view, was that with it the subject was somehow able to make use of this originary eclipse of the imaginary in verbal jouissance to forge a singular identification (and we should recall Joyce's insistent puns on 'forge' – at once the act of honest smith and fraudulent artificer). Hence the *vocational* status of the Joycean epiphany, the fact that, in the random scraps of Dublin chitchat he jotted down, the artist could hear the call of a literary destiny. The foreclusive dimension of the creative act accounts for the distortion, the linguistic impropriety it necessarily involves: the creative opening it embodies always exceeds the symbolic and the imaginary (whose coalescence Lacan writes as *sens*, meaning), disseminating itself ruinously across the systemic grid of language, undoing its established laws and conventions.

The disfigurement of the proper name is a way of indicating – but not of 'signifying' – the linguistic turbulence produced by this radical creation; as such, it is the key to Joyce's artistic invention, its sinful or erroneous 'portal of discovery'. Once again, we need to be careful to avoid wandering back onto the primrose path of a reading restricted to the imaginary domain, that of uncanny rivalry, where the distortion of names would be just another sign of the ego's paranoid assault on its mirror image. 'Great Shapeshere' would obviously fit in with such a model of identification and antagonism, with the distorted name at once a reverend and an insolent (because improper) *père-version*. But what such a reading overlooks is the fundamental Joycean 'epiphany' that sees creation itself as erroneous, as an irredeemable original sin, a jouissance foreclosed from the domain of symbolic or meaningful equivalence. Atherton notes how Joyce was able, on the basis of his reading of Vico, to figure this in theological terms: thus the Viconian 'attribution of Original Sin to God is one of the basic axioms of *Finnegans Wake*'.[8] God's creative utterance was marred, according to Vico, by nothing less than a primal symptom, a kind of divine speech impediment, making the universe originally flawed by untranslatable symptomatic jouissance (and Joyce seemed to hear as much in the ominous rumble of thunder).

The idea of a sinful God may perhaps seem a quaint theological paradox, something that Joyce found amusing. That this was very far from the case is shown most clearly by the famous sermons on hell delivered by the preacher in *A Portrait*; in Chapter 6, we shall see how the discourse of religion involves Joycean writing in a radical exploration of its own 'diabolic' coincidence of creation and sin, institution and irredeemable enjoyment. Before that, in Chapter 5 we shall consider how this devilish strand in Joyce's writing draws on the 'Zweispaltung', 'splitting in two' (*FW* 296.8), at work in some of his favourite 'egomen', namely those found in the texts of Wilde, Stevenson and Hogg; and then move on to examine in detail how it figures in Joyce's most explicit self-doubling, *A Portrait of the Artist as a Young Man*. But first we need to dwell a little longer on Joyce's enjoyment of 'shaggspick' (*FW* 177.32), his name for the libidinally invested language of Shakespeare; for it will provide us with the clearest matrix for understanding what follows.

THE GREEN-EYED LOBSTER

When Joyce closes a letter to Nora with the 'hysterical' question, 'How am I to sign myself?', he himself (perhaps knowingly) raises the spectre of literary identity that has been haunting Joycean criticism ever since. The list of critical preoccupations that we can trace back to Joyce's question – forged signatures, Circean sexual masquerade, lost identity papers, and so on – is of course profoundly relevant to Joyce's work, with its endless reflexive self-questioning. But perhaps these classic themes of Joycean interpretation, broadly speaking *comic* themes (and, in particular, themes of Shakespearean comedy), have served to draw critical attention away from a more troubled and troubling version of the problem of identity: namely the question – introduced jocoseriously in *Finnegans Wake* as 'the first riddle of the universe' – 'when is a man not a man?' (*FW* 170.5).

And it is again Shakespeare who opens a portal of discovery allowing us to think about the crucial difference between these questions of identity – as well as their uncanny resemblance. A single phrase – 'I am not what I am' – marks both ends of the spectrum here: spoken first by Viola in *Twelfth Night*, where it archly designates the ironic masquerade of sexual roles,[9] the line recurs more famously in *Othello* as the satanic self-presentation of Iago. This latter, tragic inflection of the line gives it an enigmatic dimension absent from Viola's domain of mirrors and trickery; indeed, Iago's impossible *sum* marks a veritable inversion of the philosophical subject, an *anti-cogito*, which, we shall argue, makes him the diabolic forebear of Joyce's 'naysayers' from the juvenile 'Nego' to the incarnate negativity of the Wakean 'Ondt'. Perhaps in a similar way, the riddle posed in the *Wake* by Shem, 'when is a man not a man?', is greeted first by a list of wrong answers with a tangle of comical literary and theatrical connotations, before what the text explicitly dubs the 'correct solution' (*FW* 170.22–3) is given by Shem himself – the name or noun or adjective 'Sham', a version of the questioner's own identity. If a man's not being a man, or perhaps not being only *one* man, merely corresponds to feminine masquerade or the ludic dissembling of identity, we might still be in the domain of comedy, of pleasurable revelation and resolution. But, we shall argue, this Wakean 'Sham' also points to a more radical moment of self-dissembling, of uncanny selflessness, that emerges in Shakespearean tragedy and becomes a central element in Joyce's writing.

'When is a man not a man?' could indeed serve as the subtitle of several of Shakespeare's tragedies – but perhaps above all of *Macbeth*. One of the answers given to Shem's question may remind us of how the collapse of identity in that play is linked to a radical evacuation of human time: 'when yea, he hath no mananas' (*FW* 170.20) echoes the vaudeville song 'Yes, we have no bananas' but also, with its *mañanas* or Spanish 'tomorrows', recalls Macbeth's famous repetition of 'tomorrow' (v.ii.19), where the mechanical iteration of the signifier marks the complete absence of meaningful time. In *Finnegans Wake* Macbeth's despairing line is re-served as a 'quashed quotato' – 'Toborrow and toburrow and tobarrow!' (*FW* 455.13); both recited and undone, its dead rhythm rephrased as a rich variation on the anguish and rapture of Joycean reinvention. The borrowing or purloining of Shakespearean letters is also a textual burrowing, like that of the 'old mole' at work beneath *Hamlet* and a raiding of grave or barrow, a barrowful of borrowed buryings.

Yet if the self-declared 'tombstone mason' (*FW* 113.34) in the *Wake* thus busies himself with mortuary art, with redelivering dead letters, perhaps he too 'hath no mananas', is doomed to eternal repetition. The quasi-Nietzschean problematic of the 'now', of the impossible struggle of the *Jetztpunkt* to overcome its fleeting contingency in time, is at the core of Joyce's return to Shakespeare. As we argued above in the Prologue, this is not simply because of a sense of irredeemable artistic indebtedness that would make the ostensible modernity of Joyce's work, its 'now', nothing but a sterile repetition of past literary glory. Rather it derives from a perception that *within* the Shakespearean text itself we encounter a first, and perhaps unsurpassable, version of the crisis of human time and representation later to be formulated by Nietzsche as Eternal Return. Thus, in *Macbeth* a vertiginous encounter with the transgressive dislocation of time and history is linked to the disruptive moment of the *act* – 'I feel now / The future in the instant,' as Lady Macbeth murmurs (I.v.46). The *Wake* gives this crisis of temporality a comic Nietzschean spin, via some schoolboy Shakespearean puns: 'Yet's the time for being now, now, now. For a burning would is come to dance inane' (*FW* 250.16) An impossible 'would' would have to come to pass, or Birnam Wood would have to come to Dunsinane, for time to surpass itself in Lady Macbeth's fantasmatic 'now' ('Yet's' punning the German *jetzt*), with the gap between the actual and the possible overcome, obliterated. Instead, the infinite creative or apocalyptic potential of the future, its 'burning would', is reduced by Joyce's text to a bathetic parody of Dionysiac affirmation, an endless frisking around of typographical characters. Just as the inane repetition of Macbeth's 'Tomorrow' speech, with its rhythmic emptying of signifying potential, is equivocally redeemed in the *Wake* – brought back to a certain semantic valence, if only as a name for imitation and grave-digging – so, conversely, the impossible happening that spells out Macbeth's doom is robbed of its fatal grandeur and exposed as mere verbal trickery, a trivial 'dance inane'.

The Shakespearean text often hides its secrets in stray lines, uttered at seemingly insignificant moments. When Macbeth, precariously instated as king at the beginning of Act III, dismisses his court with the words 'Let every man be master of his time' (III.i.40), it is easy to miss this line as a vital clue to understanding the play – in particular, to how it links the problem of self-identity to a fantasmatic act of overcoming time. To be a man, according to the fantasy gripping Macbeth, is to master one's time in two senses: first, to dominate the contemporary situation – something at least within the horizon of possibility – but also to appropriate time itself, an impossible 'act' and therefore, Lacan would argue, a figure of the fantasmatic real. The key moment occurs in Act I scene vii, which we could read as a struggle between opposing responses to Shem's question, 'when is a man not a man?' Macbeth's effort to make a conclusive statement on that question is undermined by a fatal ambiguity: 'I dare do all that may become a man; / Who dares do more is none' (I.vii.46–7). A man who is too much a man is thus no man at all, according to a strange sum that leaves the definition of a man (or rather what 'may become a man', hinting at the possibility of failing to become one) wide open to rhetorical manipulation, to the dangerous duplicity of the signifier. And Lady Macbeth's rebuttal makes full use of this semiotic potential in suggesting a bond between male identity and the fantasmatic control of time:

> When you durst do it, then you were a man
> And to be more than what you were, you would
> Be so much more the man. Nor time, nor place
> Did then adhere, and yet you would make both.
> They have made themselves and that their fitness now
> Does unmake you.   (I.VII. 49–54)

Being a man, Lady Macbeth implies, entails measuring up to a specific fantasy: that of *making* time, dominating history through a masterful act that would encapsulate 'the future in the instant' and do away with the castrating subjection to contingent temporality. We recall how Maurice Blanchot linked Nietzsche's idea of Eternal Return to the act of suicide: as the ultimate act, suicide corresponds for Blanchot to the 'apotheosis of the instant', an unparalleled affirmation of the *now*.[10] Juan-David Nasio re-situates this suicidal act in psychoanalytic terms as 'an act that breaks through to a limitless jouissance'. But the act of suicide, continues Nasio, 'is only one example of the subject's confrontation with the Other-jouissance, an example among others that shows the subject opening a door onto a place from which we are forcibly banished'.[11] For Lady Macbeth, the act of regicide is a similar confrontation with absolute jouissance in an act of total self-affirmation – the only problem is her husband, who is shown by Shakespeare in the characteristically neurotic position of one who seeks to enjoy, to experience absolute jouissance, *only in fantasy*. And when that fantasy 'passes to the act', to use Lacan's terminology – that is, when it transgresses the limits of the psyche, no longer belonging to the appropriative 'I' but spilling over into the ecstatic real of jouissance – Macbeth's ego of course recoils from it, and his constitutive masculine fantasy falls apart.

Slavoj Žižek puts forward the hypothesis that 'the act as real is "feminine", in contrast to the "masculine" performative'.[12] If for Austin the performative entailed a tightly codified speech act, ineffective outside the rules of a given social scenario (such as marriage or ceremonial rite), the speech-*act* as Lacanian conceives of it would comprise the power to 'do things with words' but outside any such rhetorical regulation. The *passage à l'acte* opens a space 'where words no longer oblige', as Žižek puts it (36): where the contractual, inter-subjective dimension of the performative is radically lacking. It is almost, we might say, as if the performative ritual were instituted precisely to control the anarchic potential of the speech act, to bring its rhetorical, seductive force back into the sphere of subjective responsibility.

But why does Lacan's account, according to the gloss offered by Žižek, imply mapping these different kinds of speech act on to sexual difference? There is clearly a risk of reproducing an old misogynist figure of woman as seductive transgression versus man as responsible law-bearer; but if we look more closely at how sexual difference operates in *Macbeth* we shall see how such an easy opposition effaces a crucial ambiguity – 'th'equivocation of the fiend', Macbeth calls it (v.v.42) – that Joyce will exploit to the full.

Act I, scene vii is again the key moment. There, Macbeth begins by con-templating what Blanchot calls the 'apotheosis of the instant': his impossible fantasy would be to stall the momentous act 'upon this bank and shoal of time' (I.vii.6), suspend the significance of the act by hiding it from the gaze of the socio-symbolic Other. But he immediately acknowledges that such a withdrawal into self, into the immediate instant of jouissance, is for-bidden by the symbolic consistency of reality itself; because 'We still have judgement here' (8), the innermost reality of subjective desire is always socially mediated, formed by the Other. Thus, unless we are mad and have abandoned 'judgement here', we cannot escape from the circuits of the signifier, from the 'even-handed justice' (10) that returns our own message or poisoned chalice to us. And it is at this moment of 'dialectical' resolution, when Macbeth seems to have concluded a classical philosophical argument 'against the deed' (14), drawing on the authority of Seneca and Aristotle, that the crucial Shakespearean *act* takes place:

> I have no spur
> To prick the sides of my intent, but only
> Vaulting ambition which o'erleaps itself
> And falls on th'other – How now? What news?
>
> *Enter* LADY MACBETH
>
> (1.vii.25–9)

The sudden appearance of the spur that will prick Macbeth into action (with a contorted sexual pun heavily implying that it is she who wields the 'prick')[13] does more than simply burst the airy bubble of his philosophising; it literally interrupts the signifying economy of the Other, its 'even-handed' or symmetrical structure. The rupture of male discourse and phallic authority is thus also a rupture of meaning, indeed a breach in the symbolic fabric of reality (and we can see this spelled out in the ellipsis: what is lost is one whole 'side', leaving everything skewed, unbalanced). Nor is the text content to represent or name this breach of symbolic reality: it *enacts* it. Scholars have laboured to make sense of Macbeth's figure of 'vaulting ambition which o'erleaps itself', some picturing a rider who fails to leap into the saddle properly, while others prefer to imagine both horse and rider falling together.[14] Such efforts to return the text to full legibility risk overlooking the crucial significance of the Shakespearean trope here: for in this impossible figure the text itself 'o'erleaps itself', gesturing towards the unfathomable jouissance of its own poetic invention (its 'baseless fabric', as a later play will famously call it). How, after all, can anything actually leap over itself – without, that is, splitting apart, doubling itself and thus forfeiting the very unity that is supposed to constitute identity?

'Vaulting ambition which o'erleaps itself' thus marks a point of inconceivable textual self-division, an 'overplus' or *plus de jouir* that is precisely beyond identification and cannot therefore be integrated with the 'even-handed' signifying economy pictured by Macbeth in his attempt to represent, theorise or render legible his own moral position. It is therefore entirely appropriate for the phrase itself to be robbed of the other 'side' needed to maintain its semantic balance, to make it 'just' – and that this semiotic breakage takes place not in discourse, but in act; it is Lady Macbeth's sudden apparition, her sheer bodily presence, that interrupts her husband's line and shatters his attempt to salvage a consistent theoretical self and reality.

It is here, then, at the point where *Macbeth* dramatises the implosion of the reflective subject in the face of an uncanny act beyond its imaginary self-representation, where we can begin to reconceive the central significance of Shakespearean tragedy for Joyce's writing. And the key to grasping that significance is to link it – in a characteristic Joycean reversal – to *humour* (perhaps even with some help from Freud's theory of jokes). The special function of *laughter* in Shakespearean tragedy particularly fascinates Joyce; it is bound up with the unprecedented textual self-reflexivity of that tragedy, its capacity to address the question of the rich and troubling semiotic gap between authorial script and performance 'in act', on stage.

In particular, as Cheng notes, 'Joyce revels in notably fouled-up Shakespearean performances'; and two such 'maimed acts' (*FW* 325.32) from Dublin theatre legend were first identified as sources for elements of the *Wake* by Fritz Senn.[15] In the first, a production of *Hamlet* has to be halted during the performance because of the lead actor's illness, only for the cast to resume with *She Stoops to Conquer* (and in the *Wake* the two plays are therefore intermingled: *FW* 325.25ff.). But the second of Senn's accidents offers a more powerful image of how Joycean laughter can disrupt the institutional *gravitas* of Shakespeare, and in the process generate an irresolvable semiotic complexity. In an eighteenth-century performance of *Othello* at Dublin's Smock Alley Theatre, the part of Iago was played by an actor named Layfield, who suffered a curious tragicomic *peripeteia*: 'When he came to the lines: "Oh, my Lord! Beware of jealousy; / It is a green-eyed monster," – he gave the latter as "It is a green-eyed lobster." He was at that moment struck with incurable madness, and died [later].'[16] Layfield's 'fall' is both comic and terrible: his variation of Shakespeare's line is first an inspired witticism that transforms Iago's trite sententious cruelty into 'something rich and strange', the embodiment of a submarine, inhuman otherness – and at the same time it marks the irruption into the drama of something senseless, unspeakable. And of course the moment is peculiarly apt in *Othello*, whose script has the very same scene – complete with falling down, loss of linguistic control, inversion of established power relations – waiting to occur later in the play (iv.i), but with the roles of master and victim switched. It might thus seem as if the classical prescription for tragedy, an accordance with the 'even-handed justice' named in *Macbeth*'s soliloquy, had been observed with grotesque irony in this reversal that sees Iago hoist by his own verbal petard – were it not, that is, for the complete disruption of dramatic space caused by the unfortunate slip, its disastrous and yet laughable irrelevance to theatrical meaning. As we shall see, it is the fall out of the artwork, across its spatio-temporal frame, into the *actual* dimension of reality, that turns this into a supremely Joycean event.

The 'grand old greeneyed lobster' (*FW* 249.3) thus appears in the *Wake*, where it becomes a Joycean name for the point at which a regime of representation collapses and something monstrous appears – something that precisely does not belong to discourse, that breaks the chain of signifiers. But what appears is also funny; and here Freud's account of humour may prove useful. 'Any uncovering of unconscious material', writes Freud in his 1905 joke-book, 'strikes us in general as "comic"', adding in a footnote that his patients often laugh during analysis 'even when the content of what is unveiled would by no means justify this'.[17] It is thus the very act of unveiling, the *alethia*, that generates laughter, beyond any traceable pattern of meanings.

But how can something 'outside' discourse appear within it? For Freud, the *Witz* is a thoroughly 'social' phenomenon, in contrast to the raw, asocial fantasy embedded at the core of a dream; indeed, in Freud's account a joke is a subtle discursive ruse whereby something 'contraband' can be smuggled into the law-governed domain of inter-subjective language. Freud draws freely on this metaphor of customs and excise in describing the relation between the taboo kernel of fantasy and its discursive 'envelope': a *Vorstellung* or thought, he writes, 'seeks to wrap itself in a joke . . . above all because this wrapping bribes our powers of criticism and confuses them' (182). In other words, although a joke has something illegal in its baggage, it gets into the lawful domain of social reality by bribing the customs officer – that is, by offering a distracting intellectual pleasure in its verbal 'cover'. The joke is thus both fully discursive and entails – somehow in the very rhythm of concealment–disclosure – something *irreducible* to discourse, an asemic pulse of forbidden, fantasmatic jouissance.

If we return to Joyce's greeneyed lobster, we could therefore read it through Freud's idea of the *Witz* as at once fantasmatic and discursive. But if a joke is to be successful, Freud implies, there has to be a certain performative expertise, the canny rhetorical ability to defer and displace revelation and so cause fantasmatic enjoyment to flicker up momentarily without disrupting the semantic coherence of (the ego's) reality. Shakespeare's name for this devilish comic talent is of course Iago, that arch-manipulator of discourse and disclosure, whose very name encodes a sort of performative tautology: *I* + *ago*, Latin for 'I do', being the perfect title of one who

knows very well 'how to do things with words'. And the Joycean significance of the actor Layfield's unfortunate-fortunate slip bears precisely on
its creative undoing of such rhetorical mastery. If the Shakespearean text
embodies in Iago its most extreme figure of seductive language – and perhaps even of its *own* theatrical language[18] – as a cunningly sealed vessel
for nameless and deadly fantasy, Joyce's enjoyment of the greeneyed lobster signals his sense of the vast literary potential waiting to be released
by the self-unravelling of that masterly performative language. After all,
Layfield's fatal slip is both 'rich and strange', to repeat Ariel's line: that is,
it is not only alien to the semantic fabric of reality, a laughable or uncanny
showing-forth of mute jouissance – but is also *rich*, an evocative and mysterious literary symbol. When Layfield in the guise of Iago fails to tell
the joke properly, as it were, his variation of Shakespeare's line undermines
both the coherence of his character and the subtle force of rhetorical suggestion it depends on. What emerges, however, is not merely some meaningless
squawk but a *name* that figures forth metonymically a fantasmatic, undersea
otherness.

Here it might be worth recalling another famous literary lobster: the one
taken for a walk in the Palais Royal gardens by the 'mad' poet Gérard de
Nerval. Joyce had first come across Nerval in Arthur Symons's *The Symbolist
Movement in Literature* (1899), where the poet's work was declared to be 'the
particular origin of the literature which I call Symbolist', which Symons
went on to define as 'a literature in which the visible world is no longer
a reality, and the unseen world no longer a dream'.[19] For Symons, that is,
Nerval's poetry was visionary in a special sense: it saw through reality and
made visible an occult fantasmatic domain masked off by that reality. And
if the extravagances of aesthetic *folie* were later made merely fashionable by
decadent Parisian *flâneurs* out strolling with their turtles, Nerval's literary
madness was no trivial pose of eccentricity. As Gautier reports, the poet
defended taking a lobster for a walk by claiming that, unlike a dog, it
embodied something foreclosed from human reality: these clever creatures,
as he put it, 'know the secrets of the sea'.[20]

If both Nerval and Layfield had their lobsters, then, both also stand for an
uncanny awakening; the moment when a character falls out of the fictional
frame, be it a Shakespearean text or a constrictive 'reality', marking the
emergence of something socially unacceptable, indigestible. Yet the mad
poet and the inept actor are also supremely funny; it is once again 'poison
in jest' that characterises the literary act. How does Joyce take up that fertile
and dangerous self-undoing without covering over its traumatic breach of
discursive legality?

SANT IAGO

First we must examine how Shakespeare himself deals with the intrusion of comical and uncanny lobsters on to his stage. We should take careful note of Hamlet's words to the players prior to the performance of 'The Mousetrap':

Let those that play your clowns speak no more than is set down for them – for there be some of them that will themselves laugh, to set on some quantity of barren spectators to laugh too, though in the meantime some necessary question of the play be then to be considered. That's villainous, and shows a most pitiful ambition in the fool that uses it. (III.ii.38–45)

Like ham-fisted Freudian jokers, such villainous clowns fail to provide the critical faculty (or the 'judicious' (26) members of the audience) with the necessary intellectual distraction that would allow enjoyment to be smuggled invisibly into the domain of social meaning, and instead they simply fall back on laughter as a crude, carnivalesque subversion of theatrical propriety. Note how Hamlet sees an antagonism between extended textual interpretation and the immediacy of performance: the fool's actorly excesses, his unauthorised or impromptu variations, precisely distract from 'some necessary question of the play', impede the audience's engagement with the significant textual message being launched by the playwright. The key point about this clownish laughter, which threatens the symbolic integrity of the play, is that it is unrepeatable: like all true comedy, it is an unscripted event, forming no part of a quotable text but depending entirely on the instance of the living voice and the singular, accidental rapport between player and audience. The clown's impromptu enjoyment ruptures the artwork by showing that its authorial signifiers are mired in the sinful particularity of an utterance.

Moreover, Hamlet's advice to the players manifests a certain faith in language as mimetic representation (Austin's 'constative') – a faith that is, in an oft-noted irony, completely undermined by *Hamlet* itself. If 'any camelot prince of dinmurk' is pictured in *Finnegans Wake* crouching 'hapless behind the dreams of accuracy' (*FW* 143.7), one such dream would surely be to imagine 'The Mousetrap' as offering a definitive solution or truthful representation of the riddles of *Hamlet* (and the same could be said of Freud's Oedipal 'solution' of those riddles, as we saw in Part I above). The idea that sticking to the script is enough to ensure faithful delivery of the authorial message is notably undone later in the play when Hamlet encounters the gravedigger (v.i). 'We must speak by the card or equivocation will undo us' (v.i.133–4) is the prince's prim response to the clownish wordplay that dares to unravel his authority; and here 'equivocation', as an editorial note tells us, already carries connotations of occult or diabolic trickery, later to be made explicit in Macbeth's 'the equivocation of the fiend'.[21] Equivocation stands more generally for the way that language exceeds and subverts the semantic control of the ego, causing meaning to slip from my grasp: once again, it is verbal *performance* that displaces any prescribed role or stable self-identification. Like the 'quick lie' that refuses to take a single subject – ''twill away again from me to you', the gravedigger quips (124–5) – discourse is revealed to belong to the Other: in other words, it is drastically at odds with the ego's urge to achieve final semantic self-appropriation. Even speaking rigorously 'by the card', with complete fidelity to the script or grammatical rule-book, may not be enough to protect the ego from the transformative play unleashed by the linguistic act, its fundamental effect of error, of going astray.

Here, we should note how Hamlet's response to the verbal clowning of his social inferior, for all its tight-lipped irony, makes a definite link between an encounter with the otherness of verbal enjoyment and the disintegration of the subject: 'or equivocation will *undo* us'. And this is of course precisely what occurs in the quasi-Kafkaesque 'transformation scene' (*FW* 222.14) of Layfield's green-eyed lobster: an accidental verbal slip, the uncanny metamorphosis of 'monster' to 'lobster', somehow coincides with – perhaps triggers off – the unknotting of the 'I', the hilarious but disastrous loss of self-possession.

To explore this scene of self-unravelling further, and to confirm its central significance for Joyce's writing, we shall augment our Joycean readings of Shakespearean tragedy by turning to Lacan's seminar *Le sinthome*. As we saw in Part I, by the mid-1970s Lacan has come to conceive of the human subject as precisely a knot or chain in which real, symbolic and imaginary are linked together, allowing the unconscious and the ego to attain different degrees of signifying coherence in the face of the asemic force of jouissance. But what would happen, Lacan asks his seminar on 11 May 1976, if the knot were not tied properly, if it contained an error or *faute* (a term deliberately chosen to echo 'sin')? It would, of course, come undone – and the Joycean 'epiphany' is testimony, in Lacan's view, to just such disintegration. For Lacan, the epiphany records a quasi-hallucinatory encounter that entails the unknotting of real, symbolic and imaginary, although the act of writing itself then 'makes up' the knot, offering it *suppléance*. A moment in *A Portrait of the Artist as a Young Man* serves, in Lacan's view, to illustrate this topological reading of the epiphany: there Stephen, having been beaten by

Heron and his friends because of a disagreement (on the question of the literary merits of the 'heretic' Byron), experiences a sudden loss of feeling, as if 'some power was divesting him of that sudden-woven anger as easily as a fruit is divested of its soft ripe peel' (*P* 82–3). Pierre Skriabine offers a useful topological sketch of this reading:

It is now possible to locate the fault, to trace it on the knot of R, S and I, and it is there, at the point where it takes place, that Lacan situates – this is how he formulates matters in the case of Joyce – the ego as *sinthome*, as a corrective sewing-together.[22]

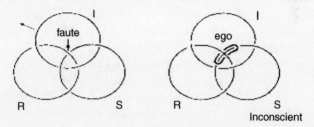

What 'falls out' of the knot is thus the 'I', the imaginary register that conveniently doubles the English personal pronoun; and then the 'I' seems to return with a different name, as 'ego', to carry out the *raboutage* that will reconstitute the knot. We shall return to this falling-away of meaning and the restoration of the knot in Chapter 6 below.

For the time being, it seems that 'I am not what I am': if the ego is to be relocated at the point where meaning collapses, it must have undergone some radical transformation, for, in so far as it coincides with the imaginary, the ego is – according to Lacanian orthodoxy – the locus *par excellence* of semantic mastery. But we should note that Lacan is careful here to avoid using the term *moi*, the standard French translation of Freud's *Ich*, instead choosing the Latin *ego* to designate this transformed point of identification. Now, the self-appropriation of the ego in a meaningful image, position or role is the very definition of the imaginary, as Lacan had first spelled out long before in 'The Mirror Stage'; so again, the peculiarity of what is written as 'ego' in the right-hand diagram must be that it identifies without meaning, somehow appearing to itself at the point where human discourse dissolves, and with it the social bond that it inscribes.

The Wakean question, 'When is a man not a man?', which we have seen to be a central 'necessary question' of Shakespearean tragedy, thus returns in Lacan's exploration of Joyce as *sinthome*. Among the puns that cluster around this reinvention of the psychoanalytic symptom are *saint homme* – sainthood entailing a transcendence of the limits of human, or perhaps merely of masculine, subjectivity – and *synth-homme*, with a Greekish prefix perhaps suggesting an artificial or fabricated, fictitious manhood.

What is at stake here is an identification with something outside the discursive bounds and bonds of social reality – in other words with what refuses to be subject to the constraints that constitute that reality (and above all, Lacan insists, those constraints bear on jouissance). Such an identification might thus take the paradoxical form of pure selflessness: either that of the saint who abandons all egoic investment in worldly matters, or that of the actor whose rapid changes of role and costume signal a radical withdrawal from the everyday social-discursive consolidation of identity. In both cases, the *sinthome* is the site of a 'disinvestment' (Lacan's term is *désabonnement*, literally 'withdrawal of subscription') from the repetitious social circulation of signifiers; an act that entails a mysterious or terrifying apparition beyond the forms of identity imposed by the Other.

Critics have pointed out the radical ambiguity of the self-evacuation at stake in Lacan's theory of the subject, and have traced its roots back to contradictions in the first attempts by Enlightenment thinkers to envisage subjectivity as a 'free particular'. If, as Joan Copjec notes, 'Kant's innovation was to link evil to human freedom',[23] Slavoj Žižek sees in critical philosophy a veritable *coincidentia oppositorum* where the subject, robbed of a substantial ego by being posited as a moment of pure, groundless 'self-relating', returns as nothing less than an uncanny spectre or monster.[24] In Lacan's *sinthome*, a kind of postscript added to his theory of the subject, perhaps we see a certain *nachträglich* or delayed effect of this unresolved or irresolvable Enlightenment question. The selflessness of choosing what lies beyond the limited interests of the 'pathological' ego may entail either obeying the moral law or pursuing what Kant calls 'radical' – which is to say groundless, diabolic – evil. But who or what is it that chooses?

Perhaps these questions, or something uncannily like them, are already being enacted and explored on the Shakespearean stage. In *Macbeth* we witness a split between the ego as reflexive self-representation and its 'anamorphic', spectral double, and see that split being clearly linked to the fateful moment of the act. When, immediately after the killing of Duncan, Lady Macbeth urges her husband to relinquish the unmanly pleasures of reflective selfhood – 'Be not lost / So poorly in your thoughts' (II.ii.74–5) – he has to confront a stark alternative between his familiar self-conscious ego and some unrecognisable other self who has committed murder: 'To know my deed, 'twere best not know myself' (76). Macbeth's formula in effect inverts the famous inscription above Apollo's temple at Delphi,

gnothi se auton, 'know thyself', which had governed Western thought since
Plato first noted it in the *Protagoras* (and which Lacan will dismiss as a
'futile adage': *E:S* 165). With the *passage à l'acte* of regicide, Macbeth has
put himself beyond the space of representation, a space where the subject,
even if it was in thrall to the desire of the Other, had at least been able to
find some shelter in the ceaseless *différance* of signification from the sheer
immediacy of jouissance. And *Macbeth* seems already to know all about
the psychical economy at stake here, as the fatal act triggers off a hallucinatory transgression of the barrier between ego and fantasmatic double:
'Methought I heard a voice cry, "Sleep no more: / Macbeth does murder
sleep"' (II.ii.38–9). The 'I' that is awoken by the voice is split off from – and
precisely *by* – the 'Macbeth' whose deed has breached the protective barrier
between fantasy and symbolic reality, causing unrepresentable jouissance
to flood into that reality and render it unreal, nightmarish. Lady Macbeth
quickly grasps that the only way to respond to such a traumatic breach of
reality and maintain a coherent self is to forbid it access to the psyche, to
foreclose it: 'These deeds must not be thought / After these ways; so, it will
make us mad' (36–7).

   The transformation of what Lacan writes as 'ego' in his topological reading of Joyce's epiphany, its unimaginable identification with a refusal of
the symbolic constraints on jouissance that constitute social reality, is thus
already in question for Shakespeare's tragic protagonists. Macbeth's initial
inability to identify with his 'own' act marks his stubborn attachment to
worldly meaning, to the familiar shape of his social reality with its protective
semantic protocols. To seek to appropriate, to enfold in a self-representing
subjectivity, an act that smashes apart the semantic ground of that egoic
reality would be, at least according to Lady Macbeth's shrewd diagnosis, to
be mad.

   The question of quotation, and here in particular of Joyce's quotation of
Shakespeare, might offer us another way to approach the *sinthome* at this
point. An actor who properly quotes the dramatist's lines identifies with a
coherent imaginary world governed by clear semantic laws – one of which
(as Hamlet stresses) is to speak 'by the card', to give a faithful rendition of the
script without disfiguring it through anything accidental (or 'pathological',
to use Kantian language) such as improvisation or laughter. To maintain
the fictional consistency of the 'I' who speaks in character is one way
of guaranteeing the stability of the artistic frame, the border separating
artwork from reality. When a character falls out of character – as in the
theatrical anecdotes so relished by Joyce, but also less straightforwardly
within Shakespearean drama itself, as when Macbeth begins to unravel

after his murderous act into Macbeth, Glamis and Cawdor (ii.ii.44–6) – what is revealed is an unruly burst of jouissance, either laughter or anxiety, signalling an uncanny breach of the representational law; something has occurred that is precisely *against the rules* that govern the meaning of a theatrical event by distinguishing it from a real one.

Critics have often dwelt on the overwhelming predominance of *Hamlet* in Joyce's reworked Shakespearean universe; and certainly, as Cheng notes, there are far more allusions to that play in *Ulysses* and *Finnegans Wake* than to any other Shakespearean work. But it is another Shakespearean tragedy, *Othello*, that will provide the key to our exploration of Joyce as *sinthome* – and notably to Lacan's problematic of 'radical foreclosure', of ego-unravelling, which in our view can best be thought of by linking it to 'maimed acts' (*FW* 325.32) or performative catastrophes.

One such maimed act, indeed, would be a textual hybrid of *Hamlet* and *Othello*. It is perhaps no surprise to see Joyce, who delights in disfiguring the integrity of Shakespeare's texts through literary collage, suturing together *Hamlet* and *Othello*; but he does so in a particularly revealing way. The most striking instance of this comes in the 'Circe' episode of *Ulysses*, when the face of William Shakespeare appears, deprived of beard and crowned with cuckold's horns, and screeches 'Iagogo!' (*U* 15.3828). Both Bloom and Stephen gaze at this image in the mirror, each seeing something of his own reflection: for Bloom, the castrated bard perhaps serves as a nightmarish reminder of his wife's adultery, while Stephen sees the image as a projection of his own Hamlet-like obsession with traduced paternal authority. But he might also hear in its strange utterance – 'Iagogo!' – an echo of another of his obsessions, with the (castrating) desire of the mother: for Hamlet's shrill rebuke to his sinful mother, 'Go, go, you question with a wicked tongue' (iii.iv.12) is distinctly audible in the distorted name of Othello's tormentor. If 'Iagogo' thus brings a devilish Shakespearean seducer into the 'dance inane' (*FW* 250.16) of 'Circe', at the same time it bears traces of the irreducible, unspeakable sexuality revealed when Hamlet encounters his mother.

The textual phantasmagoria of 'Circe' makes manifest many of the potential, implicit or unconscious elements from earlier in *Ulysses*, and there are plenty of hints from the very beginning of the book that identifications are never stable, nor are Shakespearean roles ever fixed. When Stephen tells himself on Sandymount strand, 'you will never be a saint' (*U* 3.128), the reader is reminded that it is above all the narrative 'I', its 'manshape' (*U* 3.413) as ineluctable as the modality of the visible, that dominates Joyce's mocking self-portrait. If Stephen sees on the beach 'signatures of all things

I am here to read' (*U* 3.2), constantly re-inscribing himself at the phenomenal and artistic centre, he is nevertheless painfully aware of the limitations of such a vision, and of his inability to escape from a single, fallen
existence. Nor does his ironic identification with Hamlet help; for that
role itself amounts to little more than a redoubled crisis of identity, of
the 'mind's eye' (1.ii.185) becoming acutely conscious of itself as arbitrary,
contingent, transitory. Playing at being Hamlet can never amount to an
escape from a narcissistic *Innenwelt* into saintly self-transcendence; but
Joyce's intricate intertextual web here allows us to link sainthood, madness and Shakespearean drama as related questions of self-overcoming or
self-abandonment.

'The essential element in saintliness', declares Lacan in his seminar on
The Ethics of Psychoanalysis, 'resides in the fact that the saint consumes the
price paid in the form of suffering.' This would clearly imply overcoming,
or simply relinquishing, the ego; the goal of a saint is 'access to sublime
desire and not at all his own desire, for the saint lives and pays for others'.[25]
If saintliness thus entails the sacrifice of the 'I', it seems entirely apt to read
in *Finnegans Wake* an invocation of 'Sant Iago by his cocklehat' (*FW* 41.2):
that is, the name of a true saint, a saint minus 'I'. But we should pay close
attention, with an eye on both Shakespeare and *Ulysses*, to this I-less Saint
Iago. 'By his cockle hat' is a line from one of Ophelia's mad songs in Act IV
of *Hamlet*; the 'true love' is identified there as a pilgrim who has visited the
shrine at Santiago de Compostela, and thus wears a scallop or cockle shell
on his hat as a symbol of repentance and regeneration.[26] Once again, then,
Joyce is weaving together *Hamlet* and *Othello*, Ophelia's dissolving identity
mingling with Iago's 'I am not what I am'. But the line from the *Wake* also
refers us back again, more subtly, to 'Proteus': first to the moment when
Stephen sees two 'Cocklepickers' (*U* 3.342) on the beach and notices the
woman glance up at his 'Hamlet hat' (3.390). Perhaps donning a role or
'manshape' (3.413) – and a submerged pun on 'cock' in 'cockle hat' goes
back to Ophelia's deranged singing – stands as a metaphor for self-infidelity,
for the lack of 'proper' identity. This is confirmed at the end of 'Proteus',
as Stephen's thoughts hark back to Ophelia's song: 'My cockle hat and staff
and his my sandal shoon' (*U* 3.487–8).[27] Just as his headgear – both his
thoughts and his hat – are borrowed from Shakespeare, so Stephen's shoes
are 'a buck's castoffs' (*U* 3.446), they used to belong to Buck Mulligan.
From head to foot, it seems, Stephen finds himself declaring, 'I am not
what I am'; he is stiflingly conscious of the *otherness* of his 'own' identity,
of the intimate relations between owning up to or taking responsibility for
an identity and being in debt to another.

We should pause here to consider the question of Joycean debt more closely; we shall see again how indebted the question itself is to Shakespeare. 'He who stealeth from the poor lendeth to the Lord,' japes Buck Mulligan (*U* 1.727–8) before attributing the sentiment to Nietzsche's Zarathustra, according to the clichéd view of that philosopher as a supreme 'egoarch', in Stephen's phrase. Indeed, the opening section of *Ulysses* (the 'Telemachiad') is centred on the psychical and philosophical implications of ownership, payment and debt as experienced and theorised by Stephen. When the *Wake* mocks Nietszche by writing his 'egoarch' as 'Zerothruster' (*FW* 281.11–12), we are also given a perfect name for Mr Deasy, the pro-British schoolmaster of 'Nestor', whose *I owe nothing* (*U* 2.253–4) is thrust aggressively in Stephen's face: a staunch denial of any symbolic debt to the Other. Deasy's sum (both his all-round 'philosophy' with its closure of accounts and his self-declaring *sum* or 'I am') might be written, following the ominous triadic rhythm of *I owe nothing*, as *I O O*; and we could see the same sum inverted, its even circularity made odd, in Stephen's sum 'nought, nought, one' (*U* 3.39–40). The theological notion of 'creation from nothing' (3.35) leads the Joycean artist to conceive of existence, not as an economic transaction to be settled, rendered even – but as a singular *gift*, something unaccountable, irredeemable. We shall see that creation *ex nihilo* and symbolic debt will be central elements in Lacan's reading of Joyce.

What is most significant in Deasy's declaration of debt-free self-integrity – especially in the contexts we have examined of Lamb's 'Sanity of True Genius' and Joyce's complex relation to 'Great Shapesphere' (*FW* 295.4) – is how it seeks support in the authority of Shakespeare:

But what does Shakespeare say? *Put but money in thy purse.*
– Iago, Stephen murmured. (*U* 2.238–40)

The reflexive question of Joycean quotation returns here as another version of the preoccupation with debt, responsibility and ownership. What does Shakespeare actually say? Who is to say who speaks in this line, spoken, in a play signed by Shakespeare, by a character called Iago, who defines himself as not identical with himself? If, among the many ironies in play here, · we quickly perceive one in Deasy's attempt to find moral self-justification in a line given to Shakespeare's most hated villain at a moment of vile skulduggery, the question cannot be limited to a single misappropriation of authority. Deasy's reading is, to return to the term we explored in Part I above, a *traduction*: by ascribing the quote unilaterally to a single authorial voice, Deasy cuts out its constitutive performative dimension, completely erasing the uncanny *jouissance* of Iago's seductive villainy, his insidious ear-poisoning.

Another Shakespearean theory discussed at the beginning of *Ulysses* provokes a similar question about the origin and end of its utterance:

He proves by algebra that Hamlet's grandson is Shakespeare's grandfather and that he himself is the ghost of his own father.
–What? Haines said, beginning to point at Stephen. He himself? (*U* 1.555–8)

Buck Mulligan's mocking *précis* of Stephen's theory of *Hamlet* deliberately plays on grammatical ambiguities, which the rather slow-witted Haines seeks at once to clarify: is Stephen 'himself' in some sense a character involved in his own theory, perhaps because his relation to his own father has somehow been revealed or altered by his reading of Shakespeare's play? The ambiguity of 'he himself' returns us to Stephen's footwear, labelled 'his my sandal shoon' (*U* 3.488): if they are 'his' (Buck Mulligan's) as well as 'my' (Stephen's) shoes, they are also *and at the same time* 'his' (the character Stephen's) and *mine* (James Joyce's). In other words, the subject of the utterance – the one who thinks, speaks or writes – oscillates between authorial signature and 'portrait of the artist'; the personal pronoun marks a point of uncanny ambiguity where reality and its apparitional double seem to alternate. The infidelity or metempsychotic instability of the Other and the self thus blend in this Joycean maimed act or disfigured Shakespeare; and the loss of secure identity in language is refigured *en abîme* in a text riddled with the texts of another, with the 'I' of the other.

If *Hamlet* is thus grafted on to *Othello* (or more precisely, as we have seen, on to Iago) in Joyce, how can we read this unfaithful rendition or textual cuckoldry in relation to Lacan's *sinthome*? First, in terms of self-representation and self-division, which is to say: as another version of the Joycean 'first riddle of the universe' (*FW* 170.4). At the very beginning of *Othello*, we learn that the play will turn on the question, 'When is a man not a man?' We should pay close attention to the following exchange:

IAGO   These are the raised father and his friends,
       You were best go in.
OTHELLO   Not I, I must be found:
       My parts, my title, and my perfect soul,
       Shall manifest me rightly: is it they?
IAGO   By Janus I think no.

(1.ii.28–33)

Othello's naive faith in the constative power, the mimetic fidelity, of his self-representation is figured in the tautologous self-designation of the 'I'. The 'I' in question here refuses to 'go in', to withdraw from the fully visible scene where signs are supposed to function properly as truthful representation (note the contrast with Hamlet's 'I have that within which passes show'). Language, Othello is sure, will properly quote the 'I'; and of course every word of Iago's response suggests, with diabolic accuracy, how wrongheaded such faith in language will prove to be. 'By Janus I think no' is a subtle variation on 'I am not what I am'; both statements point to Iago's utter rejection of the model of language – indeed, of the whole representational world, with its implicitly self-identical space and time – manifested by Othello. Unfortunately, in one sense the play will show Iago to be right: his sceptical nominalism ('love', he declares, is just a name for 'a lust of the blood and a permission of the will': 1.iii.335–6) turns out to be a far shrewder approach to the signifying economy at work in Shakespearean drama than Othello's purblind faith in mimesis.

Now, our Joycean riddle is already being eloquently addressed in the contrasting visions of language thus set out by Shakespeare. We recall how in *Macbeth* the fantasy of full, integral masculine identity – 'my unhoused free condition' is Othello's version (1.ii.26) – is bound up with a fantasmatic mastery of *time*, the appropriation of temporal otherness by the global ego. A real man – this was Lady Macbeth's view – should be able to *make* time, rather than being unmade by the mere accidents of history; and a man is no longer a man when he ceases to enjoy this transcendent *poesis*, this undivided 'I' whose activity dominates the 'now', making it *his* time. The key to this fantasy is its hyperinflation of reflexive consciousness, of self-knowledge and self-possession; and this reflexive 'I', as *Othello* will show, is a matter of blind faith.

If Othello has faith in language to 'manifest me rightly', by contrast Iago has a wary sensitivity to the equivocations and slippery reversals of the signifier. But what Iago does have absolute faith in – and this is where he looks like an uncanny forebear of Lacan's *sinthome* – is the *act*. The act, as Lacan conceived it, corresponds to a central enigma of Shakespeare's tragedy; indeed, it allows us to respond to the notorious critical problem of Iago's character, his infamous 'motiveless malignity'. For the asemic jouissance of the act is something that Iago lives for – indeed, is willing to sacrifice his very 'self' to; and it entails the very antithesis of Othello's fantasmatic self-appropriation in a frozen temporality. Iago never pauses to reflect on himself (perhaps, like a vampire, he has no mirror-image), but flickers into visibility despite himself in stray lines:

''tis here, but yet confus'd; / Knavery's plain face is never seen, till us'd'
(II.i.306–7).

Knavery – we recall Hamlet's outraged reaction to the gravedigger – is
an act that both inhabits and eludes representation: it is impromptu, an
unscripted one-off, *ex nihilo*. Note how Iago's declaration of faith in such
an act dispenses with conscious reflection: ''tis here', he *feels*, and there is no
need to know just what 'it' is. This lack of knowledge is indeed essential to
Iago's act; line 307 should therefore be read literally: the identifiable 'face'
or truth of the act fully coincides with the instant of its occurrence (which
amounts to saying that it has *no* 'face'). The act can never be prescribed
or represented; it has no before or after; it always occurs as radically new.
One Shakespearean answer to Joyce's riddle, 'When is a man not a man?',
would therefore be 'When he acts' – or better, since the subject of the act
is always fundamentally passive, 'When the act occurs.' In one sense, this
corresponds to Shem's answer, 'When he's a sham': 'act' here designating
what is unreal, fantasmatic, non-existent. A sham, however, is also a Shem,
a Wakean poet: the act, by breaking out of faithful representation into a
moment of unaccountable madness or knavery, constitutes an essentially
creative and innovative event. But how is an artist to identify with such
a moment of creation *ex nihilo* without entering into satanic rivalry with
God the Father? How am I to sign myself?

CHAPTER 5

Egomen and women

A human truth, which is always very much a lie, hides as much of life as it displays.

Robert Louis Stevenson[1]

Language sup-poses and hides what it brings to light, in the very act in which it brings it to light.

Giorgio Agamben[2]

s.d. (*sic*)

Lionel Trilling reports that when Freud was greeted, on his seventieth birthday, as the 'discoverer of the unconscious' his response was to disclaim that title, remarking that 'the poets and philosophers before me discovered the unconscious'.[3] This was to return 'discovery' to its literal sense: an act of making visible, of unveiling. So the unconscious had previously been revealed, Freud implied, but anonymously, without the involvement of a self-theorising ego like himself: its *alethia* had, paradoxically enough, been blind. The many questions immediately raised by Freud's ambiguous tribute to poets and philosophers – to do with how we might locate the unconscious subject thus posited, how we can identify the source and end of this alleged participation in Freudian truth – have continued to bedevil psychoanalysis, above all in its repetitive attempts to shed light on the artistic object and its creation.

Lacan's reading of Joyce as *sinthome* might, however, provide us with ways to rethink and clarify certain aspects of this artistic dis-covery; above all, the question of how art can embody or conjure up the fantasmatic enjoyment that is excluded – or foreclosed, to use Lacan's term – from reality. In this, however, Joyce's writing is in no sense reduced by Lacan to a mere vessel of psychoanalytic truth; rather, the *sinthome* marks a limit of articulate, theoretical truth (although we shall examine below some attempts – by

104

Wilde as *agent provocateur*, by Morton Prince as psychological authority –
to make it truthful).

One of the first problems of reading Joyce involves identification. His
early struggle with editors and printers to remove from his texts what he
saw as the 'eyesore' of quotation marks was a deliberate effort to break with
the restrictive typographical conventions of Victorian publishing: inverted
commas, as Joyce put it, 'give an impression of unreality' (*JJ* 353). If the
reader is therefore often unsure about who is supposed to be speaking
in the Joycean text, we can immediately see how this difficulty rejoins
that of psychoanalysis in its search for the agency or source of the artistic
message. (Who is speaking, through Hamlet's mouth, of Oedipal desire?)
And the question of identification is always bound up in Joyce with that
of quotation: how can we situate a subject in language as identical with
its utterance? Our act of reading itself is already implicated in the same
question, as the text constantly reminds us; for we occupy the central
place in it, as those who quote and question it, who identify with it and
through it.

Joyce's writing explores the same questions in its celebrated moments
of critical self-reflexivity, most of all in *Ulysses*. Our exploration above of
Iago as a forebear of the *sinthome* – a character centred on a deliberate non-
response to the hysterical-critical question 'What does it mean?' or 'Who is
speaking?' – leads us straight into Stephen's theory of Shakespearean authority and identity. In *Othello*, Stephen concludes in 'Scylla and Charybdis',
Shakespeare is both 'bawd and cuckold. . . . His unremitting intellect is
the hornmad Iago ceaselessly willing that the moor in him shall suffer'
(*U* 9.1021–4). But this notion of an impossible textual site – 'unremitting'
in the sense of impossible to deliver to stable legibility – does nothing to
deter John Eglinton, a character given the epithet 'undaunted' (*U* 9.1027) to
mock his application of solid realism to the most otherworldly. If Eglinton
immediately seeks to restore Iago to realistic plenitude – 'And what a character is Iago!' he exclaims, re-punctuating Stephen's question as an affirmation
of identity – his next comment nevertheless returns us to Joyce's preoccupation with creation *ex nihilo*: 'After God Shakespeare has created most' (and,
significantly, Eglinton cannot decide whether this line belongs to Dumas
fils or Dumas *père*) (*U* 9.1027–9).

The idea of the act of divine creation being itself a transgression, an
original sin – once again, an idea Joyce discovered in Vico – returns here in a
Shakespearean setting. If Iago is 'hornmad', he resembles the 'shrewridden'
(*U* 15.111) or devilish bard we see in 'Circe', with a head crowned with

horns like Freud's Moses – and the resemblance is confirmed when Joyce has Shakespeare crow, 'Iagogo!' (*U* 15.3821–8), the distorted name itself perhaps an encrypted signature (I + *ago*, Latin for 'I act'). The line from Dumas might thus have to be revised, so that Shakespearean creation would be not so much divine as diabolic; or perhaps the very act of creating 'after God', seeking to rival or double the original *ex nihilo*, would be a defining characteristic of the devil.

Long before Coleridge's identification of Iago with a quasi-Kantian 'nihilation' of the substantial subject, the search to explain Shakespeare's most notorious villain had already linked the character to the idea of absolute evil and its diabolic incarnation. Indeed, we could identify the first 'critic' to make such a link – and we shall return to this crucial self-reflective turn in Shakespeare – as Othello himself. Unable to look Iago in the face during the play's agonising denouement, he can only mutter, 'Will you, I pray, demand that demi-devil / Why he hath thus ensnar'd my soul and body?' (v.ii.302–3). This demand for meaning sets a template, we might say, for literary criticism in its desire for a responsible Shakespeare, as paradigmatic literary-ideological father. The key for our argument here is therefore Iago's refusal to speak: it marks the instance of what Lacan will term 'radical foreclosure'. Iago seems to withdraw his 'I' from social circulation, to subtract it from the institutional chain of subjectivation (of the kind analysed in Foucault's early work; note how Gratiano threatens to use the apparatus of state violence to induce the subject's self-enunciation: 'Torments will ope your lips': 307). But the crucial point is that Iago's gesture of satanic defiance (or saintly resistance) is a double bluff, a final card played by his 'sham' subjectivity; for the demi-devil has no inner truth to yield up that would have made sense of 'his' act, he cannot take responsibility (literally, is unable to answer) for it, and so in refusing to do so he is being at last – and somewhat paradoxically – honest.

How does this radical irresponsibility relate to Joycean creation? Iago's faceless knavery, an essentially unaccountable or asubjectal act, resembles nothing so much as Joycean paternity, at least as it is explicitly theorised by Stephen in his discussion of Shakespeare. The famous passage beginning with Stephen's notion of a father as 'a necessary evil' (*U* 9.828) reads differently, a darker note sounding beneath its self-conscious rhetoric, if we refer it to the foreclosure of meaning embodied by Iago:

Fatherhood, in the sense of conscious begetting, is unknown to man. It is a mystical estate, an apostolic succession, from only begetter to only begotten. On that mystery and not on the madonna which the cunning Italian intellect flung to the mob of Europe the church is founded and founded irremovably because founded, like the world, macro- and microcosm, upon the void. Upon incertitude, upon unlikelihood. (*U* 9.837–42)

If the only link 'in nature' between a father and his creation is 'an instant of blind rut' (*U* 9.859), fatherhood does not exist as a consistent, psychologically meaningful act, a 'conscious begetting'. And for Stephen this non-existence is originary, foundational: not only is it the basis of the patriarchal institution of the church, it even subtends divine creation, whose 'mystery' speaks less of the Father's inscrutable will than of the random collision of atoms.

Stephen himself, Joyce's most famous artistic double, is caught up in the same impossibility of 'conscious begetting', the split between self-reflecting 'I' and the creative novelty of the act. As a 'portrait of the artist', Stephen is a means to reflect upon (to re-mark) the impossibility of unitary representation – and hence, doubly, of self-representation. But the cracked artistic mirror in which Stephen contemplates this self-division offers a double vision; the integral 'I' may be threatened by reduplicative fragmentation, but it is equally tempted by the vertiginous possibilities of innovation and invention lying outside egoic closure. In a crucial sense, as we shall see, the literary act constitutes precisely an escape from a single identity, and thus offers to enrich the existence of the ego vastly – or else to unravel it fatally. When Stephen contemplates his 'own' act of self-doubling, it is with an acute sense of this ambiguity: 'As I am. As I am. All or not at all' (*U* 3.452). The doubled self posited here is either an 'Allfather' (*U* 9.61) – exempt, as absolute creative singularity, from signifying difference – or is 'not at all', a fantasmatic void masked by fictitious, supposed authority. Eglinton, having heard Stephen's talk on Shakespearean identity, has no doubt that he has witnessed the second of these two possibilities: '– You are a delusion,' he tells Stephen, before mocking him by asking, 'Do you believe your own theory?' (*U* 9.1064–6).

Here, the subtle use of equivocation, of semiotic duplicity, is characteristic of Joyce's 'portrait' of Stephen. 'Your own theory' is thus both a theoretical account of Shakespearean identity *and* the identity of the theorist himself – for the self, as Stephen's cogitating has made clear, is finally nothing but a theory. And the equivocation amounts to a hint (not necessarily one being dropped by Eglinton) that the young artist's will to theorise his literary patrimony is very closely linked to his 'own theory', his self-belief. The fact that Stephen answers 'No' to the question might therefore imply a confirmation of Eglinton's first accusation: not that he *has* or suffers from a delusion but that he *is* one, his identity a Wakean 'spoof of visibility' (*FW* 48.1) no less ghostly than his imaginary self-engendering Shakespeare. Stephen's struggle to believe in his theoretical self is articulated in an internal debate fraught with paradox: 'I believe, O Lord, help my unbelief. That is, help me to believe or help me to unbelieve? Who helps to believe? *Egomen*. Who to unbelieve? Other chap' (*U* 9.1078–80). The Lord – God the Father or his Shakespearean double – is invoked to 'help my unbelief'. The ambiguous phrase from Mark's Gospel (9:24) makes Stephen wonder whether it is faithful identification with the ego – or rather a distance from the seeming certainty of self-enunciation – that the prayer is advocating. And this ambiguous belief in 'me' is ascribed, in an oft-noted irony, to *Egomen*: both an accentuated 'I, on the one hand' and a cast of ego-men, perhaps the Shakespearean characters listed earlier, or the ego-theorists explored earlier still in 'Proteus', or even the (male) staff at *The Egoist*, the magazine where *A Portrait* first appeared. As we shall see, the question of the limits of the self raised by Joyce with Stephen's character returns as a central problem in Lacan's conception of the *sinthome*.

Now, the Joycean key to Stephen's 'own theory' is its *economic* dimension: his discourse is immediately a question of payment, of gifts and debts. 'I don't see why you should expect payment for [your theory] since you don't believe it yourself,' carps Eglinton (now ironically dubbed 'Eclecticon' as editor of the esoteric *Dana*). If Stephen's 'I' moves with bathetic rapidity from thinking itself 'entelechy, form of forms' (*U* 9.208) to being scribbled on a grubby debtor's note – 'A.E.I.O.U.' – then the same trajectory is also reversible: that is, the indignity of owing George Russell a guinea does nothing to stop the 'I' from avowing that debt by inscribing itself at the very heart of artistic invention, as a poetic 'quintessence' (in the Theosophical jargon parodied in 'Scylla and Charybdis'). The artistic 'I', in other words, is precisely lacking any given substance, founded on the void, with nothing but its own act of literary invention to rely on for its subsistence. In a crucial sense, for Stephen the 'I' is nothing but a letter: it can be inscribed on an IOU, just as it can serve as philosophical subject or as lyrical voice, without the need for any underlying psychological consistency or plenitude.

Stephen's economy of the literary 'I' recalls the discordant encounter between sums – versions of 'I am', mathematical formulae – in 'Nestor'. Mr Deasy's motto or self-authenticating *cogito*, 'I paid my way', still echoes in Stephen's ears as he contemplates his own indebted existence (*U* 9.202–12). The fundamental question returns to 'all or not at all': is literary self-creation a balanced account or an irredeemable debt, an even or an odd sum? The childhood memory of being taunted with the rhyme

'Stephen, Stephen, cut the bread even' (*U* 9.940) inevitably makes him recall Deasy's advice, his money-slicing equipment and his well-cut 'piece de Shakespeare' (quoting Iago, of course, a great settler of debts). The fact that Deasy rhymes neatly with 'easy' is an apt emblem of this 'even' economy, whose equivalencies and formal patterns precisely cover over, in Stephen's eyes, the lack of any accountable meaning, the universal void left by a non-existent 'Allfather'. Thus the mere verbal trick of a rhyming couplet can make the singular seem predictable, and mask the nonsensical with specious authority:

> Riddle me, riddle me, randy ro.
> My father gave me seeds to sow.
> (*U* 2.88–9)

A riddle is supposed to have a solution (this one does, although we don't read it in the text of *Ulysses*: 'Writing a letter'), a response to convert its musical babble into a legible text. But such a pleasurable semiotic device serves only to cover up a point of illegibility, itself figured here in the seeming nonsense of the first line. 'Riddle *me*' indicates the first stumbling-block for Stephen: namely, the enigma of self-representation – of writing not any letter, but precisely the letter 'I' or the final mark in the series 'nought, nought, one' (*U* 3.39–40). The second line of the riddle, with its connotations of patrimony and insemination, states the problem of inscribing the 'I' as one of inheritance, or more particularly of receiving a gift. Stephen will never be able to say, 'I paid my way', in the business of writing, since the seminal source of his literary 'gift' derives from the Other (from his father, or perhaps from God the Father). And so, the riddle seems to imply, literary self-invention can never be truly *self*-invention, a groundless or divine act of creation.

For Stephen, however, the notion that a seminal gift from the father could be the solution to the riddle or sum of the self is simply more rhyming nonsense. For the 'seeds' inherited by the son are, as the *Wake* will put it, 'doubleviewed seeds' (*FW* 296.1); both abstract diacritical effects and material phonographic traces, either discursive sense-units or asemic waste products. This oscillation between letters and litters becomes a leit-motif of *Finnegans Wake*, where the 'doubleviewed seeds' are also 'WCs', confirming the 'sinse' or obscene sense of litter; as a footnote added to the phrase 'writing a letter' reminds us: 'And when you're done push the chain' (*FW* 278 n. 5).

What is thus required from the son – at least, so Stephen thinks – is not some docile subjection to a pre-given semantic patrimony, the faithful

sowing of meaningful seeds for the Other, but a groundless and thus *original*
act: the inscription of 'I' as a 'selfsownseedling' (*FW* 160.10) at precisely
the point where the Other is lacking. Which is to say: the foundation of
the self as litter, as verbal refuse, as 'poor trait of the artless' (*FW* 114.32) –
or, as Lacan will write it, as *sinthome*. The act of self-inscription would
thus entail a radical autonomy, an almost autistic act. As Stephen's unsaid
riddle continues (in a kind of textual unconscious), 'The seed was black
and the ground was white'; that is, the letters have to be inscribed on a
blank surface, a *tabula rasa*, starting 'from scratch' (as does the 'original
hen' that appears in *Finnegans Wake*: *FW* 110.22). Indeed, as the deduction
of 'one' from 'nought', this act looks almost like a 'conscious begetting'
(and as such – we shall have to return to this – it would be 'unknown to
man'). But what are the limits of this Joycean self-invention?

SATAN'S SIGNATURE: DOUBLES AND DIABLES

'Stephen is Joyce, in so far as he deciphered his own riddle.'[4] Lacan's declaration may seem a trifle brusque, given the mass of problems we have
seen to be raised by literary identification in Joyce. If Stephen is a solution
to a Joycean riddle, this can hardly be in the Freudian sense of an analytic
Lösung, the restoration of a full, properly representational account. We shall
explore Joycean riddle-solving further in Chapter 6, but our first approach
to Lacan's idea of Stephen as Joyce's response to *sa propre énigme* – to his
'own' riddle but perhaps also to that of the proper itself – will be to examine
the broader question of the literary double in three classics of the genre by
James Hogg, Oscar Wilde and Robert Louis Stevenson, and to explore how
Joyce adopted and adapted what those texts reveal. The notion of 'the double' itself, deriving from the *Doppelgänger* of German Romanticism, will
be in question as we investigate the varied textual sources – including the
different psyches imagined by Freud, Jung and Morton Prince – on which
Joyce drew in writing his 'multiplicity of personalities' (*FW* 107.24–5).

James Atherton includes in his list of Structural Books for *Finnegans Wake*
works by various 'egomen', including Morton Prince and James Hogg, and
he remarks that 'all the characters in the *Wake* split up into parts at some
place in the book'.[5] The idea of a character – in a literal sense, letter or trace –
being itself divisible, as well as the more 'freudful' (*FW* 411.35) notion of
a person decomposing into multiple constituents or identities, will be in
question as we try to shed light on the specific problematic that Atherton's
generalised picture of splitting risks obscuring. One comment from *The
Books at the Wake* should be noted at the outset, however, as it will prove

crucial: 'What is now called dissociated personality', notes Atherton, 'would not long ago have been described as demonic possession' (41). He goes on to cite Issy's letter about 'castoff devils' (*FW* 273 n. 6) before concluding nonchalantly that 'it is not usual in the *Wake* for women to be possessed by devils. This is a thing which happens to men while women simply split up into parts' (ibid.).

If the devil is another name for the double – *le double et le diable*, in Sarah Kofman's punning title, where *et* doubles as *est* – this further turn of doubling might in turn have something to do with sexual difference, at least in Atherton's reading of the *Wake*. Kofman takes the equation of double and devil literally in her reading of Freud's *The Uncanny*, but she sees the double figure as an allegory or *mise en abîme* of an originary difference at work in *all* representation, and of which sexual difference would be a mere secondary effect: 'A "diabolical" literature is no longer a literature of illusion or deception: it mimics the double as illusion . . . introducing within the text a structure of duplicity which does not allow itself to be reappropriated into, or mastered by, a problematics of truth or falsehood.'[6]

The multiplication of selves would thus be only a radical exposure of how all language 'doubles' the world, triggering the philosophical anxiety – as old as Plato – that its simulacra constitute a 'structure of duplicity' and thus obscure or dismantle the truth. Joycean writing, of course, is an exemplary site of truth-dismantling – also known as deconstruction – and has been ascribed a privileged status as such by Derrida.[7] When Joyce signs a letter to a friend using the initials of his fictional alter ego – S.D. – and then repeats that cryptic signature with a confirmatory *sic*, he opens (perhaps without knowing it) the question of representation *en abîme*, of how writing can re-mark itself as mimetic or duplicative act (*SL* 22). But when in 'Ithaca' Stephen 'himself', now installed at '7 Eccles street', obliges his host Bloom 'Doubly, by appending his signature in Irish and Roman characters' (*U* 17.775), Joyce surely confirms himself as a deconstructionist *avant la lettre*.

If the 'structure of duplicity' bound up with what Freud identifies as the uncanny is, then, from a deconstructionist perspective, a quasi-transcendental effect of representation itself, it is no surprise that psychoanalytic theory saw it differently. Freud's search for the specific core of meaning proper to 'the uncanny' (*das Unheimliche*, with a definite article) is in Kofman's eyes precisely not diabolical enough for its putative object; by looking *through* language, and thus overlooking its mimetic surface, Freudian theory wished to posit as unitary concept something that marked precisely the fracture of any such logocentric economy.

Here, Atherton's remark cited above, for all its apparent lack of theoretical sophistication, is worth recalling. If possession by the devil can be seen in the *Wake* as a distinctively masculine mode of Joycean *Ichspaltung*, this might make it, as it were, less 'diabolical' than the more radical, 'feminine' fragmentation of identity. In other words, the identity or name of the devil, supposed to be a discrete entity with a 'core of meaning', might perhaps serve as a defence against the very 'structure of duplicity' in question. Lacan will use the term *phallic* to identify the register of signification as such, and in his later work will associate phallic jouissance with the ego's urge to master its object.[8] In this perspective, identifying *the* uncanny, or being possessed by *the* devil, would comprise a certain degree of phallic enjoyment: the reduction of mimetic, reduplicative excess to a coherent, legible figure. And our critical pursuit of meaning itself would of course be yet another 'phallic' endeavour, if we accept Lacan's terminology here. But in our effort to follow Freud's pursuit of a specific fantasmatic structure in the literary multiplication of character – a structure that Joyce adopts and transforms – we shall discover not some overall, unifying meaning there, but a distinct way of treating the *collapse* of meaning.

We might begin with Joyce's letter to his grandson Stephen on 10 August 1936. He includes a story for the little boy, apparently written in a momentary break from the labour of his *Work in Progress* – although, since the story features a Faustian contract with a bilingual devil, and is signed by 'Nonno' (a grandfatherly 'Nayman of Noland': *FW* 187.28), it is clearly more of the same, the 'seme asnuh' (*FW* 620.17). And a critical clue to Joyce's diabolical final work is given in a PS, where he explains to Stevie that 'The devil mostly speaks a language of his own called Bellysbabble which he makes up himself as he goes along' (*SL* 384). The devil's language, then, is improvised: like Iago's plotting, it emerges *ex nihilo*, less an act of conscious deliberation than an almost bodily pulsation, a 'belly's babble'. This kind of language would correspond to what Lacan writes as *lalangue* – speech embodying an infantile *la-la* – or *jouis-sens*, the coalescence of meaning and enjoyment. The crucial point is that, for Lacan, language 'normally' prohibits jouissance, so that Bellysbabble should be truly diabolical in transgressing the signifying law, breaching the fundamental barrier between signification and the real. *Jouis-sens* – or Joycesense, as we should perhaps write it – is thus above all (as Nonno warns Stevie) something naughty: in other words, both nothing-at-all, founded on naught or the void, and a childish or impish defiance of paternal authority.

But how does this 'shamebred music' (as Joyce will disfigure his own *Chamber Music*: *FW* 164.15–16), this transgressive or comical language, bear on the question of multiple characters? It is again the Lacanian matheme for fantasy, $ \lozenge$ *a*, formulated in 1957 – partly, we have argued, via an engagement with *Hamlet* – that proves useful here. Serge André makes that matheme more comprehensible by linking it to the normalising function of the paternal metaphor: it is only the Name of the Father, claims André, that 'renders the fantasy liveable for the subject, by introducing a lozenge [the mathematical symbol for "greater than or less than"] between $ and *a*'.[9] In other words, the distance between the fantasmatic object and the subject is set up by the very effect of signifying substitution that first comes to install the subject. Symbolic identification, the process that allows the subject's desire to emerge as a consistent structure, simultaneously opens an unbridgeable gap between it and the treasured or fatal *agalma* of its libidinal object.

Now, the bridging of this 'unbridgeable' gap is precisely what is at stake here. (We should not forget the devil's bridge in Stevie's story.) If a fantasy is rendered 'liveable' only by its obedience of the 'Law of desire' (*E:S* 324) that stipulates the non-coincidence of $ and *a*, what would a defiance of that law entail? Without the mediating function of the *nom du père*, the constitutive lack in subjectivity could not take effect; the two terms of the matheme would therefore fall together, stranding what was situated as the subject in an unspeakable (although not necessarily psychotic) real. And on the other side, the object *a*, fantasmatic embodiment of the jouissance excluded from the reality of speaking-beings, would fall into that reality, becoming perhaps one of its characters or 'egomen'.

Here, we should recall Lacan's aim in the last period of his work to map real, symbolic, imaginary and *sinthome* in a complex quadruple chain-knot. The collapse of fantasy into reality would thus entail a topological denouement leading to the formation of a new knot, a fantasmatic realignment organised not by the repressive semantic protocols of the Name of the Father but by a singular *savoir-faire*. We shall have to return to the question of how 'liveable' whatever transformation of fantasy is involved in the Joycean *sinthome* might be.

For the time being, we should note how the lozenge or mark of non-coincidence between $ and *a* in Lacan's matheme designates the possibility of signifying substitution in the fantasmatic relation: in other words, neurotic fantasy is articulated in discourse, it takes place within a semantic scenario. What occurs when the matheme collapses is thus something unspeakable, impossible to enchain in discourse; something outside social reality. But what cannot be spoken can of course sometimes be shown, and here we come back to the starting-point of Freud's discussion of the

uncanny, namely Schelling's definition of the latter as 'the name for everything that ought to have remained secret and hidden but has come to
light'.[10] It is therefore no surprise that the texts by Hogg, Wilde and
Stevenson dealing with double existences (or 'doublin existents', *FW* 578.13)
are profoundly embroiled in the apparitional problematic of truth, of *alethia*
or revelation. How does Joyce take up the revelation in these texts and, by
doing so, as we hope to show, radicalise its unspeakable or diabolical effect?

Joyce acknowledges his literary debt to James Hogg's *The Private Memoirs
and Confessions of a Justified Sinner* (1824) by daubing *Finnegans Wake* lib-
erally with 'hogsfat' (doubling 'Hogg's fact', a deed or document perpetrated by Hogg: *FW* 483.23). The *Justified Sinner* is both an astonishing
premonition of Freud's discovery and a turbulent proto-modernist stylistic
experiment. At the end of the text, we can read an 'account' presented by
a crooked attorney – a fraudulent will bearing forged signatures – as an
allegory of narrative self-fragmentation:

I seemed hardly to be an accountable creature; being thus in the habit of executing
transactions of the utmost moment, without being sensible that I did them. I
was a being incomprehensible to myself. Either I had a second self, who transacted
business in my likeness, or else my body was at times possessed by a spirit over which
it had no control, and of whose actions my own soul was wholly unconscious.[11]

The narrative ego grapples with its own inability to reduce itself, split
away from proper self-recognition, to a theoretical truth: 'This was an
anomaly not to be accounted for by any philosophy of mine . . . To be in a
state of consciousness and unconsciousness, at the same time, in the same
body and same spirit, was impossible' (181). This untheorisable self-division,
identified as an anomaly (the Greek *anomalos*, 'not identical with itself',
etymologically encodes a lack of 'law', *nomos*, and of 'name', *onoma*), cannot
belong to a reality governed by the spatio-temporal unity of 'mememormee'
(*FW* 628.14), where the French for 'same' doubles into a surplus 'I' (like
Stephen's repeated 'As I am': *U* 3.452).

But Hogg's inspired move is to incarnate this lack-of-reality, to make
it into a character with a 'feminisible name of multitude' (*FW* 73.4–5):
Gil-Martin, McGill, Gil (thus, Atherton claims, 'The word "gill" in the
Wake has the meaning of "devil"': 41). 'Gaping Gill' (*FW* 36.35), as he or she
is renamed in the *Wake*, is precisely a hole, a point of visible lack – in other
words, the anomaly is no longer confined to the theoretical domain of the
ego's reflection, but made to appear in the outside world: in a world carefully
constructed by Hogg, through references to parish records and historical
documents, as authentic and 'realistic'. The effect of this apparition is a

collapse of the representational laws governing such a world and its history – laws prescribing the integrity of acts such as bearing witness or signing a document. In other words, once Gil has entered the world (and Hogg clearly intends this to be an allegory of the fall of man), the self-identity of the subject, its ability to testify to a rational social reality, is in doubt – and indeed *doubt* is precisely the point: as Fritz Senn points out, the word's Latin root *dubium* derives from *duo*, 'two', indicating the loss of single identity.[12]

In *Finnegans Wake*, Joyce spells out an intricate response to Hogg's *Justified Sinner*, with 'a multiplicity of personalities inflicted on the documents' (*FW* 107.24–5). The semantic duplicity of 'characters' – veritable 'open doubleyous' (*FW* 120.28) – is insistently exploited at every turn in the *Wake*, so that identities and letters can never be untangled or properly ascribed. In particular, Joyce relishes Hogg's invention of a character to embody the fall of a formerly stable or 'realistic' world into a condition of multiplicity, of *dubium*. Such a character, after all, could be a 'portrait of the artist'; as supreme actor and master of fictive ruses, Gil emblematises the literary artificer as creator of that which is not, as disseminator of sinful nothingness. Gil is thus a Joycean 'Nilbud' (*FW* 24.1) in a mass of senses: the satanic inversion of Dublin turns the factual solidity built up in *Ulysses* into its negative, a place where things lack (as in Stephen's cry of 'Nothung!', *U* 15.4242). But if nil-bud is the source of nothing (for Aquinas, that is, of evil) it could also be the source of the Nile, of a fertile 'riverrun' that begins and flows through the *Wake* itself.

If 'Nilbud' thus marks the very opening of the *Wake*, its 'devlinsfirst' (*FW* 1.23–4), it also inscribes what Joyce purloins from Hogg and 'adopts' himself: the figure of satanic rival and lover. 'Devlin' again encapsulates Joyce's diabolical franglais pun *double/diable*, so that, in a neat reflexive twist, 'the devil in Dublin' can double 'doubling devil'. And in 'devlinsfirst' we have not only 'Dublin's first' – perhaps 'the premier terror of Errorland' (*FW* 62.25) – but also 'the first doubling'; in other words: who comes first in a double? It is precisely this question of rivalry and priority that Gil embodies in Hogg's text, and we have seen that it subverts the very basis of identity there.

When 'Gaping Gill' re-emerges in *Finnegans Wake*, he or she (we shall return to this uncertainty) is 'swift to mate errthors, stern to checkself' (*FW* 36.35): the tendency to multiply errors, inherited from the rival Irish punmen Swift and Sterne with their polysemic names, is sown into the very description. If Gill is thus 'stern to checkself', rigorous in blocking or cross-hatching identity, this is coupled with being 'swift to mate', keen to copulate or make friends; and when we read later of an 'everdevoting fiend' (408.18) it is clear that a 'freudful mistake' (411.35) has caused the letter 'r' to slip away, making an erstwhile friend into a nil-bud or no buddy at all ('nobodyatall', *FW* 73.9).

What is crucial here is to move beyond the level of meaning and consider the problematic of loving rivalry in Joyce and Hogg as an effect of the literary *act*: here the subtraction of a letter turning friend into fiend is, we might say, 'the last word in stolentelling' (*FW* 424.35) – for it is stolen by Joyce from Hogg (although a more subtle view might see a playful reflexive irony in this purloining of a purloined letter, an irony that mocks the very ideas of ownership and priority).[13] At the end of Hogg's tale, the 'justified sinner' of the title tries to conceal his identity by declaring his name to be not Colwan but Cowan, using what will be written in the *Wake* as an 'assumptinome' (assuming a name or an alter ego that is 'no me', *FW* 153.20). And Hogg heavily implies a link between this alteration of name or identity and a subversion of the very status of the text as trustworthy representation of the world:

'There cannot be such a thing in reality,' said I, 'as the story you were mentioning just now, of a man whose name resembles mine.'
    'It's likely that you ken a wee better about the story than I do, maister,' said he, 'suppose you do leave the *L* out of your name. An' yet I think sic a waratch, an' a murderer, wad hae taen a name wi' some gritter difference in the sound. But the story is just that true . . . (207)

If a friend can turn into a fiend simply by dropping a letter, the very integrity of the reality supposedly rendered by a faithful mimetic story or history is in doubt (is more-than-one). By writing 'misses in prints' (*FW* 20.11) into the text of 'Dyoublong' (a question of self-possession, doubling or being-possessed, *FW* 13.4), Joyce will make 'multiple characters' less a matter of psychological knowledge than of the spiral of fantasmatic paradoxes triggered off by the 'selfabyss' (*FW* 40.23). In this, Joycean writing will be echoed by Lacan when he insists that the desire to make the psyche *talk*, to provide itself with discursive content, is a pre-eminently neurotic symptom, and that rigorous theory should seek instead to *show* what that constant psychobabble risks obscuring.

It is above all this *mise en cause* of psychological meaning that Joyce reads or raids out of Hogg. For the letter 'l' to be dropped from a name, or 'r' to fall from 'friend',[14] makes a decisive counter-intuitive or anti-psychological point: namely, that the subtraction of a letter entails the multiplication of characters. What occurs when a letter 'falls' or is 'stolen' (it is always a sinful or criminal act) is something unspeakable; the revelation of lack-in-the-Other, of the sheer absence of any overall 'sense' or guarantee of truth in language. And this revelation is an experience of what Lacan writes as *jouis-sens*, recalling Schelling's definition of the uncanny as forbidden revelation: a rupture of the egoic pleasure principle with its repressive constraints, an ambiguously creative or evil act that breaches the semantic integrity of 'I'. When George Colwan declares his name to be 'Cowan', we should note what kind of response he produces: 'The man stared at me, and then at his wife, with a look that spoke a knowledge of something alarming or mysterious' (206).

The fall of the letter, then, opens a hole in reality that allows something forbidden, uncanny or unspeakable to emerge. The possibility that this might offer an escape from what Lacan terms 'symbolic castration' – the sacrifice of jouissance to the limited pleasures and sterile coherence of 'I' – seems to open up before a subject caught in this rapture (or 'epiphany', as Joyce will call it). If Hogg's Gil incarnates such an impossible escape, and is thus a pure fantasmatic double without any substantial identity, George Colwan, as narrative 'I', is bedevilled by it: that is, both seduced into believing in it, imagining it to be embodied in the powers of his ubiquitous 'friend' (a word repeated with ominous regularity throughout the text, as if anticipating Joyce's 'theft' of the 'r') and eventually wrecked by it.

The hole embodied by 'Gaping Gill' thus engulfs the ego, leading to the implosion of its semantic world, the unravelling of its topology. Joyce incorporates this fantasmatic collapse in the *Wake* as part of a merciless parody of academic discourse with its search for meaning and psychological 'content', the text degenerating into a barely legible barrage of typographical sigla and punctuation marks that culminates in 'a notion of time' being introduced 'by pùnct! ingh oles (sic) in iSpace?!' (*FW* 124.10–12) The obsessive professorial desire to invent some punctilious notation for the inscription of scientific truth is both mimicked and dismantled, as 'iSpace' – both egoic I-space and epistemic eye-space – has holes literally punched in it, the unspeakable beyond of that space invoked, as it were, performatively in the dumbfounding of the reading voice.

This playful and risky hole-punching in 'iSpace', in scientific enlightenment and the imaginary geometry of the ego, therefore constitutes Joyce's chief interest in multiple personality, with its famous tales and celebrated cases. The *coincidentia oppositorum* at work in this 'psychological literature' – on the one hand, a scientific discourse obsessed with its rigid constative framework; on the other, the 'selfevitant subtlety' (*FW* 186.33) of introspective cogitation – makes it a fertile domain for Joyce to explore and dismantle the labyrinths of scientific or fictive self-construction. In that domain, the moment of discovery is always poised between the swift, traumatic ecstasy of revelation and its stern reduction by scientific or moral law (to recall Joyce's improper literary names). What seems above all to be promised by such a discovery is, once again, 'selfevitant': that is, the possibility of *avoiding* (in French, *évitant*) the self, shirking off the bond or debt that both prescribes and limits its single existence. A passage from Wilde's essay *The Critic As Artist* (1891) offers a theoretical sketch of the fantasy at stake here, a sketch that had been developed in the scandalous *The Picture of Dorian Gray*:

The soul that dwells within us is no single spiritual entity, making us personal and individual, created for our service, and entering into us for our joy . . . It fills us with impossible desires, and makes us follow what we know we cannot gain. One thing, however, Ernest, it can do for us . . . It can teach us how to escape from our experience, and to realize the experiences of those who are greater than we are.[15]

As we shall see, this will be rendered 'doriangrayer in its dudhood' (*FW* 186.8) in the *Wake*, where 'Dorian blackbudds' (*FW* 450.18) offer further variants of nil-bud or no-buddy. But back in 1906, when, as a frustrated young bank clerk in Rome, Joyce had read Wilde's novel in translation as a way to mug up his Italian, he wrote to his brother Stanislaus that although the book's style was rather *à la* Huysmans, 'the central idea is fantastic'. He went on:

I can imagine the capital which Wilde's prosecuting counsel made out of certain parts of it. It is not very difficult to read between the lines. Wilde seems to have had some good intentions in writing it – some wish to put himself before the world – but the book is rather crowded with lies and epigrams. If he had had the courage to develop the allusions in the book it might have been better. (*SL* 96)

Literary apparition is again the question: Wilde's 'wish to put himself before the world' – where Joyce hints (with perhaps unconscious irony) that the writer may have considered the world to be less important than himself – is a matter of breaching social taboo, making visible naughty or nocturnal discoveries, 'nightinesses' (*FW* 51.5). The central 'fantastic' idea is obscured or diminished, in young Joyce's eyes, by Wilde's busy, mendacious style, as though the book itself were as 'doubleviewed' (*FW* 296.1) as its hero, split between a disruptive creative source and an illusory semantic surface (an opposition that certainly structures the debate Wilde stages in *The Critic As Artist*). Wilde's notion of learning 'to escape from our experience' might seem somewhat ironic if his own work lacked the moral courage to be true to its fantasmatic 'experience' or inspiration, preferring to escape into the comfortable realm of literary pastiche. But Joyce's writing itself will later fall – and willingly – into self-division by styling itself 'doriangrayer'; that is, both derivative of Wilde's novel and *more like* that novel than itself – because more courageous (which is to say, less derivative) than it. It is this paradoxical topology of self and other that defines the *Wake*'s 'dudhood'; Joyce's youthful ambition to be wilder than Wilde and 'put before the world' the naked truth behind *Dorian Gray* returns in the last work as a self-mocking (or even 'self' mocking) enjoyment of doubling 'itself'; as truly, ineluctably diabolical.

Here we should pause over 'dudhood', in which McHugh reads the Welsh *hud* (magic, illusion, trickery) and the Danish *dødhud* (dead skin). Being 'doriangrayer' would thus be a matter of defunct magic, a dud spell or failed illusion; but also of being wrapped in dead skin, like the body of Dorian exposed in its truth as 'withered, wrinkled and loathsome' at the end of Wilde's novel[16] – and again, like the 'fantastic' central idea Joyce had thought covered up by the 'dead skin' of stylistic parody. McHugh reads in 'chagreenold' (*FW* 186.8) another subtle Joycean dig, with Dorian's lovely green-gold made into an object of *chagrin* (as it proved to be for Wilde, Joyce imagined) by being linked to another letter allegedly purloined by Wilde, namely Balzac's *Le Peau de Chagrin*. The dead skin of literary pastiche, a skin made shameful or loathsome in Balzac's title, would thus have served Wilde as a way to mask off or screen the fantasmatic revelation of his book; in a word, to *hide* from it. This last term is of course the key: when a 'jackal with hide' (*FW* 211.31) appears later in the *Wake*, Joyce folds Stevenson's novel (clearly another possible source for *Dorian Gray*: it was published a mere five years before Wilde's book) into the same 'dudhood' or sham textual skin. As its pun-laden title already announces, however, *The Strange Case of Dr Jekyll and Mr Hyde* is by no means innocent of its own *hud* or verbal trickery: indeed, the spellbinding power of 'hides and hints' (*FW* 20.11) forms an essential part of what it reveals.

One link between Wilde and Stevenson is that both were intrigued by the rediscovery of age-old literary problems in contemporary science. (We should bear in mind that both *Dr Jekyll and Mr Hyde* and *Dorian Gray* were written in the high era of psychological breakthroughs, of William James, Janet, Charcot and Freud.) Wilde's speaker in *The Artist as Critic* sees modern science as the bearer of 'complex multiform gifts' for the 'critical spirit', the principal one being the dissolution of the formerly self-identical self (glossed with provocative mockery as liberation from 'the self-imposed and trammelling burden of moral responsibility').[17] If the new freedom seemingly offered by the discovery that the soul is 'no single spiritual entity'

threatens to traumatise established codes of social and personal meaning –
once again 'pùnct! ingh oles . . . in iSpace' – then that turbulence could
be absorbed into the ecstatic *affirmation* of the new knowledge, its identification as an unavoidable revelation of human truth. This involvement
or identification with science as truth-bearing 'gift' marks the jouissance
of Wilde's break with the unitary ego as precisely phallic, in Lacan's sense;
that is, as meaningful, the stripping away of dead skin to reveal a 'complex
multiform' inner truth.

Although Stevenson centres his famous tale of *Ichspaltung* on the same
'phallic' revelation of multiple personality, he is careful to ascribe it to a
character firmly distanced from authorial identity (indeed, the name Jekyll
may be a deliberate 'Joycean' pun entailing the negation of ego: 'I kill' or
'killer of the I'). The title of the story's concluding chapter, 'Henry Jekyll's
Full Statement of the Case', summarises that character's main ambition:
namely, to deliver a quasi-Freudian *Lösung*, to 'put [the] mystery to rights'
(as had been promised by a letter found earlier in the book). The doctor's
account of the psychological discoveries made possible by his 'solution'
(both a mixture of drugs and a successful interpretation) reads very like the
Wildean embrace of the 'gifts' offered by truth-bearing science. Despite the
limits of his 'partial discovery', Jekyll speculates that the future will confirm
it as the first moment of an epochal shift in human self-knowledge: 'Others
will follow, others will outstrip me on the same lines; and I hazard the
guess that man will be ultimately known for a mere polity of multifarious,
incongruous and independent denizens.'[18]

This premonition of today's multiple personality disorder forms the
core of Jekyll's revelation, and he sees it as an ultimate – and ultimately
comforting – truth: the rightful property of the Other. The Other, crucially,
is supposed as the bearer of knowledge (in a clear instance of 'transference',
as Lacan will rethink that psychoanalytic concept), a knowledge – even
if still only potential, waiting to be discovered by future scientists – that
would function as a guarantee of the subject's reality. The first line of the 'full
statement' gestures mockingly toward this taking command of reality with
its conventional autobiographical opening ('I was born in the year 18–');
only the inclusion of everything, a genuinely 'full' account, can supply a
subject worthy of identification with Truth itself, with a knowledge borne
by an Other able to restore the integral representation of reality that Jekyll's
'solution' has jeopardised. The doctor is thus convinced that it is possible to
'right' matters in his final statement, just as Stevenson's narrative, wracked
by puns, ascribes a special status to writing: 'Then I remembered that of my
original character, one part remained to me: I could write my own hand;

and once I had conceived that kindling spark, the way that I must follow became lighted up from end to end' (*JH* 93).

Jekyll's sense of himself as a phallic totality, as one self-consistent subject – something gravely undermined by the unscheduled appearances of Mr Hyde – is thus to be salvaged by a graphic proof of self-identity, this hand writing itself as 'original character' (as if the fatal ambiguity of that very phrase did not already point to the dissemination of identity). We recall that in Hogg's *Justified Sinner*, one effect of Gil's diabolic presence was the subversion of the legal validity of a signature; and likewise, when the autograph of Jekyll is compared with that of Hyde, a decisive differ- ence is visible: 'the two hands are in many points identical; only differently sloped' (*JH* 55). The 'hand of right' or bearer of the law is thus robbed of its phallic authority by its sinister double, a 'hand of write' making it doubt- ful, perhaps fraudulent; and likewise Jekyll's conviction that the 'right' way, the full truth of the subject, can be authenticated in writing is uncannily subverted by Hyde's sinister disfigurement of 'his' character.

An almost identical signature, only improperly forged: Stevenson's text already dramatises the whole problematic of plagiarism and rivalry that the *Wake*, with its lashings of 'quashed quotatoes' (*FW* 183.22), will at once the- matise and enact. What becomes apparent, moreover, is that the scriptural disfigurement that subverts identity in *Dr Jekyll and Mr Hyde* will be repre- sented primarily as an *assault on speech*. The well-meaning lawyer Utterson – another punning name, clearly suggesting a 'phonocentric' character – confronts in Mr Hyde an incarnation of representational impropriety, and he struggles to re-establish the legitimacy of signification by naming what he encounters. Having accused Hyde of using language that 'is not fitting,' he strives to bring this linguistic deformity back into the domain of consistent symbolic truth:

'There must be something else,' said the perplexed gentleman. 'There *is* something more, if I could find a name for it. God bless me, the man seems hardly human! Something troglodytic, shall we say? . . . O my poor old Harry Jekyll, if ever I read Satan's signature upon a face, it is on that of your new friend!' (40)

Hyde is thus the bearer of the ultimate forged or sinister signature, the apparition of writing as an occult, unspeakable dimension; something incommensurable with the speaking 'I'. Like the honest country folk in Hogg's tale, Utterson immediately names this uncanny revelation as the work of the devil, but he identifies the Evil One specifically with writ- ing – with a signature that paradoxically entails nothing but the making- sinister of a rightful signature, the subversive doubling of proper, God-given authority. Hyde's status as 'original character' is thus doubly ironic: on the one hand, he is nothing but a flawed simulacrum, a parasite or plagiarist; but on the other, this very lack of substantial identity, the sheer absence of a signifier, makes him wholly original as a character. Note how Utterson slips between searching for something absent (the right name) and trying to deal with something excessive, too present (or 'pressant': *FW* 221.17): 'There *is* something more . . .'

The 'diabolical' excess embodied by Mr Hyde is therefore precisely what lies outside, remains irreducible to, reality. And it is this that constitutes the most self-seductive aspect of Jekyll's transformation, promising him access to a 'sea of liberty':

In my impenetrable mantle, the safety was complete. Think of it – I did not even exist! Let me but escape into my laboratory door, give me but a second or two to mix and swallow the draught . . . and, whatever he had done, Edward Hyde would pass away like the stain of breath upon a mirror. (*JH* 86)

This unchecked enjoyment is precisely what is illegal, what can find no place in reality: Jekyll's impish delight in impunity masks the more profound and troubling exultation provoked by an escape from reality, the absolute irresponsibility of embodying the transitory fantasmatic 'stain' of enjoyment. Further on in his account, Jekyll comes up with an apt formula for this escape into jouissance; as he lapses into Hyde's character, he says: 'I began to be aware of a change in the temper of my thoughts, a greater boldness, a contempt of danger, a solution of the bonds of obligation' (*JH* 92).

So Jekyll's 'solution', in yet another of its senses, serves to dissolve 'the bonds of obligation'; the latter tautology (since 'obligation' is already rooted etymologically in the Latin *ligare*, 'to bind') only redoubles the notion of the bonded or bound condition of the 'reality principle', in which being a subject immediately entails social ties. (Language, as Lacan puts it in 1973, functions as a 'bond between those who speak'; this was to give a linguistic emphasis to the Freudian motif of *Bindung*, the bonding or binding together that results in psychical and social formations.)[19]

The possibility of freedom from the social bond recalls the Freudian theory of the joke: that is, as a momentary lifting of the repressive censorship imposed on fantasmatic enjoyment by the reality principle. Indeed, with the 'unspeakable' Hyde Stevenson recasts the traditional role of the devil in carnivalesque comedy: an incarnation of forbidden enjoyment. Our first glimpse of the character comes in a scene of grotesque black comedy; Hyde encounters a little girl at a street corner and in a moment of diabolical sangfroid he 'trampled calmly over the child's body and left her screaming on the ground'. But Hyde is in effect an improperly told joke: that is, the emergence of jouissance is too crude, it lacks the narrative fore-pleasure necessary to divert censorship. And the narrator's outrage reflects this sense of obscene, forbidden enjoyment, its very occurrence otherworldly, supernatural: 'It wasn't like a man; it was like some damned Juggernaut' (*JH* 31).

The grammatical transformation here – 'he' becoming 'it' – is a crucial point in the relation of written character to multiple personality; it corresponds, we should note, to the shift from one sense of 'character' to the other: personality ('he') to letter ('it'). In Jekyll's account, the writing subject strives to retain control over the increasingly slippery pronouns – 'He, I say – I cannot say, I. That child of Hell had nothing human' – while the narrative constantly undoes his efforts, forcing him into the position of identification with 'it': 'it was always as Hyde that I awakened' (*JH* 94–5). It is thus Jekyll's inability to say 'I', to identify with Hyde as 'assumptinome' (*FW* 153.20), that is decisive; he awakens as a pure 'character', a letter that marks a jouissance devoid of subjective meaning. After all, as Jekyll put it earlier, in the rapture of his fantasmatic act, 'I did not even exist!' In the act of passing into the forbidden domain of fantasy, Jekyll-Hyde (and Joyce will sneakily swap around the 'Dr' and 'Mr', *FW* 150.17) has *inverted* the formula of symbolic castration – that is, sacrificed the 'I' and its coherent 'iSpace' for full, lethal jouissance. Hyde thus constitutes an obscene reversal of the Freudian ethic 'Wo Es war, soll Ich werden': the 'I' loses control to a character that is finally revealed as simply 'it' or id, an anamorphic libidinal stain.

But the crux of Stevenson's text – and perhaps why it gives us pleasure as readers rather than making us turn away in revulsion – is that this collapse of identification is immediately coupled to the most easily legible, formulaic act of naming: 'That child of Hell . . .' Clearly, to identify 'it' as a diabolic character brings with it a thrilling, uncanny quota of phallic jouissance; above all, it entails a restitution of *meaning*. The devil is evidently an element in the most familiar or *heimlich* of discourses; it is a signifier, not a *hapax* or singularity, and as such is reassuringly bound into a chain of other signifiers. To that extent, Jekyll's recourse to religious language, like that of Hogg's characters, constitutes what Lacan writes as *père-version* or turning to the semic patrimony: precisely an attempt to make what has emerged *legible*, to restore the semantic scenario governing neurotic fantasy (where the lozenge separating subject from fantasmatic real is, as Serge André made clear, an effect of the Name-of-the-Father).

This reversion to a neurotic structure – where the relation to fantasy is articulated, caught up in the signifying movement that allows the subject to emerge as a structure of desire – is a frantic response to what is revealed in these haunting texts of 'Zweispaltung' (*FW* 296.8). And of course the discourses of religion and science offer the most authoritative, the richest symbolic networks within which the text or its characters can precisely hide from its fantasmatic core; thus 'the devil' for Hogg's characters or Utterson – or a scientific 'truth' awaiting future discovery, for Harry Jekyll – serve as ways to escape back into subjectivity (to escape, that is, from the illusory 'escape' offered by Jekyll's fantasmatic 'solution'). In Wilde's case, critics often claim that his partial rewriting of *Dorian Gray* between its first appearance in *Lippincott's* and its later publication as a book was an attempt to pacify Victorian conventional opinion (a sign, the young Joyce thought, of a lack of moral courage). But the 'original' idea – entailing what Joyce considered the book's 'fantastic' centre – already sets up a structure of moral allegory, with a veritably superegoic (that is: sadistic, vengeful) balancing of accounts; Dorian's portrait itself serves ultimately as a deadly guarantee of consistent, truth-governed representation. The final scene of the novel, with Wilde's fantasy idol at last exposed 'doriangrayer in its dudhood' (*FW* 186.8), shows the Other fully vindicated as the site of the subject's truth: despite the mask of dead skin, Dorian's servants 'recognized who it was'.[20]

We can thus see the central 'selfevitant subtlety' (*FW* 186.33) in Hogg, Stevenson and Wilde to hinge on a fantasmatic reversal of symbolic castration, and the consequent emergence of an obscene enjoyment that threatens to engulf both reality and the desiring subject or consistent 'I'. But all three texts offer their characters (and in turn us as readers) ways of shying away from this fantasy – or else suffering allegorical damnation if they yield to it – via conventional, 'neurotic' discourses of moral authority. What distinguishes Joycean writing, Lacan will claim, is that it abjures this re-inscription of neurotic fantasy, manages to re-sow the fantasmatic seeds scattered by his predecessors without reproducing their subjection to a vengeful, superegoic Law. How does Joyce achieve this, and what are the consequences for his readers?

Here, the psychoanalytic notion of transference, as Lacan reinterpreted this crucial aspect of Freud's discovery, will provide a useful perspective on Joyce's singular writing practice. Before it became Freud's term for the key inter-subjective link between analyst and patient, *Übertragung* was first, as Lacan writes in 1957, a formula for the general economy of the signifier, governed by the laws of connection and substitution (*E:S* 161). Transference later becomes one of the 'four fundamental concepts of psychoanalysis' treated by Lacan in his seminar of 1964, where he redefines it as the specific effect of symbolic supposition: in analysis, a 'supposed subject of knowledge' (a position occupied by the analyst) functions as the guarantee of the subject's certainty and the precondition of analytic interpretation. It is only on the basis of this supposition that what Lacan calls the 'Gordian knot' of the analyst's interpretation can take shape, and the laws of the signifier come into effect.[21]

How then can such a notion of transference shed light on the fantasmatic scenario involved in the double-dealing literature of Hogg, Stevenson and Wilde? First we have to situate the fantasy of 'reversing psychoanalysis' – writing Freud backwards: where I was, it shall come to be – in its fundamentally ambiguous 'naughtiness' (or 'nightiness': *FW* 51.5). Such a fantasy finds its perfect embodiment in Stevenson's Mr Hyde; that is, it is both a nebulous phantom without any 'reality' and something *more* real than reality itself. In other words, when the jouissance constitutively foreclosed from reality is let back into reality through Jekyll's 'solution', the obscene anamorphic revelation of Hyde is both an imaginary spectre of the 'I' and an exposure of something *outside* the 'I' that is masked by 'reality' itself: the unspeakable revelation of lack-in-the-Other. The double is thus an incarnation or imaginary version of what must be excluded from reality if the fictional institution of that reality (we recall Stephen's world 'founded on the void') is to be maintained.

Transference can therefore be situated as a response to this forbidden revelation, a desperate effort to restore the imaginary consistency of reality by symbolising – as 'the devil' or as 'true' selfhood; in signifiers authorised by the Other's supposed knowledge – that which in its very emergence renders reality improper or fraudulent. Transference puts in place (literally, sub-poses) an Other that functions as the guarantee of the normal-neurotic economy of desire and signification, knotting together the subject and reality to produce 'psychical reality'. And this takes us back to Lacan's matheme $ \$ \lozenge a $, where the central lozenge indicates the possibility of signifying substitution, of *movement* in the fantasmatic relation, the redeployment of semic gifts from the Other ('My father gave me seeds to sow'). The characteristic mark of Joyce's writing, as we have already glimpsed and shall see in more detail in Chapter 6, is that from the beginning it is profoundly invested in the moment before the 'translation' of what emerges into an identifiable or plausible discourse: a moment, that is, when reality is disfigured, exposed as improper, its 'authority' travestied.

The duplicity of character in Hogg and Stevenson – made manifest in the narrative incidents of the letter, of name-changing and sinister handwriting – is rendered still more literal, as it were, by being subtracted from any imaginary supposition of reality, in *Finnegans Wake*. The 'iSpace' that is dismantled in that text is always a product of a transferential supposition of the Other: to punch holes (or 'pùnct! . . . oles') in that space would thus be to defy transference, to turn away from its 'gift' or see through its groundless, merely 'supposed' authority. We shall see how just such a refusal of transference takes effect in Morton Prince's attempt to produce a theoretical alternative to the Freudian psyche, and how Joyce incorporates this theoretical rivalry into the *Wake*. And we shall encounter the same refusal of transference at work in the non-relation between Joyce and Jung, in which both *Ulysses* and Lucia Joyce fall foul of 'the law of the jungerl' (*FW* 268 n. 3).

MISSES IN PRINTS: RAIDING THE MIND FACTORY

'Desire = hidden identity,' writes Joyce in a notebook during the composition of *Ulysses*.[22] When he encountered the work of American neurologist Morton Prince, Joyce found that his momentary jotting had already been made into a complete theory of human subjectivity, one deliberately put forward to rival the Freudian model. Prince's 1906 study *The Dissociation of a Personality* advanced a theory of 'co-consciousness' – in clear opposition to 'the unconscious' – to account for the case of a young woman whose every desire entailed (or so it seemed to Prince) a hidden identity. Miss Christine Beauchamp, as Prince calls her, becomes as the case unfolds a proliferating tissue or text of different selves with quite distinct, often violently incompatible, wishes, styles and characteristics. Prince devises increasingly complicated schemas in his struggle to keep pace with this ever-expanding cast of personalities. The search for 'the real Miss Beauchamp' rapidly loses its way in the intricate labyrinth of Prince's case – and the labyrinth is in part an artefact of his own theory, with the collaboration of the manifold self-inventive powers of his patient (notably a personality known as 'Sally', author of the mockingly entitled 'Autobiography of a Subconscious Self').

Prince's case proved a fascinating resource for Joyce, and it is densely woven into the textual fabric of *Finnegans Wake*, as critics have noted.[23] Indeed, there were aspects of Prince's work that made it more like a writing experiment than a psychotherapy, as if it were more concerned with elaborating the symptom than 'solving' or curing it; the very notion of 'co-consciousness' already implies a certain refusal to impose theoretical hierarchies of the kind set up by Freud (unconscious/conscious, latent/ manifest and so on). More particularly, Prince's work entails a special kind of collusion between theory and its object, marked by the complete absence of any reflexive self-interrogation on the part of the doctor-theorist. Such a moment of self-reflection had of course emerged in Freud through the concept of transference (and later 'counter-transference'); the position of the analyst as an object caught up in desire, involved in the discourse of the Other, could thus be included as an element in the overall analysis. Freud was convinced that, without such theoretical self-consciousness, psycho-analysis would risk slipping back into the pre-analytic domain of hypnotic suggestion, the dangerous 'primal scene' of the Freudian institution.

That Prince's notion of 'co-consciousness' or multiple identity clearly belongs to that pre-analytic scene may have added to its appeal in Joyce's eyes; at any rate, he is certainly aware of the theoretical differences involved, and inscribes them with subtle duplicity in the *Wake*. Thus, when multiple-character Issy talks of 'prints chumming' (*FW* 280.21), we can read this either as Prince Charming – an ironic name for a psychotherapist who risks dealing in the deadly game of suggestion, only to be outplayed and mocked there by 'Laughing Sally' (*FW* 293 n. 2) – or as a specific allusion to the Miss Beauchamp case, where Sally writes letters accusing another personality, named Christine, of being too friendly (of 'chumming') with the doctor.

If Freud arguably uses *Übertragung*, both as theoretical concept and in practice, to absorb, negate or translate the uncanny pre-analytic dimen-sion of hypnotic suggestion, we can see how the lack of any such term in Prince returns in the real of the Beauchamp case as the murderous rivalry between personalities. 'Co-consciousness' marks the admission of *dubium*, of 'Dyoublong' (*FW* 13.4) or unrepresentable doubling, to psychical reality – an admission that rapidly makes that supposed 'reality' untenable (in a transformation we saw powerfully dramatised in the tales of Hogg, Wilde and Stevenson). It is no surprise that Prince saw those tales as further grist to his mill. His judgement of *The Strange Case of Dr Jekyll and Mr Hyde* is worth noting: Stevenson's tale, writes Prince, 'is so true a picture of what is actually observed in cases of double personality that it can be used almost as well as an actual case from life'.[24] The distinction between truth and fiction, or the actual and the imaginary – the pivotal stake of the Miss Beauchamp case – is thus radically put in question by Stevenson's text. In a seeming paradox, Prince is able to portray as uncanny veracity ('so true a picture') what in effect blurs the line defining the truth, separating the 'actually observed' from the merely dreamt up. If fiction can be as true to life as life itself in such cases, one implication might be that treatment of the kind Prince offers is 'in fact' fully immersed in the domain of fiction, its characters (its 'prints') as made up as those in a novel. And in his pursuit of the patient's 'real' identity, Prince does start to act very like a literary critic seeking to make legible or plausible an obscure author; he encourages 'Sally' to produce what she calls 'auto papers', to settle the account, provide an exhaustively reordered and at last comprehensible 'case'. The authentic truth of the subject is to be written (one recalls Jekyll's misguided faith in his 'hand of write'), and its veracity guaranteed solely by the authorisation of the doctor.

It is this aspect of Prince, the way his work constantly feeds off and incorporates writing, that most interests Joyce, as misprinting the name 'prints' (*FW* 20.11, 280.21) neatly indicates. The authority of psychological science, Joyce reminds us, is entirely based on printed matter – and perhaps on purloined letters, bits of text plagiarised from the creative psyche under the 'pudendascope' (*FW* 115.30) and passed off as the authentic property of a self-declared prince or master (perhaps a law-giving 'jungerl', *FW* 268 n. 3). It is thus the 'misses in prints' (*FW* 20.11) – both the multiple feminine identities in a book signed by Prince, and the dissemination at work in an error-ridden text itself – that should be recognised as the real author or authentic real (although here both notions are of course, properly speaking, inconceivable).

Around the time when Joyce was meeting with Jung to discuss his daughter Lucia's mental illness – discussions that, thinks Sheldon Brivic, no doubt 'touched on the concept of multiple personality'[25] – he divided a section of the *Work in Progress* (*FW* 11.2) into parallel columns of text. This was a specific raiding of 'Laughing Sally', whose original literary act – splitting a page of her 'auto papers' into separate columns of writing to figure simultaneous yet incommensurable sites of narrative identity – had been a prime source for Prince in developing his notion of 'co-consciousness'.[26] Alongside the split streams of text in the *Wake*, we read of THE MIND FACTORY, ITS GIVE AND TAKE (*FW* 282.3–4). If the psyche is for Joyce above all a *product* of theory, these stern capitals mark its production as an authoritarian regime of imposition and appropriation, of forced addition and subtraction. Thus, in 'Jungfraud's Messongebook' (*FW* 460.20) we might identify (alongside the psychoanalytic references we shall explore below) a text written by a Jungfrau, one of the 'misses in prints' like Sally: a messy dream book (French *songe*, dream) or a me-dream, a dream-of-me book.

If Joyce views Prince, then, as the tyrannical boss of a mind factory where the production of authoritative truth is a game of give and take in which theory both colludes with and borrows from the pathological self-invention it pretends to cure, we should not necessarily assume that Joyce's own dream-book excludes itself from that economy. Indeed, Sheldon Brivic sees Prince's work as a key element in the give and take of Joyce's writing; crucially, writes Brivic, it 'developed Joyce's ability to conceive of the relations between minds that form a unity'.[27] But the implied harmonic resolution here risks masking the traumatic nature of this 'telepathic' give-and-take; and to be precise it glosses over how the antagonistic core of sexual difference is at stake there.

The antagonism – indeed, the political struggle – in the background of Prince's mind factory is clearly exposed by Ruth Leys in a trenchant reading of the Miss Beauchamp case and the theory of multiple personality that it spawned. Prince's theoretical discourse, Leys argues, is 'entangled not only with notions of suggestion or mimesis but also . . . with questions of sexual difference';[28] the identification of 'the real Miss Beauchamp', in other words, corresponds not to a revelation but to an enforcement of feminine destiny (that of being a passive heterosexual).[29] Leys shows how Prince's account returns with symptomatic regularity to a particular scene in the diegesis, a speculative construction that ensures a certain narrative coherence: it consists of a traumatic encounter between Miss Beauchamp and an unknown man who appears outside her door. Leys argues that this enigmatic scene serves for Prince as an ultimate guarantee of the rep-resentational subject, safeguarding it from endless dissemination in sub-personalities or inauthentic copies; and she concludes that it also serves as a way to set in place a normative heterosexuality as the only possible rep-resentational economy of the subject. Theory over-invests in a key scene to cover up the points where its account threatens to unravel, reveal itself as contingent, arbitrary; to reveal, precisely, an unspeakable lack-in-the-Other.

We recall how Atherton boldly posited a split in the *Wake* between mas-culine and feminine modes of self-loss, with male characters tending to be possessed by the devil, 'while women simply split up into parts'.[30] In Hogg, Stevenson and Wilde we saw how the discourses of religion and science function as ways to make self-loss meaningful, ways to reinstate the consistent knowledge of the Other as a guarantee of the subject: in psycho-analytic terms, as modes of transference. The *Wake* ceaselessly disseminates what such 'solutions' or translations would organise as 'phallic' meaningful enjoyment; and Joyce associates this disruptive multiplicity above all with the feminine. Thus Issy writes of her 'castoff devils' (*FW* 273 n. 6), of shrug-ging off the supposed religious authority that would inflict its demons on her. The *Wake* always links femininity to a fragile moment of emergence, of birth or creation *ex nihilo* – precisely the moment of waking, before the reductive scene of phallic knowledge and authority can be imposed (thus the text's plaintive leitmotif of 'not yet').

The question of 'transference' in Joyce is often posed in terms of his ambiguous, suspicious engagement with psychoanalysis. 'It cannot be said that Joyce was *mordu par l'analyse* ['bitten' by, thought much of, analysis]', remarks Lacan ironically in his address to the 1975 Joyce Symposium.[31] But if psychoanalysis is another of Joyce's 'doubleviewed seeds' (*FW* 296.1) or ambivalent sources, the question is further complicated by his historical encounters with the MIND FACTORY; in particular, that is, the treatment of both his work and his daughter Lucia by one of that factory's famous proprietors, Carl Gustav Jung.

JUNGFRAUD'S MESSONGEBOOK: TRANSFERENTIAL TOSH

Joyce's first 'real' contact with Jung was a matter of economics.[32] His principle patroness when he was living in Zurich was Edith Rockefeller McCormick, a convinced Jungian; she attempted in 1919 to persuade Joyce – so he told his friend Claud Sykes – that he should enter analysis with Jung himself, at her expense. Whether Joyce's blunt refusal (the idea, he declared, was 'unthinkable') piqued Mrs McCormick into withdrawing her financial support, or whether Jung advised her to do so, is not known (Ellmann writes of the rich American's 'caprices'); but in October 1919 the bank in Zurich informed Joyce that his income had been cut off. In psychoanalytic terms, the triangular relation of Joyce, McCormick and Jung is clearly organised by *transference*, which is always a matter of speculation and supposition, of things given and withheld. It is easy to imagine that, in the tense transferential scenario being played out between Jung and his analysand, Joyce's indifference might have seemed worthy of punishment.

It was not until September 1930, by which time Joyce had become the famous author of *Ulysses*, that he was to encounter Jung again. And it is precisely that famous author whom Jung addresses in a letter, introducing himself as 'a supposed authority on psychological matters' called in to make an authoritative statement about *Ulysses*. We shall explore this apparently transferential scenario and its knot of Joycean and Freudian meanings below.

It was as a supposed authority on psychological matters that Jung entered Joyce's world again, shortly after their exchange over *Ulysses*. During the 1930s the mental troubles of Joyce's daughter Lucia rapidly worsened, her behaviour becoming increasingly unpredictable and even dangerous. (In 1934, she set fire to her room in a Belgian asylum.) Maria Jolas, a member of the close circle around Joyce, recommended that Lucia be transferred to the clinic where Jung worked; in September 1934, Joyce accepted this suggestion, writing to a friend, 'I wouldn't go to him, but maybe he can help her.' Recalling his earlier transferential imbroglio with Jung, he felt it necessary to state, with strange emphasis, that 'my daughter is not myself' (*JJ* 676). We shall return to this declaration in our further explorations of Joycean paternity.

A second triangle involving Jung, his patient and Joyce developed during the next four months (before Lucia was moved yet again by her father), but this time with very different transferential stakes. If, in 1919, Joyce had been caught up in some obscure trade-off between McCormick and her analyst, Jung's major challenge in approaching Lucia was to be able to intervene at all in her relation to her father, to open a minimal space in which her desire could be *überträgt*, translated away from its single, fixed investment. Jung's initial reports seemed to offer hope, and Joyce was encouraged enough to meet with him to discuss Lucia. Ellmann's account shows how the discussion soon turned to aesthetic speculation:

When the psychologist pointed out schizoid elements in poems Lucia had written, Joyce, remembering Jung's comments on *Ulysses*, insisted they were anticipations of a new literature, and said his daughter was an innovator not yet understood. Jung granted that some of her portmanteau words and neologisms were remarkable, but said they were random; she and her father, he commented later, were like two people going to the bottom of a river, one falling and the other diving. (*JJ* 679)

Lucia embodied, in Joyce's view, the creativity of *not yet*: a moment awaiting critical recognition, too fragile and subtle to be deciphered by her contemporaries. Jung's response was to work this into his own theories: there was, he decided, 'a kind of mystical identity or participation' between Joyce and his daughter. In a letter to Patricia Hutchins, Jung revealed how this fitted with his model of the psyche:

If you know anything of my Anima theory, Joyce and his daughter are a classical example of it. She was definitely his 'femme inspiratrice', which explains his obstinate reluctance to have her certified. His own Anima, i.e., unconscious psyche, was so solidly identified with her that to have her certified would have been as much as an admission that he himself had a latent psychosis.[33]

Jung transposes the antinomy of potential and actual onto a psychical topography. What is 'latent', not realised – or 'not yet understood', in Joyce's phrase – is a time of radical creative originality, the opening of the 'immarginable' (*FW* 4.19): the imaginable, the impossible-to-confine-within-margins, that which cannot be glossed by a scholar's marginal annotations. If Jung would convert this opening – and it is always, for Joyce, a temporal unfolding – into the mythic and static figure of the Anima, Joyce will respond (as we shall see in Chapter 6) with the figure of 'crossexanimation' (*FW* 87.34), where the so-called 'mystical identity' of father and daughter will be exposed as another instance of the 'misses in prints' that unravel the fabric of identity.

Jung's comments about Joyce as writer and father reveal an acute perception of his work as something transgressive, something that should be forbidden. Joyce's '"psychological" style', he continues,

is definitely schizophrenic, with this difference, however, that the ordinary patient cannot help himself talking and thinking in such a way, while Joyce willed it and moreover developed it with all his creative forces, which incidentally explains why he himself did not go over the border. But his daughter did, because she was no genius like her father, but merely a victim of her disease. In any other time of the past Joyce's work would never have reached the printer, but in our blessed xxth century it is a message, though not yet understood.[34]

Only a permissive modernity, Jung concludes, has allowed Joyce's 'schizophrenic' style to become an actual message, visible in reality if not yet assimilable to the collective psyche. In the event, Lucia's tentative glimmerings of transference soon died out, and Jung handed her back to her father, declaring, Joyce wrote, that 'nobody could make any head of her but myself as she was a very exceptional case, and certainly not one for psychoanalytic treatment' (*JJ* 681). Lucia thus remained non-interpretable for Jung, impossible to draw forth from the nebulous domain of the Anima into the enlightened world of the talking cure. 'To think that such a big fat materialistic Swiss man should try to get hold of my soul!' (*JJ* 679), exclaimed Lucia; no well-fed proprietor of a MIND FACTORY could ever grasp her 'farther potential' (*FW* 115.21), the singular identity spelled out in her father's characters.

When Jung places Joyce's writing as a message yet to be understood, therefore, he echoes the language used by Joyce himself in defence of his daughter. The idea of Lucia as the herald of 'a new literature' speaks both of her father's desperation about her condition and his sense of his *own* work as a literature in suspense, its 'messes of mottage' (*FW* 183.22–3) a message awaiting future interpretation. (One thinks of Jekyll's forlorn 'Others will follow me.') In Jung's view, Lucia's illness was due to a breakdown of the economy of identification in the relation between father and daughter

(*JJ* 676–9). The strange expression with which Joyce had sealed his acceptance of Jung as Lucia's doctor – 'My daughter is not myself' – recalls the
turbulence of pronouns we saw in the character masquerade of multiple
personality. Joyce's apparent belief that his daughter was telepathic (which
greatly intrigued Lacan, as we shall see) perhaps suggests the fragility or
osmotic permeability of psychical boundaries; and to remark such an obvious difference between identities inevitably makes it seem less obvious,
more questionable. Lucia is in effect bound up with Joycean writing: an
equivalent kind of illegibility is at the root of Jung's failure to 'get hold of'
her soul and what the analyst described as his wanderings 'in the labyrinth
of *Ulysses*'.[35] If we follow him into that labyrinth, we shall find some vital
clues to the conclusion of our argument.

FINDING THE SELF: FROM MOSES TO ELIJAH

In 1930, Jung had been approached by Daniel Brody, a publisher with the
Zurich Rhein-Verlag, who was planning the launch of a literary review; he
wondered if Jung would write an article about *Ulysses* for its first edition.
Jung agreed; but the article he delivered a month later contained such
harsh criticism of Joyce's work that Brody felt obliged to send a copy to
Joyce. Joyce's response was characteristically enigmatic; he sent Brody a
telegram that simply quoted Frederick the Great's famous command, on
seeing a political placard attacking him: *Niedrigerhängen* ('hang it lower').[36]
Ellmann understands Joyce's telegram to have meant 'Ridicule it by making
it public'; Brody could not immediately do so, however, for he had to
abandon his planned review due to increasing political tensions in the
region. Jung's article was not published until 1932, when it was used – in a
substantially revised form – as the preface to a German translation of Stuart
Gilbert's book on *Ulysses*, which Brody's press published as *Das Rätsel Ulysses*
('The Riddle of *Ulysses*') (*JJ* 628).

Jung's '*Ulysses*: A Monologue' marks a crucial point in the relation
between Joyce and psychoanalysis, on which it sheds both light and shadow.
In 1930, of course, Jung is no longer the enthusiastic young Freudian whom
Joyce had read in 1909 endorsing the psychoanalytic account of sexuality
and the father; he can even include Freud now in his condemnation of
Joyce, styling them both 'prophets of negation' thrown up by a benighted
modernity (*UM* 121). Jung writes about *Ulysses* not as a psychoanalyst, but
'as a supposed authority on psychological matters', as he tells Joyce in a
letter in 1932; it is in effect as a psychiatrist, a custodian of mental health,
that Jung feels called upon to pass judgement on the work (*UM* 133).

Just as Jung's attempts to analyse Lucia soon became implicated in aesthetic questions, so his discussion of *Ulysses*, two years before, had slipped from literary criticism into the domain of clinical psychology. No doubt Brody's request that Jung should write on Joyce derived partly from the fact that he had had some personal contact with the legendary writer in Zurich during the war, chiefly via Edith McCormick; but it was also due to Jung's broad ambition to produce a psychological theory that would be 'an object of public interest', which could be transferred from the narrowly clinical to the wider social and cultural spheres.[37]

Jung's 'Monologue' is a strangely 'doubleviewed' text, whose ambivalence seems to correspond to two different attempts to read Joyce's work. The essay in its original form, which Brody sent to Joyce in 1930 and which provoked the 'regal' telegram, is lost; Jung rewrote it extensively for the preface to Gilbert's book. (Presumably Brody had informed him of Joyce's cryptic response.) In 1932, Jung must have felt that the piece now showed sufficient respect for Joyce's literary achievement to allow him to strike a note of strained cordiality in a letter to the author. 'Ulysses', he tells Joyce,

proved to be an exceedingly hard nut and it has forced my mind not only to most unusual efforts, but also to rather extravagant peregrinations (speaking from the standpoint of a scientist). Your book as a whole has given me no end of trouble and I was brooding over it for about three years until I succeeded to put myself into it. But I must tell you that I'm profoundly grateful.[38]

'To put myself into it': Jung's slightly awkward English provides an apt formula for the relation to the labyrinth of *Ulysses* he establishes in his efforts to get through the book. The title he chooses – *ein Monolog* – seems especially germane: the 'extravagant peregrinations' of Jung's reading are, as it were, acted out in the course of his essay, as though it were a dramatic monologue (and one that at times takes on a ranting, Beckettian tone).

The first act of the 'Monologue' might be largely what remains of Jung's original article, before the revisions; it begins as a savage polemic, the opening page denouncing *Ulysses* as a 'pitiless stream' of writing, with 'not a single blessed island where the long-suffering reader may come to rest' (*UM* 110). Jung's footnotes approvingly quote the extraordinary remarks of Ernst Curtius on *Ulysses*, such as that it 'reproduces the stream of consciousness without filtering it either ethically or logically' (this concerning a book whose author was obliged to furnish schemas to help readers tackle its encyclopaedia of cultural references) (*UM* 112).[39]

If Jung relies on the critical authority of Curtius for this kind of literary judgement, however, the main focus of his essay is on his own state of mind as a reader: that is, on his *transference*. When he declares that '*Ulysses* turns its back on me', we are inevitably reminded that Jung had been treated to a similar gesture on the part of its author (in the episode of Joyce's rejection of McCormick's offer) that he may have found equally frustrating. The problem for Jung is that, like its author, the book (often playfully anthropomorphised in the article) is just not interested in his interpretation: 'Yes, I admit I feel I have been made a fool of. The book would not meet me half way, nothing in it made the least attempt to be agreeable, and that always gives the reader an irritating sense of inferiority' (*UM* 113).

'Surely,' continues Jung, 'a book has a content, represents something; but I suspect that Joyce did not wish to "represent" anything.' The striking point here is Jung's implied link between the refusal or failure of transference – clearly, since *Ulysses* makes not the slightest effort to be agreeable, the book is not neurotic enough; like Lucia, it is not a suitable case for analysis – and the refusal to 'represent' (with the word set off in scare quotes) the world, to countersign its reality principle. Does transference therefore correspond to some kind of realism, a supposition of reality?

The idea of an aesthetic beyond representation might have struck more of a chord in 1932 with readers of Joyce's *Work in Progress* (then being published by Eugene Jolas in *transition*) than among those who were still striving to assimilate the overwhelming semantic *summa* of *Ulysses*; but Jung places it within a broader conception of modernism: Joyce's art is '"cubistic" in the deepest sense because it resolves the picture of reality into an immensely complex painting whose dominant note is the melancholy of abstract objectivity'.[40] So, while the portrait of the artist in Joyce's early work maintained a certain figurative coherence and thus offered the reader a legible textual surface – invited him to meet it 'half way', in Jung's phrase – the later writing now embraced a cubist aesthetic that turned its back on the 'picture of reality' where the reader felt at home, by refusing to endorse, re-present, its familiar self-evidence.

We can understand Jung's frustration as a reader of *Ulysses* in terms of our discussion of transference and authority; his sense that the reality supposed to govern the encounter between reader and author has broken down in Joyce's work, leaving a 'supposed authority on psychological matters' like himself feeling a fool, will result in the blindness – but also, strange to say, the insight – of his reading. By placing Joyce in the wider context of aesthetic modernism, with its turn away from an idea of the artwork as agreeable to an audience (later to be theorised by Roland Barthes as the turn from a 'readerly' to a 'writerly' aesthetic),[41] Jung's argument at least detaches itself from the strident denunciation of a Curtius (for whom *Ulysses* is nothing less than 'a work of the Antichrist': *UM* 110). It nevertheless remains trapped by its insistent psychologisation of the aesthetic; modernism corresponds for Jung to a special kind of affront to the domain of the 'soul': the 'abstract objectivity' of cubism is 'melancholy' only because it leaves the ego, with its craving for meaningful content, stranded. Thus, in Joyce's writing, Jung writes, 'everything is desouled, every particle of warm blood has been chilled' (*UM* 114). The reader is not engaged by this writing: its icy stream rolls out before his eyes, not inviting him into its eddying textual currents or interesting him in the bits of flotsam, like the insignificant 'crumpled throwaway' in *Ulysses*, that float past.

Now, the crucial Joycean point, as *Ulysses* makes crystal clear, is that the crumpled litter is also a *letter*; so that, if the reader makes the effort to unfold it, a highly significant, even perhaps rewarding and enjoyable, meaning will emerge. We recall Joyce's conviction that readers are like alley cats, valuing only what they have to steal, so that the author would be wise not to offer them meaning like a pork chop on a saucer (*JJ* 495 n.).

But Jung is no alley cat: overwhelmed by boredom with *Ulysses*, he falls asleep. Special mention is made of 'the magic words that sent me to sleep', with page reference, in a footnote. They occur in the 'Aeolus' episode, where Joyce divides the text up with newspaper-style headlines (suiting the setting in the offices of the *Freeman's Journal*); the words in question come under the headline 'A POLISHED PERIOD' and exemplify the 'divine afflatus' (*U* 7.774) or windy rhetoric being doubly enjoyed and mocked at this point in the book. For Jung to admit that he was left 'dizzy with sleep' by the awful, long-winded bombast of the sentence perhaps confirms Joyce's remark that 'he seems to have read *Ulysses* from first to last without one smile' (*JJ* 628); a book that laughs at its reader, and makes a fool of him by turning its back on him, can hardly afford Jung any amusement. But we should look carefully at these magic sleep-inducing words:

A POLISHED PERIOD

J. J. O'Molloy resumed, moulding his words:

– He said of it: *that stony effigy in frozen music, horned and terrible, of the human form divine, that eternal symbol of wisdom and prophecy which if aught that the imagination or the hand of sculptor has wrought in marble of soultransfigured and soultransfiguring deserves to live, deserves to live.* (*U* 7.766–71)

The words are quoted in 'Aeolus' as a remarkable piece of legal oratory: they first 'fell from the lips of Seymour Bushe' (*U* 7.748), Stephen hears from J. J. O'Molloy (note those initials). For Stephen, of course, preoccupied as he is with his Shakespearean ruminations, the mention of rhetorical mastery merely recalls the fatal acts of ear-poisoning in *Hamlet* and *Othello* (and Jung too finds the eloquence deadly boring; it held, he admits, 'the narcotic that switched off my consciousness': *UM* III n.). But we shall find in this Joycean word-magic a dense cluster of allusions and meanings – in fact a veritable semiotic *bush* – that will prove to be of the utmost relevance to our argument.

First of all, the celebrated piece of legal rhetoric recited by J. J. concerns nothing other than Freud's favourite piece of sculpture: the 'horned and terrible' *Moses* by Michelangelo. Had Jung been more wakeful, he might have seen something in *Ulysses* here that, far from showing it to be 'desouled', revealed the book as 'soultransfigured and soultransfiguring' (the statue certainly was so for Freud, as we saw in Chapter 2 above) – or better, revealed its representation of *soul itself*; for the 'divine afflatus' that arises here is nothing but *psuche*: spirit, breath. It is as if the soul or psyche of Jung's former father-substitute and satanic rival breathes forth, so to speak, from the very 'freudful' sentence that sends him to sleep.[42]

But there is much more to be said about this 'polished period'. Ellmann reports that Joyce, at the age of eighteen and 'in pursuit of rhetoric' (*JJ* 91), had been to hear the famous barrister Seymour Bushe KC speak in court. The letters after the name, which stand for 'King's Counsel', serve to trigger a significant confusion of characters in 'Aeolus': the newspaper editor first takes them to be the initials of another famous barrister, Kendal Charles Bushe. Both Bushes reappear in *Finnegans Wake*, where indeed the reader may often feel hopelessly 'lost in the bush' (*FW* 112.3); and where Joyce's breezy Aeolean laughter blows on another bush-fire: 'cease your fumings, kindalled bushies!' (*FW* 256.12). As Atherton explains, K. C. Bushe was the author of a book entitled *Cease Your Funning* (a phrase from Gay's *The Beggar's Opera*) – but that title, Joyce discovered gleefully, was misprinted in the *Concise Dictionary of Irish Biography* as *Cease Your Fuming*.[43] Joyce's 'funning' with all this in 'Aeolus' is therefore very much also a matter of 'fuming', as the assembled characters strike matches and light cigarettes amid the rising 'divine afflatus' of eloquent speech or rhetorical smokescreen.

And the punning names of these Bushes give us a further vital clue, which will take us back to Freud's 'Anonymoses' and Jung's switched-off consciousness. If Kendal Bushe could easily provide Joyce with a kindled or flaming bush, his namesake Seymour could likewise be misread without too much effort as a 'say more' Bushe – to mark his Aeolean eloquence but also to echo Moses' effort to 'interpellate' the burning bush, his plea that Yahweh 'say more' by yielding up his name and thus entering the worldly domain of the signifier.

What is visible here, then, behind the smoke of legal oratory and the foliage of puns, is a scene of the Law and its Mosaic foundation (and Lacan will link that Law to 'the very laws of speech').[44] The representation of that scene, moreover, is set in a *mise en abîme*, a representation of representation itself, of language naming itself as a way to name the world correctly. The contrapuntal rhythm of the passage, with its final, seemingly 'tautologous' repetition, recalls Joyce's enjoyment of Giordano Bruno, whose habit of saying 'tautaulogically the same thing' (*FW* 6.30) is celebrated in the *Wake*. And of course the problem of abyssal representation glimpsed here is also a major philosophical topic: the 'absolute identity' that Leibniz wrote as $A = A$ marks a philosophical dream or ideal, the attainment of a language of pure denotation (but one that risked sliding into empty tautology).

In his own terms, Freud sees the Mosaic Law as a paradigmatic representation of human truth. His obsession with Michelangelo's statue had led him, in the article he considered an illegitimate 'non-analytic child', to link the truth of the psyche to the self-redemption of the father; only the lordly self-transcendence of the original lawgiver had made possible the spoken or spiritual, the representable domain of human truth. But, as we saw in Chapter 2, this primal scene of Mosaic Law had to be forged by Freud as a lesson in self-overcoming; while Michelangelo's work showed that Law tangled up in an obscure knot of possible meanings, Freudian theory sought to redeem both the work and the signifying legitimacy it threw into doubt by supplying a conclusive, curative interpretation. Thus psychoanalysis sought to oppose to the dubious revelations of art the redemptive plenitude of its psyche – its vocal truth – and replace the 'horned and terrible' or diabolic apparition of the father with its own father-version or *père-version*, a guarantee of signifying Law.

Now, the fuming of the kindled bush in Joyce can be seen here as an equivalent to the problem of the *cornuta* that we identified in the *Moses*. Whereas Freud's insistent demand for a solution to the statue's *Rätsel* or enigma blinded him to the straying of sense that marks it with a diabolic symptom, Joyce will celebrate that sinful straying as the *production* of sense, the multiplication of its characters or its seeds (and its Bushes). The misprint of 'funning' as 'fuming' thus *makes* sense for Joyce: it allows him, as it were, to Seymour – both 'say more' and 'see more' – Bushe, making both the lawyer's rhetoric rise like smoke and the burning bush of Exodus fume symbolically with divine wrath. *Ulysses* can be seen here in its full ambition to inscribe itself as an 'allincluding most farraginous chronicle' (*U* 14.1412): Joyce's writing desires both to make and to unmake sense, to represent and to disfigure reality. As we shall see, this inclusive, self-multiplying and self-dividing *summa* can also be expressed as Joyce's wish to be both 'trivial' and 'quadrivial'. An examination of the second act of Jung's 'Monologue' will allow us to shed some light on these terms.

Having slept through the polished period, Jung therefore remains oblivious to the fuming of its semiotic bush-fire; but when he awakens he feels ready to begin another reading of *Ulysses* in a more playful spirit: 'my views had undergone such a clarification', he writes, 'that I started to read the book backwards' (*UM* 111). The paleographers in the *Wake* will take Jung's method a stage further when they indicate 'that the words which follow may be taken in any order desired' (*FW* 121.12–13). And Jung's claim that 'the book . . . has no back and no front, no top and no bottom' seems to be more of a prophecy of Joyce's last work – the ultimate 'open work', or so Umberto Eco will claim[45] – than a description of *Ulysses*, with all its intricate architectural patterns.

Reading backwards, however, will turn out to be just what Jung needed to get into *Ulysses*; it is, after all, a fitting way to approach 'an art in reverse', as Jung now characterises Joycean writing. If *Ulysses* had previously scandalised the reader by turning its back on him, things get even worse as it now reveals itself to be 'the backside of art' (punning on the Latin *ars*, as it were). In the absence of any 'soul', Jung sees the text sink into a form of 'visceral thinking', its 'ganglionic rope-ladder' extending into a subterranean, unmentionable domain (*UM* 115–7). But if to read *Ulysses* in reverse means that Jung *bejaht*, beginning with the famous 'Yes' at the end of Penelope, this might point to the chance of something affirmative in his second reading. We recall that, in his letter to Joyce of 1932, Jung acknowledged that after years of infuriating 'peregrinations' in *Ulysses* he had finally managed to 'put himself into it', to establish some kind of identification with it. (Self-recognition in the mirror is always, one might say, in reverse.) As we have seen, of course, the Joycean text that Jung does actually 'put himself into' is *Finnegans Wake*, with its 'Jungfraud' (*FW* 460.20), its 'law of the jungerl' (268 n. 3) and so on; but he finds in *Ulysses* a portrait or mirror-image to rescue the book's 'detachment of consciousness' from unrelenting negativism – to restore, that is to say, some possibility of its *redemption*:

Whenever I read *Ulysses* there comes into my mind a Chinese picture . . . of a yogi in meditation, with five human figures growing out of the top of his head and five more figures growing out of the top of each of *their* heads. This picture portrays the spiritual state of the yogi who is about to rid himself of his ego and to pass over into the more complete, more objective state of the self. (*UM* 126)

This portrait of the artist as a jung man, as Joyce might have described it, is the other face of the 'abstract objectivity' that has 'desouled' the text, robbed it of any neurotic transferential warmth. In so far as the writing has in Jung's view freed itself from any engagement in human interest, it embodies the possibility of a certain radical self-transcendence, where the loss of meaningful identity might be counterbalanced by a redemptive access to a higher level of being. Jung thus sets out to salvage a narrative of transcendent Eastern wisdom from what he calls the 'drunken madhouse' of Joyce's text. (He means in particular the 'Circe' episode.) This requires some carefully edited quotations (resembling the *Wake*'s 'quashed quotatoes': *FW* 183.22); Jung turns to the speech of Elijah in 'Circe', picking out in italics a single line: 'You have that something within, the higher self' (*U* 15.2198). Whatever wisdom this might entail, Jung claims, 'suffers an infernal distortion' in the toils of Joyce's text; but it nevertheless harbours the arcane 'secret' of *Ulysses*, how the detachment of human consciousness it performs and embodies might be an 'approximation to the divine' (126). Although in Joyce the speech clearly looks like a mockery of such 'wisdom' – indeed, the Elijah who appears in 'Circe' looks very like the self-proclaimed Elijah III, a.k.a. Revd Alexander J. Dowie, at once tub-thumping preacher and bawling salesman – this in no way diminishes Jung's sense of it as an index of the book's ultimate message, its secret lesson in the mystery of self-overcoming.

If, therefore, in the first act of his 'Monologue', Jung was blind to the significance of Moses and the Law (with all its 'freudful' connotations), when he comes to *Ulysses* a second time – in reverse – he is able to 'put himself into' the book as a new Elijah. The passage in 'Circe' where Jung achieves this self-recognition is certainly concerned with identification. But the identification on offer there appears fraudulent:

ELIJAH. . . . Say, I am operating all this trunk line. Boys, do it now. God's time is 12.25. Tell mother you'll be there. Rush your order and you play a slick ace. Join on right here. Book through to eternity junction, the nonstop run. Just one word more. Are you a god or a doggone clod? (*U* 15.2190–4)

There can be no doubting Jung's response to this last question. The ad-man's patter may contain the stock satanic inversion god/dog – later to be stretched into Adonai's unspeakable utterance Doooooooooooog! (*U* 15.4711) – but Jung is not deterred: 'Glad tidings,' he declares with resolute mock solemnity; 'when the eternal signs have vanished from the heavens, the pig that hunts truffles finds them again in the earth' (*UM* 120). So the 'treasures of the spirit' *are* to be found in Joyce's book after all, but only by a pig with the right editorial skills, able to clean the mud from the spiritual truffles. Further on in 'Circe', we encounter Mananaan Maclir, an Irish sea-god whom Joyce shows holding a bicycle pump (a useful 'spiritual' tool, perhaps); and here Jung is able to pick out signs of 'Buddhist, Shivaist and . . . Gnostic' lore – but only by expunging all traces of its humour. So in Jung's version the sea-god does not begin his speech with a dig at Dublin mysticism (listing the guttural noises that AE considered the primal, magical elements of speech); instead, we cut straight to an apparent endorsement of that mysticism with 'White yoghin of the Gods'.[46]

The curious double movement of Jung's 'Monologue' thus begins to become clear. Having failed (but not straightforwardly, as we shall see) to identify the scene of Mosaic Law, the site of Freud's arch-representation as recited by J. J. in 'Aeolus', Jung has to read 'backwards' – as it were, satanically – in order to reinstate a divine law of his own. The 'eternal signs' are there not simply to be read in *Ulysses*, in Jung's view; they have to be dug up, restored to the book: in other words, Joyce has to be *redeemed*.

We should pause here to note the contrasting positions of Freud and Jung before an artwork. For Freud, the statue of Moses was unquestionably the product of a 'master-hand', the full realisation of an integral (albeit conflict-ridden) artistic will, so that the work's surface ambiguity had to be finally reducible to a coherent meaning. Indeed, for Freud what finally distinguishes art from the mere scribbling of a 'primary process' is its representational function. Jung, by contrast, suspects 'that Joyce did not wish to 'represent' anything' in the 'hellish monster-birth'[47] of *Ulysses*; thus the secret of the book does not lie in its representation, which is a mere superficial distraction from, or pretext for, its 'visceral thinking'. The different positions of Freud and Jung here cannot be merely an effect of the different objects they consider; both the *Moses* and *Ulysses* constitute aesthetic riddles; it is the interpretative engagement with the riddle that has shifted radically. If Freud's relation to the artwork is governed by a manifest supposition of authority – in other words, in Lacanian terms, by transference – in Jung, by contrast, there is a marked withdrawal of pleasurable readerly engagement. On one side, Freud's love for Michelangelo's *Moses* makes him identify with it, to strive to incorporate it or affirm it; to say 'yes' to it. On the other, Jung's distaste for the 'vicious dangerous boredom' (*UM* 114) of

Ulysses shows him negating Joyce's work, attempting almost literally to spit it out. The curious thing is that this negativity, which amounts to a refusal to take in the representational aspect of the artwork, will perhaps allow Jung to see an aspect of *Ulysses* that with our veneration of the book we may risk overlooking.

We should look more closely at the footnote where Jung admits to nodding off over Joyce's work; it will clarify these questions, returning us to the Law of Moses and the second coming of Elijah. Jung notes that along with the 'polished period' it is Stephen's thoughts of Moses as 'stonehorned, stonebearded, heart of stone' (*U* 7.854) that make him fall asleep; but his comments are revealing:

> Moses . . . refused to be cowed by the might of Egypt. The two passages contained the narcotic that switched off my consciousness, activating a still unconscious train of thought which consciousness would only have disturbed. As I later discovered, it dawned on me here for the first time what the author was doing and what was the idea behind his work. (*UM* III n. 5)

The moment of dawn, of revelation, is somehow both situated in the unconscious sleeping mind and deferred, left to be discovered later by the waking 'I'. But what was it precisely that was revealed? What is the significance of Moses, his 'heart of stone' an emblem of resistance to imperial power, for 'the idea behind' Joyce's work? Jung does not tell us; the implication seems to be that 'what the author was doing' concerns something 'which consciousness would only have disturbed': in other words, that Joyce *intends* to put us to sleep, and thus to gain access to a level beyond the ego, with its unconquerable readerly resistance. But if this is the 'idea behind' *Ulysses*, what does it have to do with Moses?

Moses certainly leads a strange double existence in Jung's 'Monologue'. On the one hand, he is Michelangelo's 'man of stone' turning his back on worldly concerns and thus symbolising Joyce's 'maddening defeat of intelligent reader' (as Jung puts it in a hapless attempt to parody the style of *Ulysses*); on the other, Moses appears as the 'tyrannical demagogue' who thought up the Law on Mount Sinai and foisted it on his people (*UM* 114, 122). While the first Moses resists power, the second imposes it; and if Joyce's literary crime in Jung's eyes makes him resemble the Moses who refuses to condescend to human interests, this refusal in turn is said to make him defy the 'ideals' invented by the other Moses, the lawgiver. The imposition of the Law by the prophet served to keep in check what Jung terms 'the shadow-side' (and for Lacan, in a not wholly dissimilar way, the Decalogue preserves our distance from the traumatic pre-symbolic Thing).[48] Jung now places Joyce alongside Freud: both are 'prophets of negation' who seek to reveal something concealed by reality, its obscene underbelly – in other words, who break the Mosaic Law.

Our first objection might be that surely Freud, at least, makes every possible effort in his article on the *Moses* to *restore* the integrity of that Law: the frangible and polysemic surface of the written tablet or stone artwork was to be saved from destruction, we recall, by the redemptive voice, the 'divine afflatus' of psychical truth. If Freud's commitment to exploring the unconscious is enough to make him, in Jung's eyes, a champion of the shadow-side, this ignores a blindingly obvious point: that psychoanalysis is supposed to enlighten, to make comprehensible what it unveils. But perhaps even stranger than this manifestly one-sided image of Freud is Jung's desire to link Freud and Joyce as sinful 'Naysayers' (*FW* 108.29). In what way can the 'visceral thinking' Jung sees embodied in Joyce's writing be thought to resemble Freudian analysis, with its supremely rationalist watchword 'Wo Es war, soll Ich werden'?

The answer is that Jung sees in both Freud and Joyce the moment of a certain cultural collapse, in which the laws governing human reality give way to reveal something nameless and traumatic, the corrosive antimatter that lies beyond human *Bildung*. What Jung fails to see – and this might account for his overlooking the Moses in 'Aeolus' with its clouds of Freudian significance – is how the Law itself already entails or incorporates this lack-in-the-Other (as Lacan will call it). In other words, there are not two distinct fathers, one turned away in mute, unworldly self-enjoyment and the other sternly forbidding enjoyment to others, but one and the same Moses; the very invention of the Law is marked, as it were, by its own transgression. There is something unspeakable, as it were, embedded in the very law of speech: the authority of the father, supposedly based on the redemptive self-sublation of enjoyment in a symbolic contract with God, is compromised by its flawed, living incarnation, by the father's jouissance (and Freud's encounter with Michelangelo's statue is clearly an attempt to make that jouissance finally legible).

The father's authority, then, is only supposedly based on paternal self-redemption; it is clear that transference, the unconscious act of supposing or instating authority, serves to blind the subject to the originary fault in the Law, thus neatly making up for the deficit in the Other. The difference between the two fathers, between Moses as sinner and Moses as lawgiver, is thus entirely produced by different ways of looking. And so Freud, in love with the statue, can overlook the linguistic error marked by the *cornuta* in his struggle to set in place the law of legibility (a tautologous 'law of law', as *lex* is already etymologically bound up with *lexis*). But Jung's non-transference simply turns the tables: instead of unmasking a divided or inconsistent truth, he sees nothing but error. To consider Freud a prophet of negation, and not merely an imperfect 'supposed psychological authority' (as Jung had presented himself to Joyce), is precisely to read 'backwards', deliberately undoing the search for semantic coherence in analysis – in effect, setting aside the key Freudian conflict between unmasking trauma and using discourse as an attempt to heal, to gain understanding.

When it comes to Joyce, Jung's non-transferential reading is more subtle. The key is his (at first sight astonishing) claim that 'Joyce did not wish to "represent" anything' in *Ulysses*. Our immediate response is likely to be: on the contrary, Joyce clearly wished his book to represent *everything*. But if we look again at the acme or nadir of Jung's non-transference – his collapse from boredom during 'Aeolus' – we shall see that things may not be so simple.

The Aeolean representation of legal eloquence, as we argued above, play-fully doubled representation 'itself', portrayed itself as the representation of representation; just as Freud had found in Michelangelo's statue a principle of signifying legitimacy, Bushe's polished period had held that work up as an emblem of human truth, mirrored in the perfection of its own polished syntax. The true parallel here is therefore not between Freud and Joyce, but between Freud and a Joycean character. It is Bushe, after all, caught up in a confusion of identities – and later to be transplanted into the *Wake* as one of the 'kindalled bushies' – who is the author, the legal owner, of the lines quoted by J. J. And those lines are precisely framed as *rhetoric*, as something to be savoured for its music, its texture or fragrance. If Freud's 'Anonymoses' – in other words his nervous refusal to acknowledge his piece on Michelangelo as legitimate psychoanalysis by signing it – may ironically have entangled him in a Joycean game of alibi or ventriloquism, the central aim of the essay remains none the less to tell the truth (about the law, about truth), to represent its object faithfully (that is, representation).

It is this aspiration to mimetic fidelity or true representation that is mocked – or more properly, as we shall see, trivialised – in 'Aeolus'. The very context of juridical oratory is already enough to make us suspect that the speech may be more to do with seducing the jury than with stating the truth. But when Jung compares Joycean writing with cubism, despite his failure to make the analogy convincing by applying it to the text, he uses terms that are peculiarly suggestive:

It is 'cubistic' in the deepest sense because it resolves the picture of reality into an immensely complex painting whose dominant note is the melancholy of abstract objectivity. Cubism is not a disease but a tendency to represent reality in a certain way – and that way may be grotesquely realistic or grotesquely abstract. (*UM* 117)

The 'picture' of reality should strictly speaking be something *shown*, not an invisible rhetorical artefact; Jung's 'abstract objectivity' implies that what is made visible in reality by modernism is, precisely, unspeakable. What is unspeakable in 'Aeolus' is bound up with its performance – or rather its 'perfumance' (*FW* 219.5) (and hence, for Derrida, its status as *perfumatif*).[49] Joyce's literary act, that is, has a subversive, parodic impact on the propriety of the speech it quotes as 'polished period'; the perfumative wordplay of kindled bushes, together with the smoking of cigarettes and the striking of matches, functions to carnivalise the speech, to mock its pretended pure representation by doubling it, disfiguring it with marks of irredeemable materiality, of dissemination. Thus speech at its purest, the speech-of-speech, is both represented and undone, performed and in that very performance opened up to the asemic force of Joycean writing, to its diabolic laughter. Hence Joyce's chief objection to Jung; the latter's inability to see that 'abstract objectivity', to cite the odd formula he uses to identify the modernist disruption of representation, could be anything but 'melancholy'. *Cease Your Funning* might indeed be the subtitle of Jung's 'Monologue'; its reading of *Ulysses* completely negates the laughter released by Joyce's carnivalesque doubling of signifier and letter, his simultaneous representation and disfiguration of reality. One of the enigmas of *Ulysses* may perhaps shed light on this – it comes immediately before the 'polished period':

– A few wellchosen words, Lenehan prefaced. Silence!
Pause. J. J. O'Molloy took out his cigarette case. False lull. Something quite ordinary.
Messenger took out his matchbox thoughtfully and lit his cigar.
I have often thought since on looking back over that strange time that it was that small act, trivial in itself, that striking of that match, that determined the whole aftercourse of both our lives. (*U* 7.760–5)

Who is speaking in this last sentence? Jeri Johnson notes that it is 'certainly in the manner of the Charles Dickens of *David Copperfield* or *Great Expectations*'.[50] For Hugh Kenner, this aping of high Victorian realism – in which the writer's 'small act, trivial in itself' was enough to conjure up a whole world and to determine human fate – marks a significant turning-point in *Ulysses*; something like its farewell to realism. Prior to 'Aeolus', the narrative has found an approximate centre in the consciousness of Stephen or Bloom (and readers of *A Portrait* have thus found themselves on fairly familiar ground); but in that episode, the narrative centre of gravity is displaced – like that of Stephen himself in 'Circe' (*U* 15.4433) – giving a first taste of the stylistic extravagances to come later in the book.[51] If we have difficulty attributing this 'Dickensian' sentence to a character – we are unable to *hear* it in an identifiable voice – it could be read it as a deliberate Joycean jest (or *geste*) about the literary performance or act. To describe that act as 'trivial' could either be to designate it as 'nugatory' (as Jung thinks *Ulysses*) or to include it in the *trivium*, the Scholastic triple path to eloquence – grammar, logic and rhetoric – within the medieval division of the seven liberal arts. The 'small act' or brief performance about to be delivered by J. J. will of course be trivial in the latter sense, as a masterpiece of rhetoric – although as such, in the view of the characters in 'Aeolus', it is far from being trivial in the everyday sense.

When Joyce was told by Frank Budgen that his reliance on puns might be thought by some to be trivial, he famously replied, 'Yes. Some of the means I use are trivial – and some are quadrivial.'[52] The *quadrivium* comprised the 'non-trivial' liberal arts in Scholastic pedagogy: arithmetic, geometry, astronomy and music, grouped together as the fourfold way to knowledge. The epistemic status given to the *quadrivium* by the Schoolmen clearly made it more important than the *trivium*, which was consequently taught in the introductory stages of a student's career: the 'trivial' arts of eloquence had to be mastered before the more serious work of attaining knowledge could begin. Joyce's sly riposte to Budgen thus evokes an old opposition between eloquence and knowledge, between speech and non-discursive *mathesis*. (Arithmetic, geometry, astronomy and music are arguably not wholly reducible to language; each discipline is said to entail something unspeakable. We shall return to this.) But how can a style that relies on punning wordplay be anything other than trivial in the Scholastic sense? When in 'Scylla and Charybdis' Stephen speaks (in yet another quotation) of 'quintessential triviality' (*U* 9.287), isn't his laughter provoked by a sense that the Theosophical effort to formulate mystical knowledge using magic numbers is in reality mere talk, no more essential than the ethereal fifth element dreamt up by philosophy? We shall try to formulate some answers to these questions in Chapter 6.

What is quadrivial can only be *shown*: its 'picture of reality' is not a rhetorical fiction or representation but a direct *episteme*, an unimaginable non-metaphorical grasp of the thing itself. The quadrivial 'means' used by Joyce, then, would be non-representational, and as such not really a 'use' of language but somehow its semic event, its act. The key context here, as critics have often noted, is aestheticism – and notably the poetry and poetics of Symbolism, first discovered by Joyce through Arthur Symons and Walter Pater. Mallarmé's notion of a non-expressive 'instantaneous magic of language' and Pater's contention that 'all art aspires constantly to the condition of music' are both cited by Atherton as vital ingredients of the 'shamebred music' of the *Wake*.[53] But this last derisive self-quotation already suggests the critical circle to be squared here: how can this 'specious aristmystic unsaid' (*FW* 293.27), the Symbolist notion of a pure language unsullied by mundane human speech, persist in the midst of Joyce's unrelenting parodic carnival, where at every point truth is rendered improper, spilled, disseminated? Our critical deployment of psychoanalytic thinking is partly an attempt to make legible Joyce's simultaneous invocation and disfigurement of a non-representational literary act, a language 'beyond speech' in which he hears incessant babble.

The quadrivial, then, bears on the core problems posed to criticism by Joycean writing in its war with a certain kind of representation. By contrast, the trivial aspect of *Ulysses* might seem to be less caught up in paradoxes: the legibility of the text is bound up with its phonocentric dimension, the (often playful and parodic) centring of narrative through speaking characters. The 'polished period' in 'Aeolus' would thus mark the book's 'quintessential triviality'. (Note how the 'frozen music' named in the sentence figures the collision of trivial and quadrivial: *U* 15.768.) But here a central irony is immediately apparent: it is only in the thoroughly fictive domain of speech, of rhetorical seduction, that the 'picture of reality' can be constructed. Jung's point about modernism is worth recalling: the cubist distortion of 'reality' is both an abstraction and an excessive realism (hence the oxymoronic 'abstract objectivity').

In psychoanalytic terms, we could link the trivial in this sense to the concept of transference. Like the Scholastic *trivium*, transference provides a fictive, delusory 'portal of discovery' (to recall Stephen's aphoristic definition of error): the way in to the analytic 'thing itself', the real extimate to the psyche. If that real has to be trivialised by being spoken within transference – which is to say, within a reality where truth is assumed or guaranteed by a supposed authority – this is to prevent its unspeakable, 'cubist' disfiguration of social reality; the psyche must be caught up in a fictive web of signifiers to prevent the psychical 'thing itself' from emerging (in what Lacan terms a *passage à l'acte*).

To read 'outside transference', then, may be not to *read* at all, to fail to enter the representational portal held out by a text. But perhaps to read backwards, as Jung does, to turn one's back on the supposed authority of the text and set about reinventing its meaning, could be an attempt to affirm a higher authority: in effect, a *religious* affirmation. The law of legibility, the Law itself, must be remembered, as we read at the end of the book of Malachi (4:4). With his notion of *Ulysses* as an allegory of the 'higher self', Jung attempts to salvage the same transcendent signifying legitimacy that Freud had sought to reconstruct in his encounter with the *Moses*. When Jung identifies in Elijah a *Bejahung*, a way of saying yes to *Ulysses*, he assumes the mantle of averting Joyce's biblical apocalypse, of saving the book from its own disastrous act, its transgressive revelation. In Chapter 6 we shall consider whether Joyce's dismantling of the Law necessarily implicates his work in religion (understood etymologically as *re-ligio*, the tying back together of the knot that has unravelled). Is Joyce's epiphany, his unique self-inscription, always an act of blasphemy?

God's real name

To avoid the heresy of Sabellius, we must shun the term *singularity*, lest we take away the communicability of the Divine Essence.

St Thomas Aquinas[1]

Symbolic exchange is what links human beings to one another: that is, it is speech, and it makes it possible to identify the subject.

Jacques Lacan[2]

LIST, LIST, O LIST!

In Part I, we explored narrational and institutional modes of traduction, whereby a literary 'thing' in which language showed or performed itself as a non-representable event is exchanged for – recited as – a (fraudulent or 'freudful') scene of full legibility and readerly pleasure. In Chapter 4, we saw how Shakespearean tragedy had already staged the traumatic reversal of this exchange, its unspeakable or unquotable characters – above all, the 'demi-devil' Iago – embodying a movement of language itself beyond the representable or accountable: the thing showing forth in an act as 'a suspension of constituted reality,' in Slavoj Žižek's formula.[3] If Joyce's engagement with Shakespeare sought above all to re-ignite the explosive charge of that intraductible literary thing, to render anew the disruptive force of its apparition, we have seen that this formed part of a broader desire to produce a 'quadrivial' language – to move, that is, beyond the beauty of a 'polished period' or formal masterpiece, into the realm of *mathesis*, of a non-metaphorical bodying-forth of the aesthetic thing 'in idself' (*FW* 611.21).

The first self-evident (or perhaps 'selfevitant', *FW* 186.33) problem with this will to exceed the 'trivial' in language relates to the self-cogitating 'I': that is, how can a reflexive self-consciousness ever move beyond its merely rhetorical surface, gain a self-knowledge whose truth would be non-metaphorical, irreducible to its contingent verbal utterance? In his treatise *De magia*, Bruno wrote nostalgically of a 'language of the gods' that had been immune to the mutability of worldly languages; the hieroglyphics of ancient Egypt had been the last point of contact with this divine symbolisation, but 'when Theuth . . . invented the letters of the type we use today for other purposes, this resulted in a tremendous loss, first of memory, and then of divine science and magic'.[4] To the young Joyce, reviewing a book on Bruno for the *Daily Express*, there was far more than mere recycled Platonism in the work of a thinker he dubbed 'the heresiarch martyr of Nola', even if for the time being it seemed to have only 'a distinct value for the historian of religious ecstasies' (*CW* 134). Bruno's importance for Joyce goes beyond the dry abstractions and categories of academic philosophy, to the point where thought borders on *extasis*, straining beyond itself to give voice to what is excluded from human reality, something indeed at odds with the laws of representation. And if Bruno was 'god-intoxicated', as Joyce insisted, this surely accounts for his fate at the hands of the Inquisition; his martyrdom bore witness precisely to the social *toxicity* of his 'divine science and magic', to how the constitutive laws of reality forbid any attempt to probe language beyond its 'trivial' surface. The true literary act, for Joyce, is therefore always a crime; by breaking through the constrictive skein of social representation and repetition, it adds something new to human knowledge (and only thus might be considered 'quadrivial').

In this sense, we can read *A Portrait of the Artist as a Young Man* as an extended Joycean *sum* – both an articulation of identity and an effort to write that self-articulation as knowledge. *Finnegans Wake* will spell out and playfully *dis*articulate this Cartesian ambition – 'cog it out, here goes a sum' (*FW* 304.31) – but in so doing will only draw attention to an ambiguous, writerly mathematics already 'on the board' at the beginning of Joyce's writing. In his very first term at school, Stephen has to face up to his inability to 'cog it out':

'It was the hour for sums. Father Arnall wrote a hard sum on the board and then said:
– Now then, who will win? Go ahead, York! Go ahead, Lancaster!
Stephen tried his best, but the sum was too hard and he felt confused. (*P* 12)

Here the 'brutish empire', as Stephen will call it in 'Circe' (*U* 15.4569–70), seeks to impose its antagonistic history on the children as a matrix of identification, to give false meaning to their pursuit of knowledge. But Stephen's response is to withdraw from that pursuit, with its complex made-up meanings, into a pure phenomenology of sensation:

His white silk badge fluttered and fluttered as he worked at the next sum and heard Father Arnall's voice. Then all his eagerness passed away and he felt his face quite cool. He thought his face must be white because it felt so cool. He could not get out the answer for the sum but it did not matter. White roses and red roses: those were beautiful colours to think of. (*P* 12)

The turn from *mathesis* to *aesthesis*, from the subject of knowledge to the perceptual surface of the body, points ahead to Stephen's more articulate self-reflections, 'thought through my eyes' (*U* 3.1–2) in the 'Proteus' episode of *Ulysses*. The subject conceives an aesthetics of pleasure – and the grown-up theorist, with his Aristotle and Berkeley, still rather enjoys imagining the world reduced to a set of 'coloured signs' (*U* 3.4) – which allows him to posit his identity not as abortive sum but as irreducible singularity, as a conscious *Jetztpunkt* able to reflect on its unfolding perceptual enjoyment. This infant aesthetic is above all imaginary: thus, when Stephen recalls the impossible green rose named in 'his' song at the opening of the book, he can reassure himself that 'perhaps somewhere in the world' such a rose exists (*P* 12). Theory in this imaginary modality conjures up a world whose infinite creative potential need not disrupt the eidetic wholeness given back by the mirror image.

But *A Portrait* subsequently moves its hero through a series of epistemic crises, each of which expands the range of his theory and displaces its centre of gravity (as Stephen will eventually spell out in 'Circe': *U* 15.4433). The trouble with eidetic self-contemplation as a comforting refuge from the failure to complete a sum is that it takes no account of the Other, as Stephen soon discovers. When he opens 'his geography', a book that shows on the first page a picture of the Earth suspended in the void, he finds that another student, Fleming, has secretly interfered with this quadrivial text by colouring in the picture with crayons: knowledge is 'trivialised' by colour, by being shown to be merely rhetorical, an artificial surface that can be made beautiful, given meaning. (He thinks of the political meanings given to colours at home by a woman with the colourful name Dante.) Stephen may persist in trying to 'get out the answer for the sum' of himself and his world, but his efforts become increasingly entangled in the discourse and desire of the Other:

He turned to the flyleaf of the geography and read what he had written there: himself, his name and where he was.

Stephen Dedalus
Class of Elements
Clongowes Wood College

Sallins
County Kildare
Ireland
Europe
The World
The Universe

That was in his writing: and Fleming one night for a cod had written on the opposite page:

Stephen Dedalus is my name,
Ireland is my nation.
Clongowes is my dwellingplace
And heaven my expectation.

He read the verses backwards but then they were not poetry. (*P* 15–16)

Stephen's list has the full seriousness of a signature: it is writing as act, used to authenticate identity, to establish ownership, to set the right limits of knowledge and property. Fleming's doggerel is by contrast wholly citational, a transformation of another's discourse into a new, parodic message, almost a *Witz* (although not a very witty one). Indeed, we could see Fleming as the first of Stephen's 'anticollaborators' (*FW* 118.25–6): he transforms the list into a meaningful text – and one with a religious 'teleology', at that – by reordering it, performing it anew. If Stephen's list is an attempt to name the real without using trivial speech – non-metaphorically, mathematically – in Fleming's verse the list is 'traduced into jinglish janglage' (*FW* 275 n. 6) its quadrivial solemnity converted into deliberately trivial speech (a 'small act, trivial in itself', like that in 'Aeolus').

In the juxtaposition of Stephen's writing and Fleming's variation of it, then, we see language itself in performance, in a play of names and characters irreducible to a clearly defined psyche or individual 'geography'; the two facing texts mark the *dialogisation* of identity and consciousness that all of Joyce's subsequent writing will pursue, up to the graphic 'Zweispaltung' of the *Wake* (a textual splitting that itself, as we saw, is caught up in an occult dialogue with the 'misses in prints'). The self-representation of a global ego with its own geography is thus parodied, doubled, disseminated by aesthetic enjoyment of the trivial: colours, rhetoric, poetic rhythm. The complex problematic of the textual *host* begins to become legible in Joyce at this point. Stephen is Fleming's *hostis*, his rival signatory and claimant to the textual geography, but also one who welcomes in the guest, enjoys his playful intervention. The Other as textual invader – the reader as raider – will be hailed in the *Wake* as 'my shemblable! My freer!' (*FW* 489.28); a quashed quotato from Baudelaire (in another act of literary misappropriation that itself 'refers' *en abîme* to reading-raiding) inscribes the name of the Other as an ambiguous rival who allows the subject to escape from the closure of an oppressive truth. But Stephen's own efforts to represent to himself the act of inscribing knowledge involve him in a more strenuous wrestling match with the Other:

Then he read the flyleaf from the bottom to the top till he came to his own name. That was he: and he read down the page again. What was after the universe?

Nothing. But was there anything round the universe to show where it stopped before the nothing place began?

It could not be a wall; but there could be a thin thin line there all round everything. It was very big to think about everything and everywhere. Only God could do that. He tried to think what a big thought that must be; but he could only think of God. God was God's name just as his name was Stephen. *Dieu* was the French for God and that was God's name too; and when anyone prayed to God and said *Dieu* then God knew at once that it was a French person that was praying. But, though there were different names for God in all the different languages in the world and God understood what all the people who prayed said in their different languages, still God remained always the same God and God's real name was God. (*P* 16)

Like Joyce's Giordano Bruno, Stephen is clearly 'god-intoxicated' – but the crucial difference is that for him 'God' can never be allowed to descend to a *nom commun* written with a lower case 'g': in other words, the integrity of the proper name, of the *Nom comme Un*,[5] is the core problem in this frenzied, compulsive soliloquy. And it is equally a problem of thinking rhetoric, of how the real name can figure in the trivial domain of speech: that is, how can God both remain a self-identical *Ding an sich* and be 'wordloosed over seven seas' (*FW* 219.14), be named conclusively as such and yet remain open to the infinite colours of human speech and translation? Stephen's answer is to use the proper name as a double stitch, a self-enclosing loop that prevents the whole textual fabric from unravelling. This *nom de nom* prefigures the final loop of the 'polished period' that will make Stephen blush in 'Aeolus'; God's name is thus 'tautaulogically the same thing' (*FW* 6.30), a self-quoting signature that precisely excludes itself from being caught up in the diacritical weave of signification.

In a single line, Joyce thus sews together two ostensibly quite different kinds of speechlessness: on the one hand, Bruno's ecstatic reach for an abso-lute 'language of the gods' beyond meaning; on the other, the first struggle of the human *infans*, the child in its desperate attempt to accommodate the enigmatic discourse of the Other. 'God's real name was God' could thus indicate either a divine mystery, as uttered by Yahweh to Moses, or a child's first tentative groping towards thought, with Stephen falling back on the formulaic repetition of *religio* to suture his anxiety. By doubling the deepest 'mystery' of religion with the most primitive pattern of thinking, Joyce exposes the 'ineffable' as the effect of a certain structural impossibility in language, and as such visible at every level in discourse – although it is likely to be seen at all only by the unprejudiced *theoria* of a child. The fact that, as Agamben puts it, '*Discourse cannot say what is named by the name*'[6] – and this is arguably the central problem confronted by twentieth-century philosophy – leads Stephen to the *aporia*, the lack-of-path, marked by the concluding repetition in which his argument can only sew itself up, fold in on itself.

Such an aporia is perhaps a particular symptom of religious thought. It would have been no good for Moses to start raising questions about the meaning of the Law handed down to him on Mount Sinai; in monotheism the divine will is presupposed as the affirmation of a law that is meaningless – because structurally foreclosed from discourse, as Agamben makes clear. Stephen is puzzled to find that the Other's discourse is governed by a set of structural – and, as such, 'meaningless' – rules. Why is it that there are only certain ways of combining signifiers? When he reads Fleming's verses backwards, Stephen sees that he has undone them as poetry, made them no longer the same 'thing'. *Finnegans Wake* will make this transformative *poesis*, this disseminating reversal of letters, one of its central diabolical tricks: by thus simultaneously inscribing and despoiling meaning, the *Wake* will deliberately expose itself as an *atheology*, a quasi-transcendent *Non serviam*.

Early in *A Portrait*, however, Stephen is still framed as a thoroughly religious subject; he imagines God as a knowledge somehow able to conceive of itself outside the limits of speech. Thus, when it comes to the ultimate non-trivial thought, of 'everything and everywhere', 'Only God could do that'; the Law forbids to speaking beings such a thought, in which a self-identical *cogito* could enclose within its subjectivity – and thus identify or 'own' – the whole of creation. Indeed, such a thought would be truly quadrivial, in being not a mere representation but a real thing or act ('Only God could *do* that'). We recall St Bonaventure's decree: *Anima enim facit novas compositiones, licet non faciat novas res.*[7] Stephen's restless shuffling of signifiers betrays his fundamental frustration at the split between composition and creation, representation and thing: in other words, the fact that he will never be able to utter God's real name in a meaningful or comprehensible discourse. God will not condescend to meaning, he will not enter into a symbolic exchange with the young theorist: in sum, he will not allow the subject any *textual pleasure*.

Stephen's attempt to theorise God in *A Portrait* is the first version of an oft-repeated Joycean scene: the son's encounter with a paternal act marked as tautologous, as a 'letter selfpenned' (*FW* 489.33). In one sense, this scene is simply another version of 'An Encounter', the confrontation with the enigmatic jouissance of the Other that we explored above in Chapter 1. But in *A Portrait* it is the crucial incidence of writing, Joyce's world-constitutive act, that is brought into the foreground:

They passed into the anatomy theatre where Mr Dedalus, the porter aiding him, searched the desk for his initials. Stephen remained in the background, depressed more than ever by the darkness and silence of the theatre and by the air it wore of jaded and formal study. On the desk he read the word *Foetus* cut several times in the dark stained wood. The sudden legend startled his blood: he seemed to feel the absent students of the college about him and to shrink from their company. A vision of their life, which his father's words had been powerless to evoke, sprang up before him out of the word cut in the desk. (*P* 90)

Stephen has been taken by his father to Queen's College in Cork, where he is to be given a kind of symbolic 'gift' by being shown the paternal signature. The failure of this act of transmission is clearly figured as the contrast between impotent speech – the father's 'powerless words' are not enough to constitute real communication – and a generative or seminal act of writing: the 'sudden legend' that surprises Stephen, hitting him with bodily, hallucinatory force. For Stephen, in this enigmatic, scar-like inscription, *es gibt*: the 'gift' of language is shown forth there, an anonymous 'it' marking an absolute, meaningless act of *poesis*. But, characteristically, the Joycean text also names this emergence of language at the point of its enactment: *Foetus* is clearly the name of a *potential* being, the unborn human embodying precisely the creative temporality of 'not yet'.

It is not the actual father, then, but an unworldly, ghostly Other that is able to transmit a creative language (the 'seeds to sow' later ascribed to the father in Stephen's derisory riddle); and this act of transmission occurs in a burst of uncanny jouissance that threatens to jeopardise reality itself. We recall how in *Hamlet* the paternal ghost warns the son of the danger, the potential toxicity entailed by its speech: 'I could a tale unfold whose lightest word / Would harrow up thy soul' (I.v.15–16). This soul-destroying speech is precisely what Bonaventure's law forbids: like Bruno's language of the gods, such a speech would dispense with the round-about ways of the signifier and body forth the linguistic thing itself, in an unspeakable creation *ex nihilo*. The empty speech of the self-regarding father thus seems to be Stephen's only refuge from the harrowing-up of his soul: 'Stephen's name was called. He hurried down the steps of the theatre so as to be as far away from the vision as he could be and, peering closely at his father's initials, hid his flushed face' (*P* 90).

Note that the letters *S.D.* (the mark of the real Joyce's 'own' literary alibi) are not quoted as such but simply named as 'his father's initials'; likewise Stephen withdraws from the sum, failing to see the signifier as an interpellation, a mark of his own identity. Shrinking back from the patrimonial 'gift' of his inheritance, he identifies not with a 'portrait of the artist' but with a Wakean 'poor trait of the artless' (*FW* 114.32); it is *Foetus* that gives itself as his true 'proper' name. (Note how it is written with a capital 'F'.) The key question here turns on the extent to which the Other, what Lacan terms the 'treasure of the signifier', can be *signed*: in other words, in what sense is the subject's semiotic inheritance an actual patrimony, the legacy of a singular, 'pathological' father? It is this question that runs throughout Joyce's work in its preoccupation with paternal and authorial signatures – above all, with the ultimate 'foundingpen' (*FW* 563.6), that of Shakespeare.

What is transmitted to Stephen in the anatomy theatre, then, is neither appropriate nor appropriable; it bears no trace of a cultural predecessor or authoriser. And yet it seems to *possess* Stephen, to impose itself with superegoic authority on his psyche: 'The letters cut in the stained wood of the desk stared upon him, mocking his bodily weakness and futile enthusiasms and making him loathe himself' (*P* 91). What is most upsetting about identifying with this discursive anonymity is the way it breaches – sinfully and, worse still, *creatively* – the boundary between psyche and world: 'It shocked him to find in the outer world a trace of what he had deemed till then a brutish and individual malady of his own mind. His monstrous reveries came thronging into his memory. They too had sprung up before him, suddenly and furiously, out of mere words' (*P* 90). The boundary between inner and outer worlds turns out to be a prejudice induced by a certain way of thinking, of representing the self. Language now seems to make Stephen's psyche come at him from the outside, as its 'mere words' suddenly entail a 'monstrous' productivity (a 'hellish birth', as Iago would say). The breaching of the subject's topography (prefigured by the handwriting of the other in 'his geography') marks the 'ABORTISEMENT' (*FW* 181.33) of Stephen's attempt to give birth to himself as a self-representing subject, inscribed as a properly worked-out sum. But this theoretical aporia coincides with a bodily force in language that imposes itself 'suddenly and furiously': an aesthetic *revelation*. As we shall see, the psychological consistency of *sum* will be fed into the Wakean wordpress and come out backwards, as 'mus' (*FW* 238.22) – in one sense, that is, as the imperious *muss* of a Kantian superego.

The revelation of the anatomy theatre, however, marks only a potential encounter of Stephen with his artistic vocation – although it will be fondly remembered in the *Wake* as a decisive *felix culpa*: 'O, foetal sleep! Ah, fatal slip!' (*FW* 563.10) – and there remains the problem of how to *own* it properly, how to countersign it and so draw it into the law-bound discourse of reality. Here the Stephen of *A Portrait* is very like the Alice of *Through the Looking-Glass*, who spells things out when she declares, 'I don't like belonging to another person's dream.'[8] To be inscribed in a dream signed by another, to become one of the Other's fantasmatic characters, is, for Stephen, to be forced to identify either with the kind of tedious Dublin 'character' to be found in his father's vacuous autobiography or with the non-metaphorical character *Foetus* inscribed in anonymous, mute jouissance. His artistic self-realisation will not, however, entail simply escaping from this fantasmatic 'den of monstrous images' (*P* 90) – awakening from the Other's dream into the sober light of reality – but will hinge on the act of re-inscribing its creative monstrosity, making it his *own* dream.

Stephen's first attempt in *A Portrait* to restore the legibility of his world is figured as the search for a coherent discursive frame within which to countersign his vocation, to make the encounter with the gift of language meaningful, cog it out. The problem is that by remaining open to the interpellation of discursive reality – to the ideological practice of a specific institution, namely the church – Stephen will risk merely taking up a place in another scene of oneiric, autistic libido. In other words, the very institutions supposedly governing 'reality' and preventing it from being disfigured by surreal, untreatably singular jouissance are secretly permeated by a pathological singularity of their own: so the redemption from sin they seem to promise turns out to be nothing but a perverse hypercathexis, a redoubling, of the sinful Thing itself.

The most celebrated instance of this institutional self-division is, of course, the extended sermon on hell pulsating at the centre of *A Portrait*. There, Joyce presents language gaping in an ecstasy of rapt self-enjoyment, embodying in itself – and at the same time forcibly imposing upon its audience – the fantasmatic Thing it professes, at the semantic level, to forbid. And the discourse can even index its own utterance in the very gesture of self-transgression: '– O, my dear little brothers in Christ, may it never be our lot to hear that language! May it never be our lot, I say!' (*P* 124). The word of God that consigns the sinner to hell is precisely language – again, like that warned of by the ghost in *Hamlet* – that breaches the topography of the psyche, is unutterable, *illegal*. And the sermon does not merely represent or mention such language, holding it up before the subject with the protective syntax of quotation marks: it precisely *is* that language. The effect of hearing such language on Stephen is indeed to consign him to a fantasmatic hell, to disfigure his 'portrait of the artist', to twist out of shape the imaginary coherence of his textual world and his body:

He came down the aisle of the chapel, his legs shaking and the scalp of his head trembling as though it had been touched by ghostly fingers. He passed up the stair-case and into the corridor along the walls of which the overcoats and waterproofs hung like gibbeted malefactors, headless and dripping and shapeless. And at every step he feared that he had already died, that his soul had been wrenched forth of the sheath of his body, that he was plunging headlong through space. (*P* 124–5)

Thus, instead of identifying with the semantic subject of the sermon, falling in with what it calls in its sinister mock benevolence 'our lot', Stephen feels himself touched by the voice itself, his bodily privacy violated by the 'ghostly fingers' of a fantasmatic object. The object-voice, like the signature of *Foetus*, imposes itself as the Other's nightmare; the 'rictus of cruel malig-nity' visible on the faces of the man-goats in Stephen's lurid, Goyaesque dream is nothing but a fantasmatic echo of the obscene jouissance of the sermon's rhetoric. This transgressive speech overrides the boundaries of the psyche, imposes itself on the subject, forcing him to own it, to *eat* it:

He flung the blankets from him madly to free his face and neck. That was his hell. God had allowed him to see the hell reserved for his sins: stinking, bestial, malignant, a hell of lecherous goatish fiends. For him! For him!
He sprang from the bed, the reeking odour pouring down his throat, clogging and revolting his entrails. Air! The air of heaven! He stumbled towards the window, groaning and almost fainting with sickness. At the washstand a convulsion seized him within; and, clasping his cold forehead wildly, he vomited profusely in agony. (*P* 138)

The eating of the Other's discourse is shown to be lethal: the ingestion of toxic jouissance wrapped in the guise of a semantically proper com-munication. What is transmitted is a pathological singularity, something impossible to incorporate or identify with comprehensibly, and the effect of this is to turn the topology of the psyche inside out: hence the wrenching forth of Stephen's soul powerfully figured in the convulsive self-evacuation of his body. The 'air of heaven' – a dismally inadequate 'poetic' metaphor for Stephen's desperate urge to escape, to awaken from the stifling nightmare – is exposed as a verbal 'perfumance' (*FW* 219.5), discovered to be a 'reeking

odour'. The way out proffered by religion, in other words, is revealed to
be nothing but a way back in: into infinite sinful damnation. (And this
Escherian topology precisely figures the redoubled loop of the sermon's
discursive self-transgression; at every turn, the semantic movement away
from sin is twisted back into its own sinful enunciation.)

The vicious circle of Stephen's encounter with religion thus spins on the
'I', on his own self-vomiting self-recognition: he can truly affirm himself
as a religious *sum* only by cancelling himself out – in principle, that is,
only by killing himself. This suicidal teleology begins to become apparent
once he has succeeded in assimilating some of the institutional blindness
of religion, which allows him to see the world in a new, 'redeemed' light:

Life became a divine gift for every moment and sensation of which, were it even the
sight of a single leaf hanging on the twig of a tree, his soul should praise and thank
the Giver. The world for all its solid substance and complexity no longer existed
for his soul save as a theorem of divine power and love and universality. So entire
and unquestionable was this sense of the divine meaning in all nature granted to
his soul that he could scarcely understand why it was in any way necessary that he
should continue to live. (*P* 150)

It no longer seems necessary for the subject to include itself, with all its
mortal imperfections, in God's 'theorem'; the ultimate quadrivial knowledge has no need to entangle itself in the trivial, erroneous domain of
my speech. For Blanchot, as we saw above in the Prologue, the suicidal
act always entails an affirmative dimension, as the attempt (albeit a self-
undoing one in so far as it is carried out by the irrevocably semantic ego) to
overcome temporality and experience an 'absolute' instant. But Stephen's
self-cancellation remains entirely theoretical; it will precisely never 'pass
to the act' and thus ruin the representational consistency of the supposed
Other. We are reminded of the terrible self-contemplative monologues of
Hogg's *Justified Sinner*, where the redemptive actuality of the world, its vital
resistance to ideological appropriation, is fully negated by the vocation or
interpellation of the subject, conjured away by its magic sum or 'theorem
of divine power'. In the midst of Stephen's episode of holy self-redemption,
the Joycean text signals what is truly at risk here: 'Another life! A life of
grace and virtue and happiness! It was true. It was not a dream from which
he would wake' (*P* 147). The ambiguity of the last phrase captures perfectly Stephen's plight: that is, his new life could well be a dream from
which he will *not* wake, an institutional illusion that functions precisely
to keep the subject permanently asleep, lulling him into living within its

imaginary 'theorem'. And the dream is of course not *his* dream, although its ideological effectiveness depends on making the subject identify and find his imaginary 'true self', in it. Fortunately, however, Stephen can yield up his self and his self-enjoyment only in theory: when it comes to the decisive *act* of his religious vocation – precisely the act that will break up his imaginary theoretical wholeness – he awakens from the dream of the Other, during what Joyce describes with a touch of blasphemous mischief as his 'troubled self-communion'. The crucial force of this Joycean awakening, however, lies in its break not merely with religious ideology, but with meaning itself: 'At once from every part of his being unrest began to irradiate. A feverish quickening of his pulses followed, and a din of meaningless words drove his reasoned thoughts hither and thither confusedly' (*P* 161). Confronted by the actual religious institutionalisation of his artistic potential, Stephen responds, we might say, by imagining *Finnegans Wake*. For the obscure 'din of meaningless words' that confuses him will return, will be recited – but now with bewildering joy in place of childish distress – in the 'hitherandthithering waters' (*FW* 216.4) of the *Wake*. Stephen thus turns away from the semantic interpellation of religion into a restless linguistic jouissance, the non-signifying revelation of a language-thing. Compared with this traumatic and ecstatic calling of language itself, the 'mystery and power' of the church indeed now appear trivial, mere empty rhetoric; for Stephen, its once seductive doctrine has 'fallen into an idle formal tale' (*P* 162). But for all his pride in being 'elusive of social or religious orders', the artist's desire to found his own quadrivial knowledge – to found an institution, that is: a body of knowledge inscribed with his own signature – still seems to involve him in ambiguous dealings with the Other: 'He was destined to learn his own wisdom apart from others or to learn the wisdom of others himself wandering among the snares of the world' (*P* 162). The 'free indirect' sentence is caught up in its own 'hitherandthithering' as it switches between self and others, uncertain whether its 'or' marks a true alternative or merely an equivalency: does knowledge, that is, ultimately belong to the Other, or can it be invented by the artist alone? And if it could be written as an unprecedented 'selfpenned letter', how could it then be transmitted, made legible, to the world?

EPIPHANY: CROSSEXANIMATION

We should look again at Joycean riddles. In his seminar of 13 January 1976, Lacan quotes the riddle with which Stephen baffles his class in 'Nestor':

– This is the riddle, Stephen said:

> *The cock crew,*
> *The sky was blue:*
> *The bells in heaven*
> *Were striking eleven.*
> *'Tis time for this poor soul*
> *To go to heaven.*

– What is that?
– What, sir?
– Again, sir. We didn't hear.

Their eyes grew bigger as the lines were repeated. After a silence Cochrane said:

– What is it, sir? We give it up.
Stephen, his throat itching, answered:
– The fox burying his grandmother under a hollybush. (*U* 2.101–15)

Hélène Cixous sees in this riddle a deliberate Joycean game of hide-and-seek with authority: at once its arousal and its abrogation. 'The very genre of the riddle', writes Cixous, 'assumes as a fundamental convention that there should be a solution somewhere, the one who asks being in theory the one who possesses the knowledge'; whereas Stephen's enigmatic answer 'reveals not a positive knowledge, but the gap in knowledge'.[9] For Cixous, this amounts to nothing less than 'the author abandoning his rights over language'; the riddle would thus mark Joyce's refusal to be identified as a 'freudful' author, as the legal proprietor of a final, transcendent legibility.

It becomes clear in Lacan's very late work (by contrast with some of his better-known earlier declarations) that the Name of the Father is *not* the only way of organising or knotting together the psychical orders of the real, the symbolic and the imaginary. If the fundamental structure of Freud's engagement with the aesthetic had been its assumption of a final and redemptive legibility – of some 'positive knowledge' that will reveal itself as the definitive and curative solution of the artistic riddle – we have seen that Joycean writing both enjoys and dismantles, but is never content merely to countersign, that structure. In our exploration of Joyce's relation to Shakespeare and to the literature of the double, we saw the emergence of what from a Freudian perspective must necessarily remain invisible: a language-thing (a thing embodied in characters such as 'Sant Iago', Gilmartin or Hyde) that exceeds representation, takes place not in the domain of eternal legibility but as actual performance.

One of the central questions raised by Lacan's reading of Joyce as *sinthome* is thus: how can an asemic act, a moment in language where *es gibt*, where the defective Other 'itself' is shown forth in an anonymous revelation, become the key to the topological coherence – that is, the singular identification – of a particular subject? Such a question is of course bound up with our own critical hysteria, our demand for an authoritative knowledge to resolve or close down the enigmas of interpretation – and it is precisely this demand that Joyce, as Cixous observes, both solicits and frustrates. But why does the writing awaken our appetite for authority if it is indeed 'asemic', in some essential sense unreadable, *pas à lire*?

This question, which poses itself most urgently when we turn to the *Wake*, will be the key to our final reading of Joyce as *sinthome*: as a radically ambiguous self-recitation or performance that demands a new, singular reader or 'anticollaborator' (*FW* 118.25–6). Thus, in so far as Joyce's final work does indeed pose itself as a riddle – and is not simply a colossal literary 'legpull', as Oliver Gogarty thought it (*JJ* 722) – we shall ask what the *Wake* wants of us, how it incorporates the Other as reader into its literary act. What kind of symbolic exchange do we partake in by accepting the gift or vocation of Joyce's work?

We should first read a little further in 'Nestor'. After finishing the class and leaving the children to ponder his insoluble riddle, Stephen is approached by a lone pupil, who has been instructed to copy sums off the board and thus supposedly to acquire *mathesis*, knowledge. Stephen is of course reminded of his own failure to solve a sum at the beginning of *A Portrait*: 'Like him was I, these sloping shoulders, this gracelessness. My childhood bends beside me' (*U* 2.168–9). The subject's inability to work out the sum corresponds to a symbolic destitution, a certain closure or blindness of representation. Stephen sees this figured in the gap between language as repetition or symbolic transmission and as the site for a singular, illegible inscription of being: 'He held out his copybook. The word *Sums* was written on the headline. Beneath were sloping figures and at the foot a crooked signature with blind loops and a blot. Cyril Sargent: his name and seal' (*U* 2.128–30). The signature is an untreatably bodily act of language, like the illegible 'soft stain of ink' that marks Sargent's face – that signs it, indeed, since the stain is 'dateshaped', a punning penmark of its own act of inscription. The 'blind loops' of the writing recall the double stitch of 'God's real name' in *A Portrait*. (Allusions to the earlier text abound throughout this passage, with its 'poor trait of the artless': *FW* 114.32.) In other words, Sargent's signature embodies an immanence or non-transcendence of language where the lack of a transcendent self-authorising 'I' – the master of a *sum* – allows language to reveal itself, to give or perform itself. As Stephen tries to give his pupil a lesson on how to do things with numbers, he reflects on precisely the unutterable or incomprehensible 'thing' that emerges in and beyond language:

Across the page the symbols moved in grave morrice, in the mummery of their letters, wearing quaint caps of squares and cubes. Give hands, traverse, bow to partner: so: imps of fancy of the Moors. Gone too from the world, Averroes and Moses Maimonides, dark men in mien and movement, flashing in their mocking mirrors the obscure soul of the world, a darkness shining in brightness which brightness could not comprehend. (*U* 2.155–60)

The 'dance inane' (*FW* 250.16) of the characters is an autonomous textual movement, a writing performance that is *extimate* to speech, irreducible to discursive meaning and yet inhabiting and 'mocking' it: both less and more obscure than any possible enlightenment. (Note how the occult pun on Moor/more, along with the play on dark and light, anticipates the involvement of *Othello* in Stephen's exchange with the racist Mr Deasy.) Sargent may lack the brightness to comprehend very much about the obscure soul of the world, but his childish struggle to handle the 'unsteady symbols' (*U* 2.164) provides an apt figure for the non-discursive materiality, the unspeakable opacity, of the language-thing.

Don Gifford notes that the two mathematicians Stephen thinks of here had set out to reconcile Aristotelian thought with the revealed truths of religion, and that both were therefore crucial influences on a third key thinker for Joyce: Thomas Aquinas.[10] A passage from the *Summa Theologica* (another book we might imagine with *Sums* 'written on the headline') may shed light on what is obscure here:

When anyone tries to understand something, he forms to himself certain images [*phantasmata*] by way of examples, in which he observes as it were what he is searching to understand. And so it is too when we wish someone else to understand a thing, we propose examples to him by means of which he may form *phantasmata* so as to be able to understand.[11]

Note that when Father Noon quotes this passage, he translates *phantasmata* first as 'images' and then as 'symbols'; the act of symbolic transmission can thus be instituted as such, inscribed as precisely the difference between *phantasmata per modum exemplorum*, the provisional, visible conveyance of an invisible truth, and the final, truthful revelation *ad intelligum*, in 'symbolic' form before the psyche. But Aquinas uses one and the same word, says 'tautaulogically the same thing' (*FW* 6.30); truth for him remains irrevocably trapped in the domain of *phantasmata*, hence its revelation must always be phenomenal. It is the actual epiphany or *alethia* of language that constitutes revelation, not some gathering of symbolic or potentially meaningful content. In other words, the revelation of truth can never be turned into a discourse; it is a non-transmissible event. If the Moors invented mathematical symbols to write down this quadrivial dimension, those symbols were thus radically ambiguous 'imps of fancy': both characters dreamt up *ex nihilo* to figure the unspeakable and also devilish embodiments of forbidden fantasmatic jouissance. (What are Edward Hyde and Dorian Gray but 'imps of fancy'?)

The Joycean epiphany is another attempt to write down, to set within the framework of a certain 'quadrivial' formalisation, the blinding *phantasmata* of this language event. 'By an epiphany', writes Joyce in *Stephen Hero*, 'he meant a sudden spiritual manifestation, whether in the vulgarity of speech or of gesture or in a memorable phase of the mind itself.'[12] In this early attempt to theorise, to put up on the board, the non-trivial *quidditas* of his art, Joyce remains caught in a certain tautologous knot: the subject who is said to 'mean' something by epiphany in effect provides not so much a semantic definition of the term as a list of sites – voice, gesture, psyche – where it occurs as enigmatic signifying *event*. Epiphany is thus a name for *manifestation*, the in-itself-unrepresentable moment of apparition, which, if we refer back to Aquinas, would correspond to an attempt to grasp the basic *phantasmata* mediating the subject's relation to the Other.

For Lacan, the epiphany is an index of a constitutive breakdown of metaphor in Joyce, his work's fatal-foetal slip: in it, something in the Other is revealed that is supposed to be kept masked, kept at bay, by the laws of representation governing social reality. We recall how the encounter between Stephen and young Sargent in 'Nestor' takes place alongside an explicit thematic – emblematised by the insoluble riddle – of non-transmission, failed communication or the 'gap in knowledge', as Cixous puts it. While the child is labouring at his sum, Stephen reflects on this non-encounter: 'Too far for me to lay a hand there once or lightly. Mine is far and his secret as our eyes. Secrets, silent, stony sit in the dark palaces of both our hearts: secrets weary of their tyranny: tyrants, willing to be dethroned' (*U* 2.169–72). The self-consciously poetic diction mocks itself by speaking of non-speech, of an unbridgeable gap between self and other. Something cannot be transmitted in discourse, Stephen imagines, because it remains locked deep within an imaginary interior, where each ego hoards its semantic treasure behind the unbreachable walls of its psychical defences. But these are precisely Stephen's *phantasmata*, the mock symbolic images that allow him to make an event meaningful, to inscribe it in 'iSpace' (*FW* 124.12): in other words, both to make it visible in *theoria* and to make it 'mine', the identifiable property of an 'I'. We can glimpse something of the ironic subtlety of Joyce's self-portrait here: the crucial point is not that Stephen is simply *wrong* in what he says about language, that he merely misconceives it and remains blind to its dialogic potential – but that in his very search for meaning we are shown a certain semiotic closure in act. Yet just as the text makes manifest the restrictive structure of identification for its character, it simultaneously manifests itself for us, allows us to read through and beyond the 'dark palaces' of its hero's proper meaning; that is, to read the very surface of language that such a deep semantic gaze must always overlook. So in the line 'Mine is far and his secret as our eyes' we see Stephen supposing 'iSpace' to be non-transferable, impossible to articulate, leaving each ego marooned in its own enigmatic singularity; but the text running between self and other immediately begins to spill over, to multiply its senses and jeopardise any discrete semantic self-unity. As will be made clear later in *Ulysses*, in the 'Cyclops' episode with its repeated 'Ay, says I' (*U* 12.20), to say 'eye' is simultaneously to say both 'I' and 'aye'. If the isolated souls of Stephen's imagination can never share their dark secrets, the open secret of the text lies in its dissemination, its sharing out of the 'one' letter among various senses; and this semiotic *ouverture* is above all figured by the visible-invisible inscription of 'yes' in 'our eyes'. As Derrida emphasises, 'yes' is an inherently dialogical remark in and of language; since 'it must be taken for an answer', it is always-already bound up with the discourse of the Other, inscribed in an act of transmission.[13]

While the ego remains trapped in its own phantasmal 'iSpace', then, language will override that entrapment and breach the integrity of its identificatory castle. But by the same token the ego itself, ineluctably caught in the meaningfulness of its own viewpoint, can never grasp or theorise this language-thing: it is only as the superfluous and thus 'meaningless' repetition of that utterance – 'Ay, says I' – that it can inscribe 'itself', remark its representation. Hence the Joycean epiphany, as Cathérine Millot notes, marks an uncanny coincidence of insignificance and signifying tautology, at once the evacuation and the over-determination of meaning.[14] One of the most powerful of the epiphanies links this *coincidentia oppositorum* directly to a crisis of the body:

MRS JOYCE – (*crimson, trembling, appears at the parlour door*) . . . Jim!
JOYCE – (*at the piano*) . . . Yes?
MRS JOYCE – Do you know anything about the body? . . . What ought I do?
There's some matter coming away from the hole in Georgie's stomach . . .
Did you ever hear of that happening?

JOYCE – (*surprised*) . . . I don't know . . .
MRS JOYCE – Ought I send for the doctor, do you think?
JOYCE – I don't know . . . What hole?
MRS JOYCE – (*impatient*) . . . The hole we all have . . . here (*points*)
JOYCE – (*stands up*)[15]

The mother's voice calls the young artist away from the meaningful enclo-
sure of his 'iSpace' to confront a gap in knowledge, a semantic evacuation
figured by the traumatic 'matter coming away' from his brother's stomach.
'The hole we all have . . . here' evokes the desperate conjunction in the
body of singular and universal, of both *this* being and a general condition
of being human. Likewise, the pure tautology of the mother's anguished
gesture rebounds upon the text itself, so that the 'hole . . . here' becomes the
invisible and traumatic centre of the writing, the point where its semantic
'matter' disappears into the event of its utterance – the point where, as
Lacan puts it, the signifier makes a hole in the real.

As we saw above in Chapter 4, Lacan's reading of the epiphany marks
it as the falling away of the imaginary from the knot to reveal something
forbidden and unrepresentable in language: the meaningless *punctum* where
body and speech, symbolic and real, collide. But for Lacan the *sinthome*
intervenes to prevent the psychotic unravelling of the knot, and how it does
so is beginning to become clear: when Joyce countersigns the epiphany as
an act of signification, he identifies with its anonymous semiotic gift by
affirming it (we recall the secret 'yes' embedded in 'our eyes'). The Joycean
epiphany is, as Derrida puns it, *ouï-dire*, both hearsay and yes-saying; and
its signatory doubles itself – but crucially without representing itself – in
the same gesture: 'Ay, says I.' For Lacan, it is the subject's meaningless
choice of writing that constitutes the *sinthome*, making its hearsay also a
heresy (Greek *haeresis*, 'choice'), a turning away from the consistent fictive
domain of symbolic identification towards the dangerous, unpredictable
singularity of a language-event.

The idea of the epiphany is Joyce's first declaration of faith in language
to body forth the essential dimension of being. Whereas in Stephen's dark
vision human subjects are permanently sundered by language, unable to
translate into a collective idiom the rich, meaningful singularity of the
Innenwelt, in the *Wake* every character will come to be hailed as its own
tautologous epiphany: 'So why, pray, sign anything as long as every word,
letter, penstroke, paperspace is a perfect signature of its own?' (*FW* 115.6–8).
Here we can perhaps glimpse the basis of Joyce's hostility to the representation of the self as a site of inner psychological meaning; psychoanalysis risked colluding in the ego's self-blindness, its refusal to envisage

its own linguistic ontology, if Freudian theory supplied an unconscious rich with secret meanings before it sought to address the enigmas of consciousness.[16]

The 'matter coming away' from the semantic whole of the body in the epiphany thus allows writing to manifest itself, its own 'perfect signature' emerging in the gap in knowledge. And Joyce immediately makes clear something that from a psychoanalytic perspective will be crucial: namely, that this event in language has everything to do with the law of sexual difference. The 'matter' that comes away from a hole opens our portal of discovery here. When in 'Nestor' Mr Deasy declares, 'I have put the matter into a nutshell' (*U* 2.321), we are shown a distinctly *phallic* conception of the letter: a decisive instance of containment and totalisation, and a signifier that inscribes itself in a patrilinear semantic tradition. (The nutshell clearly alludes 'unconsciously' to Hamlet's 'iSpace'.)[17] The fundamental ambiguity of the Joycean epiphany becomes apparent here: if each enigmatic scrap of semic matter that is pasted into the young artist's notebook seems in itself wholly devoid of significance (wholly trivial), once it has been entitled 'epiphany' it is framed as a discrete literary 'thing', inscribed as an authorial signature. In one sense, then, the epiphany puts itself forward as matter-in-a-nutshell and thus remains eminently phallic, committed to the semantic unity of event and identity (in an artistic vocation). And yet what we are shown in the epiphany as text precisely fails to occur as one identifiable discursive event, remaining suspended in an indeterminable realm between speakers; it cannot be translated into another meaningful proposition, but is wholly identical with its own contingent, accidental utterance.

How then does this oscillation between the epiphany as phallic oneness, as a single 'sudden spiritual manifestation', and as textual dissemination relate to sexual difference? Millot notes that the Joycean epiphany is largely 'taken from the mouths of women'; in the text quoted above, it is the mother's voice that calls on the artist, involving him in the indeterminate textual matter of his vocation. The subject confronts the desire of the Other here in a double sense (which perhaps resembles Stephen's idea of the doubleness embedded in *amor matris*): on the one hand, a demand for knowledge – 'Do you know anything about the body?' – brings with it an implicit faith in language to represent, to *treat*, the pathological singularity of the real; while on the other, the very force of the mother's utterance itself embodies something irreducible to law, inaccessible to the Other as guarantee of meaning. At this latter point – encapsulated above all by the tautologous gesture towards 'the hole we all have . . . here' – the voice becomes a 'perfect signature of its own', as the socio-symbolic system that 'we all have' collapses into the untranslatable instance of voice or trait 'here'. The epiphany is thus a pure 'joussture' (*FW* 535.3), as Joyce will write in the *Wake*: as a tautologous semiotic act, it recalls the theory of Marcel Jousse (a name with the added charm of sounding *justement* like Joyce) that language had originated in gesture and was essentially performative.

Rather than aligning Joyce's work simply with a 'feminine' writing that would deliberately expose any phallic signifying resolution as fraudulent, then, the epiphany marks precisely an interminable movement between the Other – a scene where the artist can declare himself, have his signature recognised as a decisive act – and the revelation of lack in the Other, a revelation with disastrous effects on the stability of psychical and sexual boundaries. It is this writing-disaster that Joyce repeatedly figures as a *rupture* in the scene of legislation or authorisation, the effect of untreatable creative excess; something perhaps audible above all for Joyce in a woman's voice. Although it is not until *Finnegans Wake* that we confront the full scope of this traumatic movement between letter and voice, signifying act and bodily singularity, throughout Joyce's work it unsettles the binary representational economy that 'naturally' governs our reading habits. What perhaps distinguishes the *Wake* in particular, however, is not only that it brings the disastrous movement of Joycean writing to its culmination, but also that it turns around on that movement reflexively, repeatedly giving it names.

Critics often note how difficult it is to quote from *Finnegans Wake*, as if, in attempting to excerpt anything *per modum exemplorum* from the ever-shifting textual fabric, one risked looking as foolish as Mr Deasy with his reduction of Shakespeare to Iago. The text self-evidently refuses to present itself as any single 'identificative paper', to recall one of Joyce's first statements of his writerly autonomy.[18] Indeed, one of the main themes of the *Wake* is its own non-subjection to epistemic authority: the very gesture of critical quotation is pre-quoted, as it were, its legal authority already quashed by the textual *geste*, so that the critic can never hope to emerge from an attempt to consume these 'quashed quotatoes' (*FW* 183.22) with an intact, still authoritative metanarrative.

But it is precisely this dismantling of the reader's power to cite it or make it exemplary that Joyce's text, in a final twist, *names*: thus what was revealed at the *Wake*, we read, 'oozed out in Deadman's Dark Scenery Court through crossexanimation of the casehardened testis' (*FW* 87.33–4). The mock legal scene evoked is part children's blindfold game and part uncanny judgemental return of the dead, and in it the Other returns not properly as 'cross-examination' – as it would in the psychoanalytic lawcourts, where subjects are interpellated to a fixed place and sex in the symbolic order – but as 'crossexanimation', a twisted inscription of subjectivation that releases the *anima* from its self-enclosure, sends it out across psychical boundaries and across sexual difference.

'You have never heard of a woman who was the author of a complete philosophical system,' Joyce is supposed to have said to Frank Budgen; Atherton quotes this remark as an index of what he takes to be Joyce's belief in the innate intellectual superiority of the male.[19] Now, while we should certainly take with several pinches of salt the ostensibly 'feminist' opposition in the *Wake* between a 'vaulting feminine libido' and a 'meandering male fist' (*FW* 123.8–10) – in other words, not simply identify Joyce's text as a specifically feminist *écriture* seeking to overturn a repressive masculinity – conversely it is far from clear that Joyce considered the production of totalised philosophies to be merely a triumph of patriarchal wisdom. Indeed, in 'crossexanimation' we can read the inscription of precisely what such a 'complete philosophical system' shuts out, forecloses: that is, by enclosing human subjectivity in the 'nutshell' of the anima or psyche, it remains blind to the essential dimension of *poesis*, of language as creative performance. If cross-examination would confine the subject to a single site of truth in the gaze of the Law, 'crossexanimation' releases its semiotic polyvalence into multiple and interminable readings, from the telepathic movement of the anima across psychical and sexual borders to the incarnation of the logos in the exanimation of Christ on the cross (in what the *Wake* renames as a 'cruelfiction': *FW* 192.19).

This last reading takes us back to the specifically religious contexts of Joyce's rupture of critical and philosophical – and always paternal – authority. If we return to Stephen's encounter with young Sargent in 'Nestor', we can see that 'crossexanimation' is already at work:

In long shaky strokes Sargent copied the data. Waiting always for a word of help his hand moved faithfully the unsteady symbols, a faint hue of shame flickering behind his dull skin. *Amor matris*: subjective and objective genitive. With her weak blood and wheysour milk she had fed him and hid from sight of others his swaddling bands. (*U* 2.163–7)

The ambiguity of the Latin phrase marks mother-love as something impossible to include in the *sum*, to write into the algebraic proofs of self-enunciation (such as 'I am thy father's spirit'; Stephen has just been thinking of his supposed ability to read *Hamlet* 'by algebra': *U* 2.151–2). It is therefore impossible to *situate* 'love of mother', to give its utterance a single site or subject; it breaches the boundaries of identity, or more precisely it supplements the inadequacy of the Other as a guarantee of identity by introducing an unspeakable materiality, an act of love that overrides the law of representation. In this way, Joycean writing raises questions of filiation and tradition, of the power to give and to utter names, that return us once again to the first riddle of the universe: when is a man not a man?

VENISOON AFTER: JOKY FOR JACOB

If, as we saw above, Aquinas postulated that our relation to the Other is always phantasmatic, this insight led him into theological difficulties that must have been especially compelling for Joyce. How can the existence of God, his absolute being, be grasped by human language at all if we are able to conjure up only *phantasmata*, mere specular representations mired in deceptive worldly meaning? This question, whose primal scene we could locate on Mount Sinai where Moses demands to know the name of God (Exodus 3:13), produces the following baroque response from Aquinas:

Therefore, when we proceed in God by means of the path of negation, we first negate from him the names and the other corporeal attributes; second, we also negate the intellectual attributes, with respect to the mode in which they are found in creatures, such as goodness and wisdom; and so what remains in our intellect is only the fact that God is, and nothing else: and this remains in some confusion. Finally, however, we take away from God also this being itself, insofar as it pertains to creatures and thus remains in the shadows of ignorance; by means of this ignorance, as far as earthly existence is concerned, we unite with God very well, as Dionysus says. And this is that certain shadowy realm said to be inhabited by God.[20]

As Agamben comments, God is thus reduced by Aquinas to a pure negativity, the taking-place of being beyond human discourse – or rather, to be precise, beyond human speech. For Agamben goes on to link this notion of a pure or asemic name to the written *nomen tetragrammaton* in Hebrew mystical theology, the 'secret and unpronounceable name of God'.[21] The four-letter word YHWH, declared the mystics, transcribes the true name of God, and its pronunciation by humans is therefore forbidden (thus its lack of any vowels makes it literally unpronounceable). Agamben quotes Meister Eckhart on this unspeakable *alethia*:

Once again . . . we should note what Rabbi Moses said regarding this word: I am who I am [*sum qui sum*] seems to be what the four-letter name means, or something like that, which is sacred and separate, which is written and not spoken and that thing alone signifies the pure and naked substance of the creator.[22]

There is something irresistibly comic at work in these attempts to make a statement about what cannot be spoken, as if in them we see discourse literally tripping over itself in its effort to spell out what Agamben calls a 'grammar of the ineffable'. Thus, for Eckhart *sum qui sum* can be identified with the *nomen tetragrammaton* only in the phantasmal domain of mere appearances; God's utterance only 'looks like' (*videtur*) his *nomen innominabile*, and the theologian has to admit weakly that it may be only *proximum illi*, 'more or less like that'. And a similar rhetorical bathos afflicts Aquinas, whose grand finale evokes a mysterious realm *in qua Deus habitare dicitur*, 'in which God dwells, or so they say', with the final word reducing the divine presence to mere rumour, hearsay.

Stephen's conclusion in *A Portrait* that 'God's real name was God' can thus be seen to recall some eminent, albeit potentially laughable, theological difficulties. The point of his anxious monologue was to maintain the integrity, the selfsame identity, of God's name, while also taking account of the mysterious diversity of human discourse. The problem of the Proper Name for Stephen – and the theologians were caught in the same knot – is that it is both a separable linguistic element ('sanctum et *separatum*', as Eckhart says) and a mark of the discursive transmission of identity; if the *nomen tetragrammaton* cannot be spoken, this is because it must be excluded from the alienating transactions of human meaning, where identity is precisely an effect of the Other, of *inter*-subjective exchange (and thus of 'crossexanimation'). Thus, the name of God is paradoxically *quod scribitur et non legitur*, in Eckhart's formula: that which is written but cannot be read, that which is *pas à lire*.

The comedy of the theologians and their unspeakable four-letter word returns us to what Joyce writes as a 'freudful mistake' (*FW* 411.35): that is, the confluence of laughter and sin, as exemplified in the Freudian theory of jokes. The fall is the fall from the absolute written Name into the erroneous domain of meaningful speech; likewise, in the Freudian *Witz* something illegal falls into meaningful discourse, and is shown by that discourse as its own breach, its 'anamorphic' distortion (such as writing 'freudful' instead of 'frightful'). When Aquinas and Eckhart (and then Stephen) try to refer to what, according to their own theology, can only be written, they are caught in a performative contradiction, struggling with signifiers to indicate what is supposedly alien to discourse.

The mythical opposition between writing and speech, or the hand and the voice, thus offers a frame within which theological discourse can figure the intrusion of sin (for Joyce, also the 'fall' into meaning, *Sinn* in German: e.g. *FW* 332.28). Writing, as the absolute Thing of language, the unpronounceable *tetragram*, is entirely without meaning; it is only when the voice labours comically to utter it that its letters lapse into sinful 'nomanclatter' (*FW* 147.21), the clamorous gossip of desiring subjectivity. And this last Wakean trope – where nomenclature is renamed as no-man-clatter – offers a clue as to how Joyce takes up these questions of mystical theology in a new inscription of the 'mystical estate' or 'apostolic succession' of fatherhood (recalling Stephen's phrases from 'Scylla and Charybdis': *U* 9.838). When Stephen describes a father as a 'necessary evil', in one sense he may be merely attempting to ascribe meaning to the original sin (read *Sinn*) of language itself. If we look once again at Stephen's moment of 'paternal' authority in 'Nestor', we can see how it subtly prefigures the Wakean re-inscription of the father as source of semic errancy. When Stephen is confronted by the image of his own childhood – a scene of the son turning to the father as authority, as legal proprietor of knowledge – he has, as we saw, a little epiphany of non-communication; but we should pay more attention the language he uses:

Too far for me to lay a hand there once or lightly. Mine is far and his secret as our eyes. (*U* 2.169–70)

The repetition of 'far' is more than mere poetic affectation; *far* is the Danish for 'father' and, as such, will become a central Wakean pun, insistently folding together paternity and excess ('fartoomanyness': *FW* 122.36) as well as distance, separation, loss. But in *Ulysses*, when in the 'Eumaeus' episode Stephen finds himself cast in the role of son again, these puns are already active:

– You suspect, Stephen retorted with a sort of half laugh, that I may be important because I belong to the *faubourg Saint Patrice* called Ireland for short.
– I would go a step farther, Mr Bloom insinuated.
– But I suspect, Stephen interrupted, that Ireland must be important because it belongs to me. (*U* 16.1160–5)

Bloom is identified by a venerable tradition of *Ulysses* criticism with the desire to be a stepfather, or more precisely a Stephen-father.[23] But this kind of psychological reading often risks overlooking the structural basis of textual meaning. The scenario staged here by Joyce sets the relation of father and son in a particular structure of miscommunication, of the indefinite suspension of meaningful identity. Stephen's Wildean 'paradox' depends on the I/You matrix of the performative utterance; it requires the countersignature of the Other – even if only in a 'yes' of the eyes – to take effect as a decisive and witty reversal of the message that subordinates individual to national identity. (Yet another question of parentage; note how Stephen identifies Ireland with the patriarchal figure of St Patrick via a marked gesture of avoiding his non-Irish 'mother' tongue.) But of course Bloom does not see the point, and his attempt to extend the meaning of their conversation is a step too far, a step out of line with the role required of him by Stephen's witticism. Bloom is thus, we might say, *too far*, too father-like (and note how this Danish pun might echo another pun, used by a Danish prince to ward off a too-fatherly stepfather by declaring himself 'too much in the sun') – and hence perhaps too committed to the semantic integrity and finality of communication to comprehend the 'jocoserious' (*U* 17.369) suspension of the signifying chain in the *Witz*.

The encounter between an unseeing or blind father and a jokey or treacherous son will become a central scene of *Finnegans Wake*. The *Urszene* of this encounter occurs, of course, in the book of Genesis, where a 'bland old isaac' (*FW* 3.11) – blind father Isaac – is traduced by his son Jacob (whose Hebrew name means 'he supplants' or 'he undermines'; inscribing an original substitution or metaphor), who takes the place of his elder brother Esau at the behest of his mother Rebekah (Genesis 27). The significance of this biblical tetrad for the *Wake* is, as we shall see, crucial, and it is already made manifest on the opening page. But in 'Eumaeus', Bloom already occupies the position of an Isaac (or an 'Ikey Moses': *U* 9.607): that of a father struggling to identify the son, to *hear* the son's voice properly in order to make symbolic contact with him and bring about patrilinear transmission. Likewise, when Stephen in 'Nestor' considers it 'too far for me to lay a hand there once or lightly', the same problematic arises: that of voice and hand (or speech and writing) as the dubious media for the transmission or confirmation of identity. Throughout *Ulysses*, Stephen will be preoccupied by the semiotic duplicity of voice and hand; and these concerns are bound up with his sense of the institution of paternity being fictive, insubstantial, 'founded . . . upon the void' (*U* 9.841–2). When he explicitly casts himself in the biblical scenario it is as the disinherited son, the unrecognised 'voice of Esau' (*U* 9.981); but this self-representation is itself rendered dubious when it reappears in the 'whirligig' (as Joyce put it) of 'Circe'. There it is Bloom, addressed by Paddy Dignam's ghost in a parodic recitation of Hamlet's dead father, who rephrases Stephen by declaring that 'the voice is the voice of Esau' (*U* 15.1220): Esau – the Hebrew name meaning 'he acts' – embodies the voice as failed performative, as an objectal remainder that is impossible to incorporate within the institution. If even the father's imperious utterance to the son – 'List, list, O list!' – can be identified as the voice of Esau, a speech act as ineffectual as the ghost's command proved to be in *Hamlet*, the text is presenting a generalisation of semic non-transmission, in which the paternal voice is just as deprived of the correct response, the desired recognition, as is that of the son. The positions of father and son, or speaker and audience, become interchangeable, deprived of any fixed, substantial meaning in a scene of semic collision, a 'collideorscape' (*FW* 143.28) that entirely lacks the signifying guarantee of the Other.

In the course of *Ulysses*, then, Stephen and Bloom come to occupy alternate positions in an encounter between father and son that *Finnegans Wake* will write as a 'farsoonerite' (*FW* 171.4) – both an enigmatic moment of temporal excess (as we shall see) and, reading in Danish *far* and *sønner*, a father-son-rite, perhaps the very institution of law and legacy (of 'right') structured by the I/You performative as a guarantee of patrilinear tradition. But what is crucial in both of the encounters we have examined – between Stephen and Sargent in 'Nestor' and between Bloom and Stephen in 'Eumaeus' – is that the father-son-rite turns on an element *in excess* of its actual performance, a phantasmal figure beyond the pair of discrete male identities: to be precise, what intervenes each time to give body to or render substantial the father-son-rite is 'vaulting feminine libido' (*FW* 123.8). Thus, Stephen's notion of *amor matris* as a vital support of masculine subjectivity with its 'unsteady symbols' (*U* 2.164) is echoed later by Bloom's fantasy of pairing up Stephen and Molly to form a musical and familial ensemble to restore balance, satisfy mutual desire and do away with lack. We should note of course that it is masculine fantasy that posits this supplementary feminine 'vaulting' as at once beyond the father-son-rite and underpinning it, overleaping its performative protocols but also cradling its meagre object within a protective, corporeal arch (the mother's arms, Molly Bloom's capacious, homely body). And this fantasmatic vault of feminine corporeality, its redemptive irreducibility to any single symbolic instance, is above all figured in Joyce as *music*: as a dimension of the living voice that both inhabits and exceeds the deathly movement or 'grave morrice' (*U* 2.155) of letters. Music – in particular what Bloom describes as Stephen's 'vocal career' (*U* 16.1862), suggesting a 'vaulting' impetus of the voice itself – amounts to an indispensable and dangerous fantasmatic supplement in Joyce to the dead letter of the paternal institution.

We should pause to consider the precise status of music for Joyce here. As we saw above, in the medieval scholars' *quadrivium*, alongside geometry, arithmetic and astronomy, music constituted a step beyond the so-called 'trivial', introductory topics of grammar, logic and rhetoric. In thus moving beyond speech, music might entail a movement towards the voice as such, prior to its mediation by the Other, in language; we recall how Aquinas sought to trace a negative path towards the name of God by progressively stripping away all of the positive, worldly attributes of speech, ending up with *quaedam caligo*, a certain opacity or pure sound said to correspond to the thing itself (or God's real name). If music embodies the vocal thing before its alienation into signifying discourse, it clearly resembles the language dreamt of in the 'farsoonerite'; for what the father-son-rite attempts to institute is precisely name-giving as *non-trivial act*, as a transmission of patrilinear identity somehow wrested away from the contingent vagaries of spoken discourse.

Music would thus appear both to supervene upon the father-son encounter from elsewhere, as a vivifying 'feminine' supplement, and to touch on the fantasmatic core of that encounter: to echo its central quadrivial, non-discursive or untranslatable symbolic act. *Finnegans Wake* provides a compact *summa* of these ambiguities in 'masculine monosyllables of the same numerical mus' (*FW* 190.35–6); a satanic reversal of *sum* (both a Cartesian declaration of self-identity and a piece of quadrivial arithmetic) becomes a multiple pun evoking the semic root of 'music', as well as the German for 'mouse' (we recall the 'Mousetrap', which Hamlet used as symbolic supplement of his own ghostly 'farsoonerite') and the imperious *muss* of the superego with its senseless injunctions. If masculine identity aims to write itself as an inviolate *sum*, sealed off from the error-strewn domain of actual speech, the Wakean reversal of that fantasmatic wholeness exposes it as another 'doubleviewed seed': a musical number, to be sure, but one driven by an ungovernable libidinal impetus that threatens to breach all the canons of meaningful propriety.

We need to turn to a primal scene of erroneous paternal legation – the mythical act of 'birthwrong' (*FW* 190.12) in the book of Genesis – to explore the further ramifications of Joyce's 'nomanclatter'. The blind patriarch Isaac, we recall, sends his firstborn son Esau out into the field to hunt for meat ('venison' in the Authorised Version) while his wife Rebekah prepares her favourite son Jacob to take his elder brother's place, disguising him with kid-skins (making him a 'kidscad', *FW* 3.11) so that he will be able to double his bearded brother and receive the paternal blessing. The father-son-rite is thus breached, traduced by feminine desire; and the central medium of this scene of misidentification is the *voice*:

And he came unto his father, and said, My father: and he said: Here am I; who art thou, my son?

And Jacob said unto his father, I am Esau thy firstborn; I have done according as thou badest me: arise, I pray thee, sit and eat of my venison, that thy soul may bless me.

And Isaac said unto his son, How is it that thou hast found it so quickly, my son? And he said, Because the LORD thy God brought it to me. (Genesis 27:18–20)

The encounter of father and son here is a 'farsoonerite' in more than one sense – first because Jacob comes too soon to offer Isaac his venison, returning to his father 'venissoon after' (*FW* 3.10), at an inappropriate, excessive time. Joyce's Wakean pun inscribes a complex allusion to the biblical text: on the one hand, the son's over-hasty arrival is legible in the semantic cocktail 'venissoon' (whose ingredients include Latin *venire*, 'to come', Danish *sønn*, 'son' and English *son*, *soon*); on the other, the treacherous instance of the voice itself – Jacob's false self-declaration and, beyond it, the vocal insistence of his mother's desire – is injected into 'venison', disfiguring it, robbing it of its status as act of masculine self-identity (and note how 'venison' closely echoes 'benison', the paternal blessing sought by the son, which is itself rendered improper by the vocal imposture). The stretching of the signifier by the voice makes it into 'nomanclatter' (*FW* 147.21), the breaching of patriarchal authority by feminine desire – but it is only *through* this breach that the institution of law can be made audible or musical, can be given breath, life or psyche. If the law is mythically founded on the ritual exchange of paternal benison and filial venison, these acts, at a moment 'venisoon after', must enter the domain of vocal 'noisense' (*FW* 147.6), of linguistic performance and semiotic difference: there, the law has precisely no-eye-sense; its act of institution is *blind*. It is thus as soon as it passes into discursive actuality – immediately, 'venisoon after' – that the patriarchal institution goes astray, falls away from its mythical self-identical truth and legality.

The mother's voice, then, inhabits the 'farsoonerite' and gives body to it as 'nomanclatter' so that the constitutive patrilinear identity of name and institution – we recall how the theologians tried to preserve that identity by making the name of God unspeakable – is always already compromised. But the polysemic 'noisense' in question here entails more than this single opposition: if the law is blind, its pure act necessarily traduced by inhabiting the realm of mere representation, this is also bound up with its non-trivial status, the foreclosure of meaning (the exclusion of 'I-sense') from its utterance. The blind father who bears the law in Joyce thus appears to be radically ambiguous, at once a hoodwinked fool led astray by the duplicity of human speech and a visionary prophet embodying an unspeakable truth that seems to transcend all trivial worldly meaning. We shall return to this apparent ambiguity in our reading of 'Ecce Puer' in the Conclusion.

Questions of the transmission and status of the patriarchal institution of the law are clearly at stake in *Ulysses*, in particular for Stephen and Bloom. In the 'Lotus Eaters' episode, Bloom's recollection of his father is tangled up with a dense cluster of anxieties provoked by the undermining of the institution of paternity – above all, anxieties to do with sexual identity, conjugal rights and property. Just after Bloom bumps into his tedious acquaintance M'Coy and finds himself wondering vaguely (and rather ludicrously) whether 'that fellow M'Coy' might have secret designs on Molly, he catches sight of a theatre hoarding advertising the play *Leah*, starring Mrs Bandmann Palmer. His thoughts continue:

Like to see her in that again. Hamlet she played last night. Male impersonator. Perhaps he was a woman. Why Ophelia committed suicide? Poor papa! How he used to talk of Kate Bateman in that! Outside the Adelphi in London waited all the afternoon to get in. Year before I was born that was: sixtyfive. And Ristori in Vienna. What is this the right name is? By Mosenthal it is. *Rachel*, is it? No. The scene he was always talking about where the old blind Abraham recognises the voice and puts his fingers on his face.

– Nathan's voice! His son's voice! I hear the voice of Nathan who left his father to die of grief and misery in my arms, who left the house of his father and left the God of his father.

Every word is so deep, Leopold.

Poor papa! Poor man! I'm glad I didn't go into the room to look at his face. That day! O, dear! O, dear! Ffoo! Well, perhaps it was the best for him. (*U* 5.195–209)

Nothing less than representation itself is in question here. If *Leah* is nearly a twisted version of *Hamlet* (as well as almost rhyming with Ophelia), both plays hinge on a traumatic encounter between a father and his son, and both involve the forsaking and sacrifice of a woman. Bloom recalls how his father Rudolph held up *Leah* as a lesson for his son, pointing to the play as an exemplary scene of truthful representation (but this paternal lesson is stricken with parodic irony as Rudolph Bloom, formerly Rudolf Virag, himself a name-changer, struggles to give the play its proper woman's name using proper English). The shift from masculine to feminine name or title – from *Hamlet* to *Leah* – emblematises both the transformative and liberating pleasures of theatrical revelation ('Like to see her in that again') and the risk that this metempsychotic potential poses to the stable representation of (masculine) identity. Dramatic names are mere speech 'acts' and probably no more than 'nomanclatter', and this is already hinted at in the name of Mrs Bandmann (or 'banned man') Palmer.[24]

The problematic status of dramatic representation as a medium of truth (the old 'Mousetrap' problem) is further emphasised by Bloom's cod theory of Hamlet-as-a-woman, where the Freudian gap in knowledge opened by Shakespeare's play would be simply filled in by adding an imaginary offstage sex-change or supplementary 'crossexanimation' (*FW* 87.34). But here it is truth itself as the basis of representation that is ultimately called into

doubt, as the signifier 'suicide' causes Bloom's thoughts to veer off to one
of his least favourite memories, namely his father's death. The contrast
between authentic and formulaic, deep and superficial, language returns
us to the mythical opposition of hand and voice: if *Leah* represented the
moral triumph of a truth-bearing paternal figure, so that Bloom's father
could point to the play as an instance of language that transcended mere
speech – every word so deep as to *embody* truth itself – conversely the
traumatic impact of his father's suicide leaves Bloom fumbling with trite,
meaningless phrases whose function is precisely to ward off any contact
with truth, with the thing itself. At every level here it is a question literally
of contact between father and son: Bloom's relation to his father is represented, *mise en abîme*, by 'the scene he was always talking about where
the old blind Abraham recognises the voice and puts his fingers on his
face' (*U* 5.200–02). The ambiguity of this 'farsoonerite' is immediately
legible in its metempsychotic pronouns; thus, in a single sentence 'he'
designates first Bloom's father, then 'his fingers' belong to Abraham and
finally 'his face' to Nathan. While the scene from *Leah* may appear as the
antitype or allegorical inversion of the biblical encounter between Isaac
and Jacob, with the father's hand no longer misrecognising the son but
now confirming the symbolic gift of his identity (note that a few lines later
Bloom will be humming *Là ci darem la mano*), in the version transmitted
by the father in Bloom's memory this certification of identity becomes an
unsettling, an unravelling of characters. And in a characteristically Joycean
manoeuvre, the dissemination of identity is folded back into the reading
experience; it becomes impossible for *us* to identify the exact discursive
source of any element in this textual blend of writing and speech, event and
memory.

   If, however, we turn to the 'original' text, a translation of *Leah the
Forsaken*, Saloman Mosenthal's play of 1862, we find that the words actually
spoken there by Abraham are: 'He left his father to die in poverty and misery since he had forsworn his faith, and the house of his kindred' (III.ii).[25]
In Bloom's memory of his father's version, this becomes: 'I hear the voice
of Nathan who left his father to die of grief and misery in my arms, who
left the house of his father and left the God of his father.' The phrase 'in
my arms' is the most striking deviation from the original text: indeed, it
seems completely at odds with the sense, if Bloom is recalling his father
recalling the speech of Abraham. In effect, the phrase alters the meaning
of 'left' earlier in the sentence, switching it momentarily from an intran-
sitive to a transitive sense and hence implying that someone (Nathan?)
departed leaving the dying father 'in my arms'. The 'I' here can only be

Bloom himself, who is thinking simultaneously about being abandoned by his suicidal father and about being left behind to take responsibility for identifying the dead body. It is precisely this encounter with the dead father that Bloom cannot face; the father's suicidal act has to be excluded from the son's experience and memory; its meaningless 'noisense' cannot be allowed to invade and despoil the space of subjective signification. Yet, however relieved Bloom may be to have avoided this unspeakable encounter, that act of avoidance is inevitably inscribed – in the texts of Genesis and *Leah* as well as in *Ulysses* – as filial betrayal, as a guilty turning away from the paternal gift.

Bloom's 'farsoonerite', then, is marked by a grievous collapse of meaning and identity, in which the significance of the father is radically split between being donor and withholder of nameable experience. For Bloom, it seems, there is something in the identification of the father that remains *un*representable, something at stake in the uncanny exchange of pronouns between father and son that eludes the name-giving it purports to institute. The very ambiguity of the grammatical subject – in a phrase such as 'who left his father to die of grief', subjective agency seems to be deliberately suspended, since it is never quite clear who does the dying – is here made to correspond to the lack of any decisive meaning or signifying solution. The father-son-rite is thus always poised in a 'jocoserious' or tragicomic position, between the limited, disruptive jouissance of a *Witz* and the limitless melancholy of absolute loss. The singsong clichés of Bloom's response to his father's suicide – 'That day! O dear! O dear! Ffoo!' – precisely register this gap between infantile babble and pure 'noisense', language as an effort to recover psychical stability through basic semiotic rhythm and voice as asemic object. One moment in the jocoserious catechism of 'Ithaca' provides us with a grotesque insight into this paternal tragicomedy. Bloom's attempt to make some sort of symbolic contact with Stephen was, we read, rendered problematic by

the irreparability of the past: once at a performance of Albert Hengler's circus in the Rotunda, Rutland square, Dublin, an intuitive particoloured clown in quest of paternity had penetrated from the ring to a place in the auditorium where Bloom, solitary, was seated and had publicly declared to an exhilarated audience that he (Bloom) was his (the clown's) papa. (*U* 17.975–9)

The mock punctilious style plays at dispelling the ambiguity of pronouns that had clogged Bloom's thoughts in 'Lotus Eaters', just as the melancholy of the earlier episode is poignantly recalled by the clown's disastrous jesting with 'papa'. What is truly irreparable in the past, for Bloom, is the death of his son Rudolph, named after the father who likewise disappeared in an irredeemable breach of human meaning. The clown's jocoserious act (for he may really be, as the text solemnly declares, 'in quest of paternity') provides another version of Jacob's jokey imposture on a 'bland old isaac'; a supposed father is hailed by a fraudulent son from behind a mask, resulting in an irreparable trauma of symbolic transmission (Isaac's erroneous blessing, Bloom's paternal-filial grief). We shall have to return to this scenario when we read 'Ecce Puer' in our Conclusion below.

The clownish or macabre-carnivalesque dimension of Bloom's father–son experience returns notably in 'Circe', the episode of *Ulysses* Joyce dubbed 'hallucinatory'. Bloom now finds himself cast in a fantasmatic snippet of *Leah* as the wayward son Nathan confronted by the wrath of his blind father Abraham:

RUDOLPH What you making down this place? Have you no soul? (*with feeble vulture talons he feels the silent face of Bloom*) Are you not my son Leopold, the grandson of Leopold? Are you not my dear son Leopold who left the house of his father and left the god of his fathers Abraham and Jacob? (*U* 15.259–62)

The paternal hand that had once exemplified for Bloom's father the truthful confirmation of filial identity has now withered into 'feeble vulture talons': the father's prescription of identity is no longer stable or authoritative, as if an occult fraudulence in the paternal institution (the name Jacob, we recall, designates in itself an act of substitution or subversion) had eroded its power to give proper names. And Rudolph's vulture talons remind us of Joyce's enigmatic remark in the Linati scheme that the sense of the 'Circe' episode was *L'Orca Antropofoba* (probably meant to be *antropofago*, thinks Gifford), an allusion to the blind, man-eating orc in Ariosto's *Orlando Furioso*.[26] In other words, if the father has vulture claws he must be a 'corpsechewer' (*U* 15.4214), as Stephen brands his ghostly mother later in 'Circe'; the paternal demand for identification has revealed itself as a horrifying imposture, a cannibalistic attempt to devour the son's enjoyment, to mortify his living flesh. Bloom's response to this fantasmatic encounter is revealing:

BLOOM (*with precaution*) I suppose so, father. Mosenthal. All that's left of him. (*U* 15.263–4)

A wary half-assent that draws attention to its own performative agency – 'I suppose so' – is precisely not what is required by the paternal demand, with its insistent repetition of the son's name. Instead of obediently affirming his identity as son, Bloom identifies the authorial source of his father's discourse as Mosenthal – and his next phrase is the very antithesis of the straightforward act of identification demanded by the father: 'All that's left of him' entails, as we shall see, a complex pun. We suspect that the phrase does not really 'belong' to Bloom at all but to Stephen. (Indeed, the same might be said of the general tone of the speech.) The oft-noted metempsychotic or telepathic interrelation between the two central male characters of *Ulysses* – playfully acknowledged in 'Ithaca' with the nonsensical spoonerism of Stoom and Blephen (*U* 17.549–51) – here amounts to an unsettling of the father's power to identify, indeed a challenge to the very integrity of the paternal name. For Bloom to speak as a son in 'Circe' is in effect to speak *as Stephen*, and in doing so to utter a critique of the father's voice; in identifying the literary and Jewish patrimony behind his father's demand for identity, the son simultaneously indicates how that paternal authority is being misquoted, traduced by the father. (We recall how Stephen adopted the very same position in his 'farsoonerite' with Mr Deasy, traducer of Shakespeare.) 'All that's left of him' can thus be read as an ironic gloss on the father's mangled version of Mosenthal (and note how the playwright's name echoes that of another Jewish father, Moses); Bloom identifies the remnant of an original 'proper' source of authority in his father's misspoken discourse. And if the father can represent the patrimonial institution only in such a mutilated form, he can hardly expect his voice to constitute the guarantee of identity supposedly promised by that institution and authorised by 'the god of his fathers Abraham and Jacob'.

What is revealed in 'Circe', then, is that the voice of the real father bears no more than a feeble trace of the ancient, symbolic mandate of the Law; its insistent demand therefore amounts to a clownish or sinister parody of that sacred authority. The fact that the father's discourse is strewn with errors and faulty constructions – 'Nice spectacles for your poor mother!' (*U* 15.279) – emblematises its fallen, second-best status, the unbridgeable distance between it and the divine Logos. As lowly a word as 'left' can entail a semiotic variability that subverts the father's supposed power to name the world properly; at one point that word designates a momentous exodus ('left the god of his fathers'), at another a meagre remnant ('all that's left of him'). Indeed, 'left' is caught in a semiotic web that, throughout *Ulysses*, is specifically linked to Stephen's character: 'There is something sinister in you' is Buck Mulligan's taunt in the opening episode (*U* 1.94), before he later accuses Stephen of having 'eaten all we left' (*U* 1.524), as the abstract notion of what is not right or ethical is made to pun degradingly with the abject reality of a crust of bread left for a servant.

The son's critique of the father's voice thus resonates with a complex rejection – this time, we would argue, by the Joycean text itself – of the demand that the subject submit to a single monolithic meaning and legible identity, that he disclose himself in his whole truth before the Other. The uncontrollable equivocations of the signifier – embodied in the metamorphoses of the humble (although allegorically diabolical) 'left' – ensure that the attempt to utter the name in a single decisive act will always founder, go astray. We have seen how Bloom's encounter with his father in 'Circe' offers a fantasmatic version of the primal scene of paternal error: the founding act of misidentification recorded in the book of Genesis as the scene of 'birthwrong' (*FW* 190.12), where Isaac is deceived by Jacob and Rebekah. The split between paternal hand and filial voice provides a mythical figure for the fault in signification that disrupts the symbolic transmission of identity, as the father's authority fails to write itself outside the sinful and *sinnvoll* sphere of discourse. And in this mythical scenario it is precisely the desire of the mother that occupies the dangerous space left open by the lack of an integral, self-grounding paternal law, as Rebekah succeeds in arranging for her favourite son to hoodwink Isaac. The question then becomes: how does Joyce re-inscribe, render differently, this biblical – and subsequently psychoanalytic – tale of the paternal institution and its failure?

SECRET STRIPTURE: UNSPEAKABLE NAMES

Throughout Joyce's work, sexual difference – that fundamental social antagonism, in Lacan's view, that prevents me from loving my neighbour as myself[27] – is re-inscribed in the wake of the breakdown of paternal authority. 'Circe' figures this in its bewildering textual 'crossexanimation', both the metempsychotic disintegration of the discrete anima and the slippage of speaking subjects across sex, as Bella switches to Bello and Bloom becomes a woman (*U* 15.2829–3020). Indeed, in 'Circe' Joyce conjures up a textual scene where no character or act of language – not even the 'paternal metaphor' posited by Lacanian theory – can transcend its vacillating, discursive site in order to name things properly, to make the world legible.

It may therefore seem highly appropriate, after the hyperbolic show of authoritative knowledge the text puts on in 'Ithaca' – where, in its desire to say everything, discourse finally overreaches itself and subsides into mere prattle, its *sum* reversing into *music* – that *Ulysses* should finish on a 'feminine' note. Joyce's letters to Frank Budgen are often invoked here by critics in favour of the idea that 'Penelope' constitutes a final feminine supplement to the book, providing, as Joyce famously put it, 'the indispensable countersign to Bloom's passport to eternity'.[28] But another letter spells out more clearly the true status of this 'feminine' supplement: namely, that of a contractual signature by men on the subject of Woman. As Joyce writes to Budgen:

Penelope is the clou of the book. The first sentence contains 2500 words. There are eight sentences in the episode. It begins and ends with the female word *yes*. It turns like the huge earth ball slowly surely and evenly round and round spinning, its four cardinal points being the female breasts, arse, womb and cunt expressed by the words *because, bottom* (in all senses bottom button, bottom of the class, bottom of the sea, bottom of his heart), *woman, yes*. Though probably more obscene than any preceding episode it seems to me to be perfectly sane full amoral fertilisable untrustworthy engaging shrewd limited prudent indifferent *Weib. Ich bin der* [sic] *Fleisch der stets bejaht.* (SL 285)

Ellmann's editorial *sic* indicates a grammatical slip in Joyce's German, one that adds a nice touch of irony: that is, by mistakenly giving a masculine gender to *das Fleisch*, Joyce is perhaps betraying the eminently *phallic* bias of his notional 'clou' (a term glossed by Ellmann as ' "star turn" or topper' – but whose literal sense is 'nail').[29] Joyce is speaking from the bottom of his heart, it is clear, in sharing this list of womanly adjectives with Budgen: these are *known* feminine traits, indeed traits that precisely signify woman, or rather Woman (one half wonders whether Joyce chose to write *Weib* for the sake of the capital W). To speak of 'the female word *yes*' in such a compact equation is to adopt a distinctively *ad hominem* kind of hearsay or *ouï-dire*. For the feminist critics who have objected to the representations of femininity in *Ulysses*, indeed, these remarks by Joyce only serve to confirm the ultimately conventional – nay, clichéd – tenor of the 'last word' he allegedly gives to Molly in 'Penelope'. Thus, Karen Lawrence concludes that Molly's discourse plausibly 'represents the *problem of woman represented by the male pen*, a staging of alterity that reveals itself as masquerade'.[30] The 'problem of woman' is certainly at stake in Joyce's letter to Budgen; but above all, in our view, this is a problem of masculine pleasure, of what Lacan terms 'phallic' jouissance.

As we have seen throughout our study, Joyce's work struggles to situate itself at a point of asemic fantasmatic jouissance, where something radically excluded from social discourse comes back to haunt it, emerging as aesthetic *revenant* in breach of signifying legitimacy. We saw how this destructive-creative force corresponds to the unthinkable instant of the *act*, first glimpsed in Shakespearean tragedy and refigured by Joyce as an interrogation of representation itself, as well as of the notional coherence of the self-representing ego. For Lacan, the true act entails the dissolution of the social bond, a moment when the subject turns away from the symbolic Other, shrugs off its own signifying division and enters the forbidden zone of actual fantasmatic jouissance.[31] When in 1975 he proposes *le sinthome* as a new name for Joyce, Lacan sets out a subtle reprise of this concept of the act from within a literary framework. Thus, Joyce's writing is *pas à lire*, it must remain in a crucial sense unread or untreated; Lacan deliberately refuses to reduce the disastrous impact of Joyce's work by drawing on psychoanalytic knowledge to 'diagnose' it. In this, Lacan's engagement with Joyce contrasts emphatically with the long tradition of 'applied' psychoanalysis – and notably, in the case of Joyce, with the perspective of Jung we have explored above.

It is here that the 'problem of woman' may shed light on a key question we still have to address concerning the relation between psychoanalytic thinking and Joyce's literary endeavour: namely, to what extent can a critical intervention avoid becoming a traduction – an attempt to coerce the text into collusion with readerly pleasure by suppressing or 'translating' those of its elements that resist the codes of legibility, that remain stubbornly 'anti-hermeneutic'.[32] We saw how the central 'problem of woman' for Joyce – namely, the madness of his daughter Lucia – found a neat hermeneutical solution in Jung's theory with the idea of an *anima inspiratrix* that lurked in the obscure depths of Joyce's work and his psyche. And Jung's response to 'Penelope' is especially revealing in this respect; after all the splenetic disgust he felt for the 'vicious dangerous boredom' of *Ulysses*, the final 'clou' of Joyce's book comes to him as a redemptive, healing return of truth. As Jung writes ecstatically in a letter to Joyce: 'The 40 pages of non stop run in the end is a string of veritable psychological peaches. I suppose the devil's grandmother knows so much about the real psychology of a woman, I didn't.'[33] It is clearly Joyce's exhibition of *psychological knowledge* that gives Jung such pleasure – even if there is something diabolical and uncannily *weiblich* about this grande finale. Jung thus finds his 'supposed authority on psychological matters' – the reason for his double encounter with Joyce, and upon which the intractable riddles posed by both *Ulysses* and Lucia had seemed to cast grave doubts – finally and pleasurably re-established. Or, more precisely: it is authority itself, that conventional body of knowledge that Joyce's writing had seemed hell-bent upon dismantling, that Jung finds re-served with these tasty 'psychological peaches'. And, with this ringing endorsement of 'Penelope' as a definitive representation of 'the problem of woman', Jung provides a counter-signature to Joyce's work as a properly masculine discourse that, even if it sometimes chooses to dress up like 'the devil's grandmother', will finally return us to our true patriarchal authority.

We find ourselves faced once again with Hamlet's desire: to redeem the father by purging him of diabolic ambiguity and hearing him speak the truth about woman.

It is this literary investment in patriarchal and logocentric truth that *Finnegans Wake* will set out to demolish, at once fired with iconoclastic zeal and wracked by superstitious terror. In Joyce's letter to Budgen (and arguably in 'Penelope' too), we see the fantasmatic jouissance of his work being given a phallic name – *Weib* or *der Fleisch* – and thus made semantic, turned into enjoyable *sens*. It is this self-traductive provision of readerly pleasure that Joyce actively resists in the *Wake*, as the writing struggles to be true to its own 'crossexanimation', the disruptive impetus of its literary, cultural and semiotic reinvention. When it comes to naming a woman, we are not given a string of psychological peaches but shown something unspeakable (Fig. 6.1).

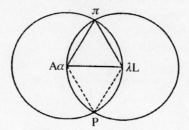

Fig. 6.1   (*FW* 293)

If discourse cannot say what is named by the name, to recall Agamben's succinct formula, then perhaps that 'thing' can be *shown*. For Lacan, the topology of knots was to become just such a silent monstration of something irreducible to the *dit-mension* of the speaking subject, something literally unspeakable. But this Wakean diagram, as McHugh informs us, comes from Euclid's first proposition;[34] it might thus be thought to embody – and its precise symmetrical form seems to confirm this – the very acme of the 'imaginary' geometry that Lacan is seeking to out-think with his knot. Yet the Euclidian origin of Joyce's figure does nothing to limit its signifying elaboration by critics, as is shown by Rose and O'Hanlon's commentary:

The intersecting spheres are symbolic as well as representative; they comprehend among other things a word (zoo), a map of heaven, hell and earth, a map of Dublin, a drawing of the pudendum and of buttocks, a letter, a mystic symbol of the harmony of contraries, the gyres from Yeats' *Vision*, a bicycle, an egg-beater, and so on.[35]

And we could extend the list to include a couple of psychological peaches or a pair of 'nice spectacles for your poor mother' (*U* 15.279). The notion that by quoting Euclidian geometry the *Wake* might be seeking to move beyond the polysemic hazards of discourse in order to figure things non-metaphorically might seem derisory. But even if its mathematical status is mocked by the Joycean text ('aristmystic'), the diagram is presented as an enigma – and notably as an enigma *for the father*: 'Coss? Cossist? Your parn! You, you make what name?' (*FW* 293.1–2). McHugh refers us to the Rule of Coss in algebra, from the Arabic *cosa*, meaning 'unknown quantity, *x*', as well as to the Italian 'Che cosa?' and the German 'Was ist?' (both phrases meaning 'What's that?'), which form an interrogative cluster with 'I beg your pardon?' But 'Your parn!' also sounds very like 'your pa', and the next phrase – with the pidgin for 'What's your name?' doubling as a question about inventing or making a name – inevitably takes us back to the reproaches of Bloom's father Rudolph in 'Circe': 'What you making down this place? . . . Are you not my son Leopold . . .?' (*U* 15.259–60). In other words, the algebraic enigma of the diagram – which may well make us exclaim 'Che cosa?' or 'Was ist?' – is immediately joined to the question of the name and of how to make it, as the wording recalls a paternal rebuke that turns on the *nom du père* and the son's alleged disregard for his patrimony.

In 'Circe', as we saw, the father's discourse is exposed as faulty, lacking in legitimacy and hence sinister or comical in its ambition to guarantee the propriety of the name or uphold its patriarchal sovereignty. We have argued that 'Penelope' serves in one reading as a final supplement to this deficient paternal-authorial institution, by which its shaky edifice can be shored up (or nailed together; recall Joyce's idea of the episode as the book's 'clou') through a return to 'knowledge of woman' that brings with it a quota of 'phallic' readerly pleasure. What we now encounter in the midst of the *Wake* is perhaps a woman's name – but one that, like the *nomen tetragrammaton*, can be only written and not pronounced. (Note how the figure bears the same number of letters as YHWH.) The list of possible 'readings' of the figure provided by Rose and O'Hanlon now looks like an attack of critical hysteria, a frantic, discursive multiplication of something that in itself eludes discourse. If we read further, we shall discover the *Wake*'s own gloss on this unspeakable collision of algebra and names:

Allow me! And, heaving alljawbreakical expressions out of old Sare Isaac's[2] universal of specious aristmystic unsaid, A is for Anna like L is for liv . . .

[2] O, Laughing Sally, are we going to be toadhaunted by that old Pantifox Sir Somebody Something, Burtt, for the rest of our secret stripture? (*FW* 293.25–8)

Algebraical expressions are jaw-breaking because they defy the human voice, must remain, like the tetragram, 'unsaid'. At first sight, with 'old Sare Isaac's universal' we are in the realm of the Enlightenment and the foundation of modern science, that of Sir Isaac Newton, for whom algebra constituted an 'universal arithmetic' – although at the same time he never relinquished an eminently 'pre-modern' belief in the hermetic, mystical significance of numbers. To disfigure Euclidian geometry and Newtonian science as 'specious aristmystic' – attractive or deceptive and mystical or mystifying arithmetic – may thus be in one sense merely to make legible an irrational residue at the very inception of scientific modernity: its faith in the mystical relation of number to the real. But the notion that scientific knowledge could ever simply circumvent the vagaries of the meaning-bound signifier is mocked by the footnote with its scurrilous puns on the names of eminent scientific authorities (Todhunter, editor of Euclid, and Sir Edwin Arthur Burtt, author of *The Metaphysical Foundations of Modern Physical Science*).

So it is once again the *name* that in Joyce becomes a way to disseminate the institution of patriarchal authority; and here this occurs most powerfully in the 'hypertext' link between 'old Sare Isaac' and 'O, Laughing Sally'. These names are at once translations of and responses to one another: if the first belongs to Newton (the 'old seer' who explored his own eye-sack and became the father of science) and to Isaac (the blind, non-enlightened father of Israel), it also evokes old Sarah, Abraham's wife, who is told by God that at the age of ninety, she is to give birth to a child; her response is to laugh, and so the son is named Isaac, meaning 'laughter'.[36] 'Laughing Sally' is thus a name for Sarah, a woman who laughs at the word of God; clearly an ideal figure to invoke in support of the parodic subversion of paternal authority and its metaphysical foundations.

It is here that the doubling of characters at work between Joyce's text and footnote gives us a vital clue as to how to treat the Wakean figure: how to see it, that is, not simply as one more endlessly interpretable element in the textual whirligig (*à la* Rose and O'Hanlon), but as the singular inscription of *the letter itself* as an instance that both produces and disrupts signification, promotes and ruins the transmission of knowledge. The Joycean paronomasia that has 'doublin' (*FW* 3.8) rhyme with Dublin is obviously relevant here; the movement between Greek and Latin, or ancient and modern, characters figured in the Wakean diagram – whereby the central triangle linking αλπ is doubled below by a dotted triangle linking ALP – corresponds to a mass of themes and tropes in Joyce's work, not least the notion that a Dublin character such as Bloom could be the double of Ulysses (that name itself in turn the double of Odusseus). The double and triple

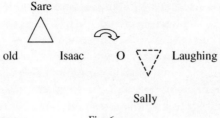

Fig. 6.2

inscriptions recited in 'Ithaca' – from Molly's inventive 'signs and hiero-glyphics which she stated were Greek and Irish and Hebrew characters' (*U* 17.677–8) to the 'glyphic comparison' of Hebrew and Irish undertaken together by Bloom and Stephen (*U* 17.731) – have prepared us to think of Joyce's doubling of ancient and modern, or of Jewish and Greek, as pri-marily *literal* acts: as transcriptions or telegraphs rather than re-imaginings or transferrals of 'psychological' meaning.

The double inscription at work in our Wakean diagram, however, will turn out to be still more unsettling. If the quotation of Euclidian and Newtonian geometry there corresponds to a rigorous banishment of the merely subjective or interpretative, by adding an inverted, hypothetical triangle Joyce inscribes a *potential* act, a supplementary gesture on the part of the reader – who is free to read the figure in either Greek or Latin, ancient or modern characters. This readerly implication in the conversion of letters into signifiers is reiterated in the hyperlink between 'old Sare Isaac' and 'O Laughing Sally'; characters that form triangles that can be mapped on to Joyce's Euclidian variation as an *Uteralterance* (*FW* 293.21; see Fig. 6.2). What does this 'specious aristmystic' enact? If the triangle on top figures the 'foundingpen' of scientific knowledge and biblical wisdom – its institution as both primal inscription and doctrinal prison – its repetition-reversal responds with an exclamatory *Witz*, a laughing sally or sudden 'jocoserious' act: an act that corresponds, crucially, to the *fall* of the proper into sinful, signifying illegitimacy. Joyce is acutely conscious throughout the *Wake* of how 'paperspace' (*FW* 115.7) is itself a signifying element, as the very layout of the page is incorporated into the writing process, becoming one of its own signatures. Here, the movement between the name-triangles is literally a *descent* from the text 'proper' to a supplementary text located beneath it in a footnote: a fall from primary to secondary, from authoritative to derivative or critical. More precisely – and this takes us back to the inscription of the lower triangle as a dotted, hypothetical textual element – the fall from the main text to the footnote depends entirely on a potential act of reading, a supplementary move by which the reader herself or himself is momentarily involved in organising the textual paperspace. The reader is above all the site of *dubium*, of the dubious doubling of the authorial act in the event of its re-inscription, a reading that may be a wilful misappropriation or raiding – or that may simply not occur. In this sense, the potential marked by the dotted triangle inscribes the moment of reading as 'passencore' (*FW* 3.4–5): both *pas encore*, not yet realised, and the central element or core of the textual and temporal flow.

Elsewhere in *Finnegans Wake* the dangerous supplement of the reader is introduced – or intra*d*uced, Lacan might say – as an element in both the production of meaning and its 'anamorphic' distortion. Thus, the opening exploration of 'this municipal sin business' (*FW* 5.14) is inflected by the possibility of the text being read 'down upown' (*FW* 5.20) or 'otherways wesways' (*FW* 5.22) – that is, with its letters rearranged down-up-down or otherwise-westwards, inverted or reversed, in an illegitimate (although paradoxically 'authorised') reading act. On the one hand, this textual mal-leability allows the *Wake* to embody a semantic relativity subversive of any politics that would situate the origin of all that is sinful in some devilish Babylon, 'bedoueen the jebel and the jypsian sea' (*FW* 5.23). But on the other hand, Joyce's deliberate disorientation of reading foregrounds the text as a site of constant readerly choice, where the authorial 'message' (whether conscious or not: *Sinn* or sense is split between egoic *je bel* and unconscious *je psychique*) is always prey to being doubled or bedevilled by a heretical reader-raider.

Now, the fall from 'proper' text to jesting footnote, which we have exam-ined, would clearly, according to a traditional quasi-Bakhtinian reading of the *Wake*, entail a carnivalesque subversion of science and the Word of the father by feminine laughter or the irrational particularity of the body – or, in only slightly different terms, the transformation of an author-centred text into a dialogic exchange with the reader. What we should be careful to avoid, however, is allowing this kind of perspective to freeze our read-ing into fixed pairs of opposing terms; for, in a crucial sense, what the *Wake* figures with its mirroring triangles is precisely the *identity* of 'old Sare Isaac' and 'O Laughing Sally'. In other words, the discovery of truth in the Enlightenment is as terrifying and laughable an event as the birth of Isaac to his ninety-year-old mother; it is not sacred scripture but 'secret strip-ture' (*FW* 293 n. 2) that determines the miraculous revelation of science to Newton or of baby Isaac to Sarah, in an uncanny or comical transgression of established symbolic protocols. In the same way, the event of reading

[sacred scripture] → secret stripture

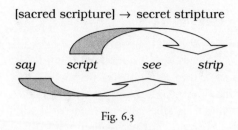

Fig. 6.3

in which the *Wake* is revealed itself constitutes a 'crossexanimation' that undoes the fixity of psychical barriers and plunges both writer and reader into a dubious – perhaps diabolical – but above all *enjoyable* rapport.

We should pay close attention to what Joyce inscribes in the signifying 'fall' here (Fig. 6.3). Something indeed *falls away* in this reflexive transition from legible text to taboo revelation, from 'saying' to 'seeing': precisely the semic self-identity and differential consistency that constitutes the signifier. Thus, 'secret stripture' figures both the laying-bare of truth and the presentation of an indecipherable enigma, so that it is at once the perfect double of 'sacred scripture' and – perhaps by that very token – its blasphemous inversion. What emerges in such a signifying rupture is, from the point of view of the interpreting 'I', both blinding and dumbfounding: something that can no more be assimilated to the visible or utterable domain of signifying legitimacy than Moses can confront the face of God, or Stephen pronounce God's real name.

WHEN A SYMPTOM IS NOT A SYMPTOM: JOYCE'S EX-HYSTERIA

How, then, does our engagement with Lacanian thinking finally allow us to attempt a new formulation of what links a woman's laughter, scientific discovery and the Joycean text? The first portal of discovery here is the *Wake*'s garbled version of the Circean father's rebuke – 'You, you make what name?' – which exactly formulates the interpellative demand of the Other: re-mark yourself, make yourself legible in discourse. The function of a discourse, as Lacan teaches in his seminar *L'envers de la psychanalyse*, is to institute a social bond where jouissance can be accommodated through a fixed set of relations between truth, knowledge and power.[37] The discourse of the Master – and for a time Lacan considered calling it the discourse of the Father – is, as Bruce Fink notes, 'unconcerned with knowledge'; its aim is simply to maintain the proper circulation of signifiers, to perpetuate existing structures of power (and hence of ideological doctrine, the domain

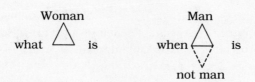

Fig. 6.4

policed by its 'servant' discourse, that of the university). It is only in the discourse of the *hysteric* that the real, the jouissance that does not fit in with any pre-established theoretical circuit, emerges as the true aim. Thus the laughter of Sarah at the word of God – or the response of that other Wakean 'laughing Sally' whose writings, as we saw above in Chapter 5, insistently undid Morton Prince's demand for a unified subjectivity[38] – finds an echo in the epistemic rupture caused by Newton's discovery, where something of the real shows itself in an asemic epiphany that is both shocking and hilarious: an utterly unpredictable event or (to pun in German) *Fall*. If the Father or the Master merely demands consistency and continuity in signification, the safeguarding of the propriety and integrity of the name, the hysteric always rejects such a demand in the name of *truth*: her or his overriding imperative is to interrogate the epistemic and ethical status of gender-bound subjectivity lying beneath the established patterns of representation and identity. Thus, for Lacan the question voiced by the Freudian hysteric Dora through her symptoms and her resistance is *What is it to be a woman?*[39] And if we entertain for a moment the idea of Joyce as hysteric, we might point to the Wakean question, 'When is a man not a man?' as an alternative formula for the disruption of scientific knowledge that catalysed the Freudian discovery. As we saw above, however, in the *Wake* that question bears on more radical problems than those of sexual identity alone: concerning creation *ex nihilo*, the creative-destructive act as a dissolution of the social bond, of time and spacing in representation. We could write the difference between the hysterical and the Joycean questions in the Wakean variation depicted in Fig. 6.4.

As we saw in Chapter 4 above, the young Joyce seems preoccupied with an eminently 'hysterical' question of self-identification when he writes at the end of a letter to Nora Barnacle in 1904: 'How am I to sign myself? I won't sign anything at all, because I don't know what to sign myself' (*SL* 25). The hysteric views identity as a senseless conventional form imposed by the Master, with no authentic purchase on the dense particularity of empirical selfhood. We could easily link this to a speculative

narrative in which the intensity of Joyce's encounter with Nora unsettles his
sense of the proper fit between representation and the world, in particular
as regards the occult or unspeakable domain of sexuality; hence everything has to be re-identified, even – or rather, especially – his own proper
name. At one level, throughout his work Joyce clearly retains something
of this quasi-hysterical urge to interrogate the basis of the subject's (sexual)
identity; but at the same time, as that work unfolds, it moves beyond an
exploration of the self and its 'true' representation, towards something far
less readerly: namely, a reflexive engagement with the literary *act* itself –
as, in effect, an annihilation of the self-representing or truth-bearing subject. In this sense, we might consider Joyce as *ex*-hysteric, one no longer
concerned with merely exposing the inadequacies of the discourse of the
Master – that is, with overturning the prejudices and conventions masking
the truth of the human subject; and we could certainly see this as the aim
of a 'modernist' artist like Stephen Dedalus or Richard Rowan, and perhaps even 'Jim Overman' – but rather with exploring how the unspeakable
apparition of the literary act undermines the very status of an integral truth,
of a single human subject.

The Joycean question, 'When is a man not a man?', thus belongs not
only to the problematic of masculinity and sexual difference, but beyond
it to the larger problem of human being-in-language, of what Lacan calls
the *parlêtre*. If Joyce's writing could indeed be considered *pas à lire* (despite
all of its author's best efforts to recruit Joycean readers), this would be to
the extent that it exposes language as irreducible to the 'social bond' of
discourse where the speaking subject is robbed of its jouissance at the very
point where it acquires meaning.

It is here that we need to look again at Joyce's quotation and disfigurement
of Euclid's geometry in *Finnegans Wake*. The parodic marginalia we read
on the figure's left (note the old theme of 'sinistrous' paperspace) gives us
a vital clue to Joyce's ex-hysteria and the transformational reflexivity of
his writing; the figure is seemingly given as its 'title' the enigmatic words
Uteralterance or the Interplay of Bones in the Womb (*FW* 293.22–5). For
'utterance' to slide into 'uteralterance' implies that the womb or uterus is
indeed involved, that the figure perhaps embodies some kind of uterine
transformation. But before we deduce that the figure therefore 'represents'
the womb, we should note how a characteristic Joycean translinguistic pun
would make 'uteralterance' a metamorphosis of *hysteria* (Greek *hustera* =
Latin *uterus*): it is the hysterical interrogation of sexual difference – and
beyond it, as we shall see, of difference *per se* – that the Wakean figure
transforms.

If the movement inscribed here in or as the letter can thus be paraphrased as *the Interplay of Bones in the Womb* it simultaneously signals a textual interplay within the matrix of Joyce's work – for in designating itself 'foetal sleep' (*FW* 563.10) the letter sends us back to what we may consider the primal scene of Joycean 'hysteria'; that is, Stephen's encounter with the 'sudden legend' of the word *Foetus* in *A Portrait* (*P* 90). As we saw above in our discussion of that passage, the encounter entails a devastating revelation: a monstrous creative force in language that traversed and ruined the father's nominal attempt to transmit – or, in truth, simply to repeat for his own self-pleasure – an identity to his son in the signature *S.D.* The Wakean figure thus refers us back precisely to a 'foetal' point in the development of Joyce's work, and one where the proper inscription of identity or 'portrait of the artist' collapses into hallucinatory *jouissens* or verbal monstrosity. But the *Wake* insists on its figure being an *Uteralterance*: that is, an altering, a mutation of the earlier utterance that left Stephen – a figure of the reader *en abîme* – floundering helplessly in the face of the fantasmatic letter. That letter now offers the reader multiple interpretative possibilities (see the list compiled by Rose and O'Hanlon quoted above); as we have suggested, however, the excess of reading triggered off by the 'alljawbreakical' enigma can itself be understood as a defence against the very interrogation of meaning enacted by the figure. How can meaning itself be put in question by Joyce's diagram?

It is crucial here to be alert at every letter to the self-deconstructive subtlety of Joyce's last text. We can see that the central triangle of the figure and its 'alterance' or potential inversion link the initials of Anna Livia Plurabelle, the maternal deity and river whose 'untitled mamafesta' (*FW* 104.4) is contained in the *Wake* and at the same time *is* the *Wake* itself. In the latter sense, the writing names nothing but itself with this figure, returning us to its first word, 'riverrun' (*FW* 3.1), which, as is often said, runs backwards from the *Wake's* last word, 'the' (*FW* 628.16). But if this reverse movement can be seen clearly inscribed in the figure's 'upown' (*FW* 5.20) or up-down letters, we are given another vital clue to its significance by the words that follow 'riverrun': 'past Eve and Adam's' (*FW* 3.1). This jokey *hysteron proteron* or rhetorical reversal – which by turning around the name of the pub or church beside the Liffey neatly suggests a river running the wrong way – also inscribes the characters in the biblical scene of primal 'sinse', of original *Sinn*. What, after all, are the triangles in Joyce's figure if not the letters A and V, designating the primal opposition between standing Adam and falling Eve? Thus, 'Eve takes fall' (*FW* 293.30), or woman bears the weight of having to embody the sinful cause of upstanding Adam's downfall: this would be the meaning of the 'strayed-line AL' (*FW* 294.2–3), the quadrivial or scientific doctrine of sin, of straying from the line.

So is Joyce merely countersigning, even if with a clownish, carnivalesque, formal inversion, the old misogynist myth of 'Eve and Adam's' original transgression? The answer, and the key to understanding the Wakean figure as a self-given textual name, lies in including the reader among its characters; for the movement of letters hinges on the potentiality entailed in reading. Thus, however straight a line is laid down in the *Wake* it will be deformed as the text falls – immediately, that is, in the very act of being written – into the irredeemable, pathological enjoyment of the Other. It is this, the fall into the worldly 'sinse' that governs reading, that is made spuriously legible in the story of Adam and Eve. And when those names are rewritten as 'atoms and ifs' (*FW* 455.16) we see how the *Wake* both makes visible and puts in question the ideological stakes of reading and meaning-making; although every letter may seem atomic, indivisible and self-identical, it is always only an 'if', a *potential* mark of meaning, entirely subject to the affirmative, creative act of eye or voice. It is thus that the letters that spell Anna Livia's name can be twisted, in a 'uteralterance' or 'strayed-line', into AV; or that the inscription *Foetus* – the name of a pure 'if', we might say – can become 'a poor trait of the artless' (*FW* 114.32), an artistic signature by way of textual or vocal error.

It is this *mise en cause* or deconstruction of sense in Joyce's work that in Lacan's view makes it such an invaluable resource for the psychoanalyst. But how can psychoanalytic theory avoid colluding with the pleasurable decipherment of literary enigmas – above all the ultimate enigma: Woman – that Joyce, as we have seen, works through and finally dismantles as a mode of reading? Doesn't every artistic *Rätsel* in Freudian aesthetics have to be 'treated', given a curative *Lösung*? Regarding Joyce, Lacan responds with his own piece of 'specious aristmystic' (Fig. 6.5). 'The Borromean

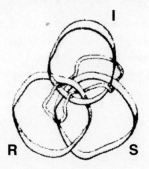

Fig. 6.5   (*Scilicet* 6/7)

knot is a writing,' comments Lacan in the 1974 seminar *RSI*, before adding that 'there is no other perceptible idea of the real than the one offered by . . . the trait of writing'.⁴⁰ We should pause to consider this statement carefully, for what it indicates is that the knot is a *mise en abîme*, that like a playful heraldic device it 'includes itself': that is, the knot both *is* the real (or at least it amounts to the only perceptible idea of it) and also situates the real as one of its four constituents, alongside the symbolic, the imaginary and the *sinthome*, the fourth term that Lacan introduces in his reading of Joyce. What is the significance of this reflexive paradox?

As Lacan insists, the coherence of the knot is not representational; it does not string together its elements as signifiers in a discursive chain, addressed to and borrowed from the Other. The register of the symbolic where such a discourse could occur is precisely only one element of the knot, which, along with the imaginary register – the site of identification and psychological 'depth' – forms the domain of meaning. The real does not form part of that domain, but nor can it be entirely dissociated from it; jouissance is irreducible to the psyche (where unconscious and ego, or symbolic and imaginary, are always at meaningful odds), but at the same time it 'condescends', as Lacan puts it, to partake in a form of subjective coherence because of the letter. In other words, the 'material support' the letter offers to signification (in the formula Derrida dismisses as patently metaphysical)⁴¹ remains as the sole bond between the unconscious – ultimately, that is, the *interpretable* – and the unpresentable singularity of the real. What the fourth term Lacan adds to the knot therefore indicates is that the act of writing constitutes the knot as such, by lending a particular coherence to the otherwise disjunctive categories of psyche and jouissance.

If we now turn to Lacan's *mis à plat* of the 'Joycean' knot, we can see how the double status of the letter (yet another 'doublin' character) features there. The figure seems to dramatise a contrast between the knot 'proper', made up of the relatively consistent, topologically stable rings R, S and I, and a fourth element which is given a more variable, elastic shape (with perhaps even a suggestion that it is mobile). This latter element appears somehow 'rogue', alien to the structure of the knot, added to it in an *ad hoc* manner. What it indicates is therefore that the writing of the knot cannot be situated in symbolic structure, psychological meaning or the mute insistence of the drive; in other words, the knot itself is irreducible to the registers it inscribes.

Lacan's Joycean knot is therefore a special kind of letter, but not one that will always – or indeed, ever – arrive at its destination. As the asemic coincidence of 'messes of mottage' (*FW* 183.22–3) or linguistic substance and jouissance, the letter has precisely no destination; it remains behind language as its *litter*. The *sinthome*, of course, is Joyce's *name*, Lacan insists; no mere predicate of a subject but its constitutive mark, its signature. And as such – this is what distinguishes Joyce's originality, for Lacan – the *sinthome* does without the Name of the Father, inscribing itself as a non-metaphorical act, a bodying forth of language without reference to the Other, *pas à lire*.

If the *sinthome* is therefore the non-metaphorical knot 'itself', it simulta-neously appears in the knot, and ostensibly as its least stable element. When Lacan declares in 1975 that 'the Oedipus complex, as such, is a symptom', he touches on the crucial point here, and in doing so identifies his very late work as a *pas au delà*, a 'step beyond' Freud. Psychoanalysis as con-ceived and practised by Freud was still, Lacan implies, in effect governed by an Oedipal symptom, its legibility bound into the paternal institution of the name; whereas the concept of *sinthome* unmasks an untreatable sin-gularity that is made invisible by institutions: the untranslatable signature of a subject's enjoyment.[42] What ties the knot of human subjectivity is therefore not some universal patriarchal law of signification, but an *act* – and this in the double character of disruptive praxis and masquerade of meaning.

The double character of the act is the key to Lacan's notion of the *sinthome* as the principle of a new, singular topology. The act corresponds to a momentary rupture in the social-discursive fabric, the obscene or hysterically funny exposure of a forbidden – indeed, properly speaking, *non-existent* – jouissance. We saw above in Chapter 5 how this act occurred in the evanescent, fantasmatic stain of Mr Hyde's enjoyment, alongside the illicit pleasures of the other 'imps of fancy' displaced and disfigured, made 'doriangrayer', by Joyce. The fantasy of enjoying experience outside history, in a zone of pure aesthetic irresponsibility, proved to be entangled with the figure of the literary *alibi*, of the Joycean 'assumptinome' or forged signature that the ego uses to protect itself from a wrathful (paternal) Law. In Lacanian terms, the act here takes place predominantly in the imaginary register, and as such it is characterised by problems of the ego – bound up with meaning and ambiguity, the assumption of identity, rivalry with the other. But crucially, an act of this kind is always a masked act, its trans-gressive edge blunted by an implication in social discourse; its exposure of jouissance is limited to an anamorphic instant, a momentary glimpse of the forbidden Thing. The *sinthome* is in this sense easily recuperable by metaphor; as we saw in our readings of literary doubles, it can be rendered meaningful in religious or medical terms as uncanny revelation or hallucinatory episode – or else be announced to the world as an artistic vocation, an 'epiphany'.

But the constitutive act of the *sinthome* also takes place away from the domain of imaginary legibility. (The knot, says Lacan, 'is best tied with the eyes closed'.)[43] As an event in language, where the register of the symbolic breaches and is breached by the real, its effects on the discursive organisation of subjectivity go beyond what can be decisively troped as a post-Romantic moment of inspiration or insanity. It is here that Lacan's idea of Joyce as a body of writing that is *pas à lire* comes into focus: if the agency of the letter 'agentlike brought about . . . this municipal sin business' (*FW* 5.13–14), its domestic-political *Sinn* (its *sin'thomerule*, as Lacan jokes) may be only a pretext for the more disruptive 'politics' in which it functions as *encaisse-jouissance*, as a receptacle for Joyce's transgressive 'sinse'. In other words, the text does not set out to be read in the same way that the Freudian joke orients itself towards the signifying instance of the Other, which prohibits direct exposure of jouissance and supposedly guarantees the circulation of the subject's truth or desiring identity. Rather, Lacan sees in Joyce a subject who sees through that 'transferential' fiction in an epiphany or 'radical foreclosure' – the collapse of 'this municipal sin business', the laws and conventions of discursive reality, and the revelation of what they mask: the void of creative jouissance-in-language.

At various points in our study, we have been able to gauge the fundamental ambiguity of the psychoanalytic exploration of literary space (to use Blanchot's phrase). We can now rearrange Lacan's letters in a Joycean-Euclidian manner to make more sense of this double inscription (Fig. 6.6).

In Freudian aesthetics, as we saw in Chapter 2, theory emerges as a *traduction*: an attempt to restore the artistic enigma to the domain of discursive legibility and thus to cure it of its symptomatic resistance, make it identifiable or co-operative – turn it into a manifestation of *transference*. Lacan's distinction between the imaginary and the symbolic allows us to understand the two aspects of Freudian traduction: the restoration of an integral, analysable psyche, on the one hand, and on the other the search for an identifiable cause underlying human creativity. If the literary act arguably reaches its fullest reflexive development in Joyce, his work can perhaps be defined as a unique point of writerly resistance to this traductive manipulation, its 'crossexanimation' mocking the notion of a

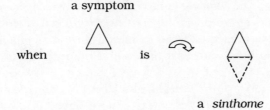

Fig. 6.6

discrete psychical site as it celebrates its own diabolic or fantasmatic creation *ex nihilo*.

But what is crucial is that psychoanalysis does not *only* collude with readerly traduction and treat any 'resistance' on the part of its literary object as a troublesome symptom to be deciphered, solved or dissolved. In Lacan's view, the analyst should never engage with his interpretative object – whether neurotic speech or literary document – in a symmetrical relation or evenly balanced conversation. Rather, Lacanian analysis is the encounter of Wakean 'anticollaborators' (*FW* 118.25–6): participants in an interpretative essay that refuses to operate by means of mutual collusion, imaginary oneness. When Lacan reads Joyce, therefore, it is as an anticollaborator, at odds with the semblance of authorial meaning – and therefore, paradoxically enough, in a sense co-operating with Joyce's self-deconstruction.

In a final twist, we might read this Lacanian anticollaborator as an 'antic elaborator': a reader who, like the fool censured by Hamlet for his 'pitiful ambition', will not stick to the script but uses it as a pretext for his own rhetorical performance. In our Conclusion, we shall examine how, both in *Ulysses* and in *Finnegans Wake*, Joyce figures this lexical anticollaboration or antic elaboration in ways with a particular bearing on the theological aspects of our reading. Regarding psychoanalysis, we might define the act of interpretation itself as an anti-collaboration: and this is precisely what distinguishes it as a disruptive textual *problem* from the various critical discourses in search of different kinds of truth (historical, psychological, political and so on). If Freud first looked to art as a confirmation of the truth of the unconscious, the *force* of his discovery took it beyond that traductive gesture, and towards a moment when psychoanalysis would attempt to learn from the aesthetic new ways to write what lay beyond its discourse of truth.

Conclusion: mememormee

Our starting-point was the idea that the attempt to read Joyce today is bedevilled by a sense of institutional exhaustion and interpretative redundancy. We should now, in the light of our double engagement with Joycean artifice and psychoanalytic aesthetics, be in a better position to grasp what might be at stake in this potential closure of reading – and to resist its becoming actual. We saw that Freud's first efforts to transfer his discovery of the unconscious to the aesthetic domain went together with a fantasy of redeeming the father as the guarantee of integral, truthful representation; and that this Hamlet-like ambition was visible in Freud's preoccupation with the 'ghost not laid' of the patriarch Moses. By contrast, Lacan's reading of Joyce's work began with what he considered its exposure of a *démission paternelle*, a 'dereliction' of paternity. Yet the effect of this catastrophic breach of the father's symbolic function was not necessarily, in Lacan's view, a disabling one; on the contrary, it could open on to an unspeakable new inventivity (as seen in Joyce's work, and then implicitly in Lacan's own topological 'writing').[1] If the Joycean epiphany appealed to Lacan in particular, this was because he saw it as a pure *écrit* or 'joussture' (*FW* 535.3) – an act of writing that manifested itself as such, as untranslatable gesture, while simultaneously functioning through that act as a revitalisation of the paternal name (a confirmation of its 'joyceture', so to speak).

At first glance, then, the *père-version* or father-centredness of these psychoanalytic responses to art seem diametrically opposed in their theoretical aims; while Freud strives to dissolve the symptomatic opacity of an artwork, and so restore the efficacy of the paternal signifier to govern meaningful narratives, Lacan takes the aesthetic thing as evidence of the terminal collapse of such meaningfulness, the emergence of an untranslatable jouissance, something impossible to theorise. But in this respect, both psychoanalysts – both father and son, we might say – are one in ascribing a unique importance to the figure of the father for the interpretation of artistic enigmas, the identification of meaning. Here, we Joyceans once again find ourselves on Groundhog Day – in other words, confronting the uncanny prescription of critical ideas in Joycean writing. At the very beginning of *Ulysses*, we are reminded once again how Joyce can make the very notion of addressing the text 'in one's own voice' – or of a psychoanalyst applying his 'own' ideas to it – seem derisory. The Englishman Haines is thinking about *Hamlet*: 'I read a theological interpretation of it somewhere, he said bemused. The Father and the Son idea. The Son striving to be atoned with the Father' (*U* 1.577–8).

These baffled remarks about reading Shakespeare point to a subtle *mise en abîme* of the very same problem – 'the seme asnuh' (*FW* 620.17) – now confronting the Joycean reader (and which psychoanalytic accounts of art usually aspire to solve). 'The Father and the Son idea' is offered as one possible way of translating, of rendering interpretable, the enduring riddle of Shakespeare's play – but note how careful Haines is to disclaim any ownership of the idea, attributing it to a safely anonymous authority. It is as if the very notion of having an original idea about *Hamlet*, of trying to say anything new about it, is unthinkable, almost verges on blasphemy. But it is precisely this predicament of non-originality, of embarrassed belatedness, that constitutes the 'Father and the Son idea'. Seeking to be 'atoned with' the father would imply, as the etymology of the word indicates, a search to identify, to be at one, with a site of authority or true paternal origin; in the same way, the reader looks for an authoritative solution or 'theological interpretation' of *Hamlet* – and now of *Ulysses* – in order both to guarantee the integrity of the textual origin and to redeem himself from the sinful novelty, the fallen waywardness, of his present reading (and, as we saw above in Chapter 2, the first such sinful reader was Hamlet himself).[2] The Joycean twist here is of course that, since the episode we are reading bears the ghostly title 'Telemachus' (there was no such title in the 1922 edition, even though the reader had no doubt heard of it), we already have 'the Father and the Son idea' in the pair Ulysses and Telemachus – and, as Haines's comments remind us, we could just as well apply that idea to the pair *Hamlet* and *Ulysses*, making the latter both a 'theological interpretation' of Shakespeare's play and an effort on the part of incarnate son or sinful reader to be at one with its divine author's meaning or will.

We shall return shortly to 'Telemachus' and to the significance of Joyce's remark to Stuart Gilbert that the 'art' of the episode is 'theology'.[3] But first let us try to focus more clearly on the question of filial and readerly atonement or being-at-one-with by relating it to the central thesis of our study: that, briefly, Joyce's writing refuses (both negates and trashes) what we have termed 'traduction', in effect preventing the central breach of discourse that marks its *poesis* – and that is rooted in a certain 'bardic memory' (*FW* 172.28) or Shakespearean inscription of the 'I' – becoming legible within a masterly narrative of identification. When in *Finnegans Wake* we read that one of the names of the father is 'papyr' (*FW* 20.10), we are given an apt Joycean reprise of the 'Father and the Son idea'; the question of atonement or identification is no longer simply a matter of characters, of representable traits or signifiers, but now concerns the very stuff of representation, the material basis and phenomenal instance – or 'inkstands' (*FW* 173.34) – of letters.

To consider the question of atonement in Joyce, critics often turn to a brief poem he wrote in 1932 and entitled 'Ecce Puer': indeed, the poem would seem almost to bear as its invisible subtitle 'The Son striving to be atoned with the Father'. Ellmann notes how in 1932 Groundhog Day saw an agonising coincidence: the recent death of Joyce's father and a severe deterioration of the mental health of his daughter Lucia ('February 2 did not prove a lucky day this year', as Ellmann drily puts it: *JJ* 645). The birth of Joyce's grandson Stephen on 15 February thus produces the emotional turbulence inscribed in the opening lines of the poem:

> Of the dark past
> A child is born;
> With joy and grief
> My heart is torn.[4]

What is immediately striking here is the almost complete lack of literary style; it is as if we have returned to the moment of Joycean birth, where an epiphany presented a language-thing 'in idself' (*FW* 611.21), a pure textual seed or vocal ejaculation. But, given that in 1932 Joyce is in fact deeply involved in the complex obscurity of his 'usylessly unreadable' (*FW* 179.26) *Work in Progress*, the sudden production of this apparently simple – above all, apparently legible – text adds a further torsion to the 'Father and the Son idea'. At one level, the son's desire to seek atonement with the father might be seen here in the wilful shrugging-off of 'Joycean' stylistic extravagance, the reduction of the authorial voice to a bare literalism. The struggle of the son to be one with the originary purity of the 'seme' or paternal seed would in this sense entail a deliberate attempt to minimise the enjoyment (again, usually a characteristic 'Joycean' signature) of the textual material in hand. This momentary urge to perpetuate the paternal line in an authentic voice shorn of all unnecessary literary complications could surely be linked to Joyce's tomfoolery (or, as Lacan would insist, his *sinthome*foolery) in apparently once wishing to hand over the task of finishing *Finnegans Wake* to the hapless James Stephens.[5]

Is 'Ecce Puer' therefore no more than Joyce's renunciation of sinful literary extravagance, a return to the straight line linking the moment of birth to the 'dark past' of a lost paternal origin? The poem's final stanza seems to suggest as much:

> A child is sleeping:
> An old man gone.
> O, father forsaken,
> Forgive your son!

The images of sleeping son and absent father are offered in a stripped-bare, denotative language, as if the poem embodied a wish for absolute mimetic fidelity or authenticity in relation to the mystery of birth and death or, in still more cosmic terms, to that of the sheer event of Being as apparition: 'The world that was not / Comes to pass.' We shall have more to say below on this link between stylistic minimalism and a certain 'theology'; but first we should dwell on the final couplet of the poem, where Joycean 'atonement' becomes perhaps more dubious.

'O, father forsaken, / Forgive your son!' might seem to be Joyce at last speaking *in propria persona*, finally voicing his actual filial remorse with the full sincerity of prayer. Perhaps so – but this heartfelt prayer is at the same time, unmistakeably, the recitation (with a characteristically Joycean, disfigurative twist) of another sacred text, one that voices the very antithesis of a prayer for paternal forgiveness: that is, filial reproach or blasphemy (from the medieval Latin *blasphemare*, 'to criticise, reproach'). The first three words of the line – 'O, father forsaken' – amount to a kind of ultimate blasphemy, as a 'quashed quotato' recalls the utterance of Christ on the cross: 'And at the ninth hour Jesus cried with a loud voice, saying, Eloi, Eloi, lama sabachthani? which is, being interpreted, My God, my God, why hast thou forsaken me?' (Mark 15:34).

We should bear in mind how Joyce's choice of title, 'Ecce Puer', deliberately plays on the infamous 'Ecce homo' uttered by Pontius Pliate before he passed sentence on Christ. The question of *imitatio Christi* takes us back both to Nietzsche and to Joyce's student essay on Michael Munkacsy's painting *Ecce Homo* (*CW* 31–7). If Nietzsche's final word had claimed to abolish the human identification with God by unmasking Christian morality and setting '*Dionysos against the Crucified*',[6] it is arguable that the biblical text itself already marked that identification as singularly precarious, if not ultimately impossible. At this extraordinary moment in the Christian 'farsoonerite' (*FW* 171.4) or father-son-rite, we are shown a dramatic split between paternal truth and incarnate filial discourse, between the metaphysical Logos and the suffering flesh of an existing 'I'. What emerges here is something that remains 'pathological', a moment of human agony impossible to sublate or evacuate in symbolic equivalence: something, that is, that does not translate (and note how Mark insists on quoting Christ's words in the original Aramaic). Indeed, the non-coincidence of 'spiritual' meaning and its material embodiment was already preoccupying the young Joyce when he found 'nothing superhuman' in the face of Christ as represented by Munkacsy (*CW* 36); like the Joycean epiphany, what the painting showed could not be translated, did not allow the interpreter to transcend its aesthetic materiality or 'passion'.

If 'Ecce Puer' constitutes a prayer for atonement, then, in its final couplet that prayer is doubled blasphemously: 'O father forsaken' inevitably evoking the Christlike *father, why have you forsaken me?* As we saw in Chapter 6, this last line is essentially Bloom's filial reproach to his father, whose suicidal act amounted to an absolute jouissance or irredeemable sin that makes it impossible for his son to remember or represent him as a single meaningful existence. For Bloom, in other words, the paternal memory is a ghost not laid: the son is unable to redeem the sinful actuality of the father's bodily existence by substituting it for – or translating it into – a 'symbolic' paternity. The Joycean son is thus always left behind, abandoned in his irreparable or unspeakable predicament (we saw how the word 'left' dogged Stephen throughout *Ulysses*); like the Wakean Shem, he is accused of being 'excruciated, in honour bound to the cross of your own cruelfiction!' (*FW* 192.18–19)

Lacan was certainly intrigued by the suggestion that Joyce may have viewed his work as an *imitatio Christi*. At one point in his seminar, he turns to his own Joycean 'anticollaborator' Jacques Aubert with a question: 'Is there, in his writings, something we could call a hint of his being or making himself into a *redeemer*?' (Lacan uses the English word.) Aubert replies that there are traces of such an identification in *Stephen Hero* (where the artist has 'an air of false Christ' about him), and mentions a period when the young Joyce was fascinated by Franciscanism with its institutional commitment to *imitatio Christi*.[7] What is crucial to add here, however, is that in Joyce the figure of Christ always embodies a *failure* of symbolisation, a point of unbearable aesthetic 'excrutiation': the Joycean 'redeemer' thus remains forever forsaken, alienated from paternal truth in mortal jouissance.

In the youthful rush of 'A Portrait of the Artist', Joyce already seems to have grasped this sense of redemption as *coincidentia oppositorum*: 'It was part of that ineradicable egoism which he was afterwards to call redeemer that he imagined converging to him the deeds and thoughts of the microcosm.'[8] There is thus something ineradicable or untreatable in the egoic 'symptom'; it marks a singular event of Being, in which 'The world that was not / Comes to pass.'

The problem of psychoanalysis for literary criticism, as we have explored it in this study, ultimately corresponds to how to treat this ineradicable jouissance or world-constitutive 'joussture' (*FW* 535.3). The Joycean critic Jean Kimball has to develop a complex strategy to negotiate this problem: on the one hand, she finds reasons to avoid the 'messes of mottage' (*FW* 182.22–3) in *Finnegans Wake* altogether, arguing – in line with Jung, as we saw in Chapter 5 above – that 'in a very literal sense [it may] be called a schizophrenic text'.[9] At the same time, Kimball works out a manifestly 'traductive' reading of *Ulysses*, in which the meeting of Bloom and Stephen turns out to be a *successful* realisation of the 'Father and the Son idea': *Hamlet*, we might say, rewritten as a comedy. And even a critic as astute as Beryl Schlossman, whose ground-breaking study was the first detailed engagement with Lacan's reading of Joyce, finds the encounter between Bloom and Stephen to be ultimately therapeutic, a dramatisation of psychical 'integration' – and finally of redemption.[10]

As we have argued, at first glance 'Ecce Puer' reads as a plea for atonement written in the simplest, least Joycean language; but a more attentive reading discovers in it an act of 'transluding' (*FW* 419.25), of parodic allusion and translation, in which we hear the blasphemous voice of the forsaken son. Joyce's literary act is shown here with exemplary clarity: as the inscription of something irredeemable or unrepresentable in a position of textual *extimacy*, somewhere beyond or beneath the text's characters (perhaps in its very 'papyr': *FW* 20.10). Throughout our study, we have encountered this uncanny coincidence of representation and its disruption in two central critical enigmas: to do with, on the one hand, the limits of translation, and on the other, the apparitional presence of the 'I'. The very title of 'Ecce Puer' indicates the entanglement of Joyce's poem with these two kinds of enigma (or with this double enigma); it offers the text as an act of testimony to the appearance of our old friend 'the seme asnuh' (*FW* 620.17) – a new incarnation of the paternal seed or ego (thus we might read 'see me as new'); what is crucial is that this event is to be shown as such in the poem, not merely enchained meaningfully in its discourse. And at the same time, by alluding to the presentation of Christ as man, the title also addresses the question of the name of God – one that, as we have seen, is at stake throughout Joyce's work.

The untranslatability of the name of God provides one possible basis for a reading of Mark 15:34 with its 'original' Aramaic quotation. When Jesus cries 'Eloi, Eloi' his words are misunderstood, according to Mark, by 'some of them that stood by' as an attempt to invoke the help of Elijah; the utterance of God's name inevitably eludes the network of human discourse, its pure tautology – note the double 'Eloi' – impossible to integrate with the realm of the signifier. The encounter of Moses with the burning bush in Exodus 3:14 had already made this point, of course – and crucially, for our argument, had shown how the unspeakable tautology of God's absolute identity could be translated into an utterance of the 'I', a *sum*: 'I AM THAT I AM.'

As we mentioned above, Joyce considered 'Telemachus' to be the 'theological' part of *Ulysses*. The episode shows clearly how the problems of translation and of the 'I' converge – or rather emerge as 'tautaulogically the same' (*FW* 6.30) – in the act of Joycean writing. For what we find here is a playful, jocoserious treatment of the same knot of questions raised by 'Ecce Puer': questions of incarnation and redemption, remembrance and re-apparition. The very first apparition of *Ulysses* – 'Stately, plump Buck Mulligan' (*U* 1.1) – is already a parodic bearer of these questions: both frisky and ponderous, he emblematises the incarnate density of human discourse, the sinful embroilment of language in jouissance. And Mulligan's clownish parody of the Mass introduces a string of 'satanic' inversions and anagrams – such as the repeated 'dogsbody' (*U* 1.112, 137) blasphemously distorting 'God's body' (and anticipating the 'bloated carcass of a dog' seen by Stephen on the beach in 'Proteus': *U* 3.286). The fallen condition of the empirical 'I' – structured by the 'ineluctable modality' of its phenomenality, as Stephen thinks (*U* 3.1) – makes it forever impossible to utter a truthful *sum*, a self-grounding 'I am'.

Stephen can only imagine an escape from this ineluctable phenomenal materiality in a moment of fantasy, when he remembers a song his mother may have once heard in a pantomime:

> *I am the boy*
> *That can enjoy*
> *Invisibility.*
> (*U* 1.260–3)

Here we should return to the idea that 'Telemachus' may be a 'theological interpretation' of *Hamlet*, for what the song re-voices (and note that it is sung by 'old Royce': 1.257) is the prince's outraged declaration 'I have that within which passes show' (1.ii.85): Hamlet's claim to be the incarnation of a spiritual essence irreducible to mere representation. In Stephen's view – or in what the *Wake* will write as 'iSpace' (*FW* 124.12) – such a *sum* is best consigned to pantomime: the 'I' can no more *possess* as an empirical object its negative potential than a boy can really enjoy invisibility. The 'bloated carcass' of contingent lived phenomena leaves no room for some inner, metaphysical, *non-bodily* jouissance that would render the world meaningful, imbue it with transcendent *Geist*.

Another boy in 'Telemachus' who playfully sings of enjoying invisibility or incarnating pure spirituality is of course Buck Mulligan. In his 'ballad of joking Jesus', Mulligan declares,

> *– I'm the queerest young fellow that ever you heard.*
> *My mother's a jew, my father's a bird.* (*U* 1.584–5)

The comical bathos here clearly hinges on the question of how much reality theologians ascribe to the body of Christ (a debate whose history is very much in Stephen's mind); and Mulligan's own 'stately, plump' presence, emphasised by minute textual attention to the details of his body, reiterates the cumbersome comedy of the supposedly divine or paternal Logos being travestied by its incarnation, its fleshly or phenomenal 'bloated carcass'.

The central Joycean *Punkt* here again concerns the name of God: for I AM, as God names himself in Exodus, is both a *sum* and a pun on the Latin *iam*, 'now'. In other words, the problem of reincarnation or re-presentation involves both the cogitating ego and its punctual manifestation in time, the bodily but also the temporal condition of the 'I'. The re-embodiment of a textual origin or remembering of parental identity in Joyce opens on to a jouissance from which the 'I' in this double sense – as self-representing *cogito* and as temporal point – is foreclosed. It is thus that the only voice in 'Telemachus' actually able to utter a truthful 'seme asnuh' (*FW* 620.17) – 'see *me* as *now*' – is the drowned man in Dublin bay, to whom Stephen silently ascribes the Jehovan 'Here I am' (*U* 1.677). Only at the unspeakable moment of death or birth – a moment Joyce struggles to occupy in 'Ecce Puer' – can the 'I' show itself as an absolute affirmation of identity, uncompromised by historical representation or the history of representation (the 'Oxen of the Sun' episode of *Ulysses* is another Joycean treatment of this problem: its 'Hoopsa, boyaboy, hoopsa!' (*U* 14.5) offering a first version of *ecce puer*).

We recall that Blanchot saw in the act of suicide something of this quasi-Nietzschean 'apotheosis of the instant', an ultimate affirmation of the *now*, of the singular occurrence of jouissance, in defiance of the meaningful or communicable space and time that govern history. Likewise Joyce's literary rupture of 'iSpace' (*FW* 124.12) constitutes, we have argued, an unaccountable *yes* or *jetzt*, the affirmation of an aesthetic 'thing' at odds with the discourse of social identity, governed by a restrictive egoic 'reality principle'.

What is crucial to emphasise here is how this asocial or unreal dimension of the Joycean literary act is also a textual *re*-embodiment, both a disfigurative memory and a blasphemous atonement. In Joyce's raids on the work of 'Great Shapesphere' (*FW* 295.4), what he seeks to reaffirm is the force of an act that is uniquely transgressive, that *breaks through* historical reality: when Lady Macbeth feels 'the future in the instant', she is caught up in that force, entranced by a jouissance that overwhelms representation. We saw how the murderous or suicidal jouissance that Shakespeare ascribes to Lady Macbeth resurfaces in the *Wake* as the force behind a tragic *passage à l'acte* – a fantasmatic drive or 'burning would' that emerges in an excessive self-affirmation: 'Yet's the time for being now, now, now' (*FW* 250.16). In this sense, the figure of Lady Macbeth embodies a veritable 'Will in overplus': both a relentlessly phallic, self-inflating desire and an uncanny spectre (something that refuses to die, is left behind like a will). Above all, at this point when the Shakespearean text exceeds itself in the jouissance of its act we are given a true portrait of the artist: the great anti-heroine figures a 'bardic memory' (*FW* 172.28) suggesting both the endless *poesis* of Shakespearean invention and even that of the literary 'thing' in general. But crucially what the *Wake* does with this traumatic literary memory is to re-inscribe it in a 'dance inane' – in other words, to reveal its inherently *comic* potential as an aesthetic disfiguration of reality.

Freud wrote that 'the essential *ars poetica* lies in the technique of overcoming the feeling of repulsion in us which is undoubtedly connected with the barriers that rise between each single ego and the others'.[11] The secret of humour for Freud likewise lay in this transgression of 'iSpace' (*FW* 124.12), of the aggressively defined topology of the ego. It is here that we can see how Joyce's ambition to render 'the essential *ars poetica*' in his work – vividly shown in his rejoycing of Shakespeare – takes us back to the Lacanian idea of the act, and in particular of its relation to sexual difference. Let us return to Stephen's memories of his mother in 'Telemachus':

Fergus' song: I sang it alone in the house, holding down the long dark chords. Her door was open: she wanted to hear my music. Silent with awe and pity I went to her bedside . . .

. . .

She heard old Royce sing in the pantomime of *Turko the Terrible* and laughed with others when he sang:

> *I am the boy*
> *That can enjoy*
> *Invisibility.*

Phantasmal mirth, folded away: muskperfumed. (*U* 1.249–63)

Stephen's memories are antiphonal; his own sad figure playing for his dying mother is echoed by the contrasting image of her as a young woman at a crowded pantomime. What it is impossible to miss in this tableau are its antithetical versions of aesthetic experience: on the one hand, a solitary, mournful artist-son (his spectral figure doubled, perhaps with ironic hyperbole, by the vanishing boy in Royce's song), and on the other a woman who 'laughed with others', her enjoyment experienced in carnivalesque self-abandonment. If the mother's 'phantasmal mirth' now appears ghostly, disembodied, this is because it has indeed been 'folded away' – but only into Stephen's inner 'iSpace' (*FW* 124.12) which is defined by the notion of artistic solitude, by a disembodied *cogito*. If, as Žižek puts it, Lacanian theory holds that 'the act as real is "feminine", in contrast to the "masculine" performative',[12] we can see how Joyce articulates a version of this difference with the problem of the artistic 'I', the ego that participates in – or else is obliterated by – the aesthetic act.

It is thus above all in Shakespearean *femininity* – a problem exemplified by Lady Macbeth with her 'burning would', but one by no means confined to nominally female characters – that Joyce finds the trace of the pure literary act. And here it is clear yet again that literary criticism, with its history of thinking Joyce's relation to Shakespeare as a 'farsoonerite' (*FW* 171.4) or father-son-write (reading Stephen as an 'Oedipal' Hamlet, and so on), has established itself as a traduction: an attempt, that is, to echo Hamlet's advice to the players by banning laughter, eliminating the unnecessary turbulence of jouissance from the space of interpretation.

Yet the notion that Joycean writing is above all a Dionysiac celebration, a gale of Rabelesian laughter, is of course also a critical commonplace. At the very end of *Finnegans Wake*, we hear in a Shakespearean echo something that encapsulates the radical ambiguity of this textual jouissance, this musical 'overplus': both its delightful and its unspeakable impact. When, in the closing monologue of Anna Livia Plurabelle, we read 'mememormee!' (*FW* 628.14), perhaps we think first of the departing words of Hamlet's ghostly father, 'Remember me!' (1.v.91). The paternal edict – and this might hold for the Shakespearean text too – constitutes an affirmation of identity that is distorted, dissolved by the vocal flux of the *Wake*, just as the child-river begins to merge with her marine father and lose her distinct identity. But this musical dissolution of the 'I' is precisely not what is involved in the spectral father-son-rite of *Hamlet*, where the prince (and Stephen Dedalus is like him in this respect, at least) remains fatally locked in a specular inwardness or 'mind's eye' (1.ii.185) that seals him off permanently from the *act*. In *Hamlet*, the one who acts – in the sense of sacrificing the 'I' to an absolute, suicidal jouissance – is of course Ophelia; and her 'pray you, love, remember' (IV.v.174–5) is likewise disfiguratively remembered at the end of the *Wake*: 'Bussoftlhee, mememormee!' (*FW* 628.14). It is her brother Laertes' response to Ophelia's madness that provides the best gloss on this Joycean remembrance: 'This nothing's more than matter' (IV.v.173). What is remembered, in other words, is precisely the excess of the Shakespearean performance: an act beyond identity, more than me, more than 'same' or *même* (and with the Hebrew *mem*, 'water', adding another note of Ophelian dissolution). And this writing excess – at once something lacking, irreducible to the text, and yet 'more than matter' – is what finally makes the Joycean *thing* impossible to read or remember in terms dictated by a solitary 'I'.

'This nothing's more than matter': we have returned to the idea of creation *ex nihilo*, that radical creativity that St Bonaventure considered a blasphemous error if allowed to enter the domain of the mortal *anima*. Our pursuit of Lacan's thought has allowed us to learn more about the transgressive enjoyment at the root of Joyce's creative vocation, its self-fabrication in a jouissance foreclosed from the ego's reality. But by exploring this sinful creativity in terms of its literary genealogy, we have seen that Joyce enjoyed and worked not in some self-enclosed fantasy but as a *participant* in aesthetic experience. For Joyce, it is above all the Shakespearean text where memory – the waking to selfhood or gathering of representation before a cogitating 'I' – becomes 'mememormee', an excess of self, the obliteration of the punctual 'I' in an ecstasy of aesthetic enjoyment. And the destruction of 'iSpace' in this literary topology makes what may seem its most repetitive feature, its endlessly recycled 'bardic memory' (*FW* 172.28), something unspeakably innovative.

Notes

PROLOGUE: GROUNDHOG DAY

1. F. Nietzsche, *The Gay Science* (1882), New York: Random House, 1974, 273.
2. F. Nietzsche, *Ecce Homo* (1888), London: Penguin, 1979, 99–100.
3. M. Blanchot, *The Infinite Conversation* (1969), Minneapolis: University of Minnesota Press, 1993, 274.
4. H. Gorman, *James Joyce*, New York: Farrar & Rinehart, 1939, 18–19.
5. G. Agamben, 'The Idea of Language', in *Potentialities: Collected Essays in Philosophy*, Stanford: Stanford University Press, 1999, 41.
6. P. Klossowski, *Nietzsche and the Vicious Circle* (1969), London: Athlone, 1997, 30.
7. For a clear summary, cf. J. Roberts, *German Philosophy: an Introduction*, Cambridge: Polity, 1988, 215–18. For a crucial exploration of the bearing of Nietzsche's thought on the Freudian discovery, cf. M. Henry, *The Genealogy of Psychoanalysis* (1985), Stanford: Stanford University Press, 1993, esp. 204–80.
8. F. Nietzsche, *Thus Spake Zarathustra* (1885); quoted in Roberts, *German Philosophy*, 233.
9. M. Blanchot, *The Space of Literature* (1955). Lincoln, NB: University of Nebraska Press, 1982, 103.
10. S. Critchley, *Very Little . . . Almost Nothing: Death, Philosophy, Literature*, London: Routledge, 1997, 69.
11. See J. Derrida, 'Ulysses Gramophone: Hear Say Yes in Joyce', in *Acts of Literature* (London: Routledge, 1992), for a discussion of the problem of *ouï-dire* to which my argument is of course endebted.
12. F. Kermode, *Shakespeare's Language*, London: Penguin, 2000, 123.
13. 'The soul makes new compositions, but it must not make any new thing.' III *Sent.* 37.1.1. Quoted in U. Eco, *The Aesthetics of Thomas Aquinas*, London: Radius, 1988, 173.
14. The German title of Freud's 1925 text has a force considerably diminished by Strachey's polite-sounding 'Civilisation and its Discontents'.
15. These references to the history of astronomy by Freud have been explored by Jean Laplanche in terms of an opposition between the fundamentally decentring force of Freud's discovery and the tendency of one strand of psychoanalytic theory to work against that force by returning to an 'ipsocentric' account of the

psyche. Although the terms of our argument are quite different, it would be conceivable to relate our reading of 'An Encounter' in Chapter 1 to Laplanche's 'general theory of seduction'. Cf. J. Laplanche, 'The Unfinished Copernican Revolution', in *Essays on Otherness*, London: Routledge, 1999.

16. J. Kimball, *Odyssey of the Psyche: Jungian Patterns in Joyce's Ulysses*, Carbondale: S. Illinois University Press, 1997, 8–11. For my review of Kimball's work, see *James Joyce Broadsheet* 62, June 2002.

17. J. Lacan, *Le sinthome* (S23), 1975–6, selections of which are published in *Ornicar?* 1976, 6: 3–20; 7: 3–18; 8: 6–20; 1977, 9: 32–40; 10: 5–12; 11: 2–9. A more inclusive text of the seminar has been produced in a non-commercial edition by the Association freudienne internationale (1997); my references are to this text. For a lucid and wide-ranging examination of *Le sinthome*, see Roberto Harari's recent study, *How James Joyce Made His Name: A Reading of the Final Lacan*, New York: The Other Press, 2002; and for some original and thought-provoking readings of the seminar, see the essays collected in my edited volume *Re-inventing the Symptom: Essays on the Final Lacan*, New York: The Other Press, 2002, especially those by Paul Verhaeghe and Frédéric Declercq, Véronique Voruz and Philip Dravers.

18. Lacan's phrase is quoted by Sheldon Brivic (who notes that it is absent from the official version of the address, published as 'Joyce le symptôme 1' in J. Aubert, ed., *Joyce avec Lacan*, Paris: Navarin, 1987). Perhaps Lacan is wittily inverting César Abin's 1932 cartoon portrait of Joyce as a giant question mark suspended above the globe (reprinted in *JJ* plate XLIX). Cf. S. Brivic, *Joyce the Creator*, Madison: University of Wisconsin Press, 1985, 9.

19. J.-A. Miller, Foreword, in J. Aubert, ed. *Joyce avec Lacan*.

20. J. Lacan, 'L'Etourdit', *Scilicet* 4, 1973, 33. For an account of Lacan's work with Borromean knots, see my 'Ineluctable Nodalities: On the Borromean Knot', in D. Nobus, ed., *Key Concepts of Lacanian Psychoanalysis*, London: Rebus, 1998, 139–63.

21. J. Lacan, 'Jeunesse de Gide ou la lettre et le désir', *E* 747. I am grateful to Dany Nobus for drawing my attention to this passage. See D. Nobus, 'Illiterature', in Thurston, ed., *Re-inventing the Symptom*, 25.

22. See Lacan's remarks on the mutual exclusivity of unconscious and writing in his foreword to Robert Georgin's *Lacan*, quoted by J.-M. Rabaté, *James Joyce: Authorized Reader*, Baltimore: Johns Hopkins University Press, 1991, 57.

23. R. Ellmann, *The Consciousness of Joyce*, Oxford: Oxford University Press, 1977; Kimball, *Odyssey of the Psyche*; idem, *Joyce and the Early Freudians: A Synchronic Dialogue of Texts*, Gainesville: University Press of Florida, 2003.

24. Kimball, *Joyce and the Early Freudians*, 13–14. Cf. M. Schechner, 'Joyce and Psychoanalysis: Two Additional Perspectives', *James Joyce Quarterly* 14, 1976, 418; S. Brivic, *Joyce Between Freud and Jung*, Fort Washington: Kennikat, 1980, 4.

25. S. Žižek, *Enjoy Your Symptom!* London: Routledge, 1992, 126.

26. Cf. J. Fineman, *Shakespeare's Perjured Eye: The Invention of Poetic Subjectivity in the Sonnets*, Berkeley: University of California Press, 1986.

27. For more on the problem of the 'unreadable' in Lacan, see my 'Introduction: Lacan's *pas-à-lire*', in Thurston, ed., *Re-inventing the Symptom*, xiii–xix.

1 'AN ENCOUNTER'

1. 'In love, as in almost all human matters, friendly agreement is the result of a misunderstanding. That misunderstanding is pleasure' (my translation). 'Mon coeur mis à nu', in *Œuvres complètes*, Paris: Gallimard, 1961, 1289–90.
2. G. Agamben, 'The Thing Itself', in *Potentialities: Collected Essays in Philosophy*, Stanford: Stanford University Press, 1999, 35.
3. J. Lacan, 'Joyce le symptôme 1', in J. Aubert, ed., *Joyce avec Lacan*, Paris: Navarin, 1987, 22–3.
4. J.-M. Rabaté, 'Joyce the Parisian', in D. Attridge, ed., *The Cambridge Companion to James Joyce*, Cambridge: Cambridge University Press, 1990, 90.
5. Ibid., 83.
6. J. Lacan, Yale University, Kanzer Seminar, 24 November 1975, *Scilicet* 6/7, Paris: Seuil, 1976, 20.
7. Cf. Joel Fineman's provocative meditation 'The History of the Anecdote: Fiction and Fiction', in *The Subjectivity Effect in Western Literary Tradition: Essays Toward the Release of Shakespeare's Will*, Cambridge, MA: MIT Press, 59–87.
8. Rabaté, 'Joyce the Parisian', 97.
9. See David Trotter's compact account of Joyce's lifelong struggle with publishers: *The English Novel in History*, London: Routledge, 1993, 95–8.
10. Quoted in M. Beja, ed., *James Joyce: Dubliners and A Portrait of the Artist as a Young Man: Casebook*, London: Macmillan, 1973, 38–9.
11. Shoshana Felman's *La Folie et la chose littéraire* has partly informed this notion of a fantasmatic core paradoxically 'extimate' (to use Lacan's coinage) to the literary work: in other words, both 'behind' it, its pulsional force or inspiration, and 'outside' it, impossible to identify with any particular element within it. We shall return to consider Felman's work in more detail in Chapter 3 below.
12. In his notebook for the *Work in Progress*, later published as *Scribbledehobble*, Joyce organises phrases and topics relating to homosexuality (and Oscar Wilde's 'decadence' in particular) under the heading AN ENCOUNTER. The 'enormity' in question in the story is, on this evidence, in Joyce's view, of a sexual, perhaps an abusive kind. It will be no surprise that we shall argue that the reading of Joyce is drastically constrained by any privileging of authorial opinion. Cf. D. Hayman, *The 'Wake' in Transit*, Ithaca: Cornell University Press, 1990, 19–21.
13. G. Puttenham, *English Poesie* III, xix. (Arb.) 213. Quoted in the *Oxford English Dictionary*, s.v. 'Traduction'.
14. Agamben, 'The Thing Itself', in *Potentialities*, 35.
15. J. Lacan, 'The Function and Field of Speech and Language in Psychoanalysis', *E:S* 44.
16. R. Grigg, 'From the Mechanism of Psychosis to the Universal Condition of the Symptom: On Foreclosure', in D. Nobus, ed., *Key Concepts of Lacanian Psychoanalysis*, London: Rebus, 58.

2 FREUD'S MOUSETRAP

1. A. C. Bradley, *Shakespearean Tragedy*, London: Macmillan, 1904, 202 n.
2. *The Complete Letters of Sigmund Freud to Wilhelm Fliess*, Cambridge, MA: Bellknap, 1985, 272–3. (Note the aptly 'Oedipal' Freudian slip: the substitution of 'Polonius' for 'Laertes'.)
3. S. Freud, *The Interpretation of Dreams*, SE 4: 264–5.
4. Idem, 'Psychopathic Characters on the Stage', *SE* 7: 309.
5. Idem, *The Interpretation of Dreams*, SE 4: 266.
6. Idem, 'Delusions and Dreams in Jensen's *Gradiva*', *SE* 9: 1.
7. P. Gay, *Freud: A Life for our Times*, London: Macmillan, 1988, 314.
8. S. Freud, 'The Moses of Michelangelo', *SE* 13: 216.
9. Quoted in Gay, *Freud*, 314.
10. *Selected Prose of T. S. Eliot*, London: Faber, 1975, 48.
11. R. M. Frye, *The Renaissance Hamlet: Issues and Responses in 1600*, Princeton: Princeton University Press, 1984, 84.
12. J. Lacan, 'Desire and the Interpretation of Desire in *Hamlet*' (S6), in S. Felman, ed., *Literature and Psychoanalysis, The Question of Reading: Otherwise*, Baltimore: Johns Hopkins University Press, 38.
13. Stephen Greenblatt gives an illuminating account of the theological and political struggles that provide contexts for the uncanny ambiguity of the ghost; cf. his *Hamlet in Purgatory*, Princeton: Princeton University Press, 2001.
14. For a related discussion of 'the ear of the other' and Derridean questions of the signature, naming and wounding in the encounter between Shakespeare and psychoanalysis, see Nicholas Royle, 'The Remains of Psychoanalysis (ii): Shakespeare', in *After Derrida*, Manchester: Manchester University Press, 1995, 85–123.
15. Cf. Harold Jenkins's Longer Notes in the Arden edition of *Hamlet*, 509–10.
16. J.-M. Rabaté, *James Joyce, Authorized Reader*, Baltimore: Johns Hopkins University Press, 1991, 1.
17. Greenblatt, *Hamlet in Purgatory*, 237.
18. Lacan, 'Desire and the Interpretation of Desire in *Hamlet*', 21.
19. *Sigmund Freud as a Consultant: Recollections of a Pioneer in Psychoanalysis* (letters from Freud to Edoardo Weiss), New York: 1970, 37.
20. S. Freud, 'The Moses of Michelangelo', *SE* 13:211.
21. *The Diary of Sigmund Freud 1929–39*, London: Hogarth, 1992, 240, 305.
22. S. Freud, *Der Moses des Michelangelo*, *Gesammelte Werke* x, London: Imago, 1946, 201.
23. Cf. B. S. Childs, *Exodus: A Commentary*, London: SCM, 1974, 604.
24. Cf. ibid.
25. S. Freud, 'A Seventeenth-Century Demonological Neurosis', *SE* 19: 80.
26. *SE* 19: 84.
27. For a development of the notion of linguistic remainder, cf. J.-J. Lecercle, *Philosophy of Nonsense: The Intuitions of Victorian Nonsense Literature*, London: Routledge, 1994.

28. 'The winter of 1913–14 . . . was the worst time in the conflict with Jung. The *Moses* was written in the same month as the long essays in which Freud announced the seriousness of the divergences between his views and Jung's.' E. Jones, *Sigmund Freud: Life and Work*, vol. II, London: Hogarth, 1957, 366–7.

29. J. Lacan, Seminar of 15 April 1959 (S6) in Felman, ed., *Literature and Psychoanalysis*, 20–1.

30. See 'The Subversion of the Subject and the Dialectic of Desire in the Freudian Unconscious', *E:S* 313–14.

31. J. Lacan, *The Ethics of Psychoanalysis* (S7), London: Routledge, 1992, 159.

32. Ibid., 135.

33. M. Bowie, *Lacan*, London: Harvard University Press, 1991, 171.

34. Cf. M. Garber, *Shakespeare's Ghost Writers: Literature as Uncanny Causality*, New York: Methuen, 1987.

35. Ibid., 132–3.

36. Felman, ed., *Literature and Psychoanalysis*, 25.

37. Cf. J. Lacan, *Encore* (S20), New York: Norton, 2000, 61–71.

3 THE PLEASURES OF MISTRANSLATION

1. G. Steiner, *After Babel*, Oxford: Oxford University Press, 1975 (3rd edition, 1998), 63. (Note that in the original 1975 edition, Steiner spoke of 'medieval' rather than 'German' Hasidism.)

2. R. Howard, 'A Note on the Text', in R. Barthes, *The Pleasure of the Text*, New York: Farrar, Straus & Giroux, 1975, v.

3. Ibid.

4. J. Lacan, *The Four Fundamental Concepts of Psychoanalysis* (S11), London: Hogarth, and the Institute of Psychoanalysis, 1977, 184.

5. R. Barthes, *Le plaisir du texte*, Paris: Seuil, 1972, 92–3; idem, *The Pleasure of the Text*, 58.

6. J. Lacan, *The Ethics of Psychoanalysis* (S7), London: Routledge, 1992, 71.

7. S. Felman, *Le Scandale du corps parlant: Don Juan avec Austin, ou, la séduction en deux langues*, Paris: Seuil, 1980, 84 (emphasis original).

8. Idem, *The Literary Speech Act*, Ithaca: Cornell University Press, 1983, 61–2.

9. J. L. Austin, *How to Do Things with Words* (1962), Oxford: Clarendon, 1975, 13 (emphasis original).

10. M. David-Ménard, *Hysteria from Freud to Lacan: Body and Language in Psychoanalysis*, Ithaca: Cornell University Press, 1989, 178.

11. In Beckett's famous constative statement about the language of *Finnegans Wake*: from 'Dante . . . Bruno . . . Vico . . . Joyce', in *Our Exagmination Round his Factification for Incamination of Work In Progress*; reprinted in S. Beckett, *Disjecta*, London: John Calder, 1983, 27.

12. J. Milton (1643), *Divorce* II. xii. *Works*, 1851, IV.92. Quoted in the *Oxford English Dictionary*, s.v. 'Traduce'.

13. Steiner, *After Babel*, 295.

14. Cf. L. Bruni, *The Humanism of Leonardo Bruni*, New York: SUNY Press, 1987.
15. See D. Attridge, 'The Postmodernity of Joyce: Chance, Coincidence and the Reader', in *Joyce Effects: On Language, Theory and History*, Cambridge: Cambridge University Press, 2000, 117–25.
16. See J. Derrida, 'Ulysses Gramophone: Hear Say Yes in Joyce', in *Acts of Literature*, London: Routledge, 1992, esp. 288–90.
17. See the editorial note in *CW* 132.
18. Quoted in Steiner, *After Babel*, 248.
19. G. Bruno, *Cause, Principle and Unity*, Cambridge: Cambridge University Press, 1998, 90.
20. H. Gatti, *The Renaissance Drama of Knowledge: Giordano Bruno in England*, London: Routledge, 1989.
21. C. Marlowe, *The Tragical History of Dr Faustus*, v.iv.
22. G. Bruno, *Spaccio della bestia trionfante*, quoted in Gatti, *Renaissance Drama*, 5.
23. T. Wilder, 'Giordano Bruno's Last Meal in *Finnegans Wake*', *A Wake Newslitter* 6, October 1962, 5.
24. *Le Séminaire de Jacques Lacan, Livre XI: Les Quatres concepts fondamentaux de la psychanalyse*, Paris: Seuil, 1975, 252; with Colin MacCabe's translation (modified) from *James Joyce and the Revolution of the Word*, London: Macmillan, 1979, 12.
25. J. Lacan, *Encore* (S20), New York: Norton, 2000, 37. We should note in passing that Di Jin has wholly disproved Lacan's allegation in a fascinating account of the aesthetic and conceptual challenges of his work as Chinese translator of *Ulysses*: D. Jin, 'The Artistic Integrity of Joyce's Text in Translation', in K. Lawrence, ed., *Transcultural Joyce*, Cambridge: Cambridge University Press, 1998, 215–30.
26. F. Senn, *Joyce's Dislocutions: Essays on Reading as Translation*, Baltimore: Johns Hopkins University Press, 1984, 210.
27. Steiner, *After Babel*, 47.
28. J. Lacan, 'Conférences et entretiens', *Scilicet* 6/7, 36.

4 HOW AM I TO SIGN MYSELF?

1. C. Lamb, 'Sanity of True Genius', in *The Essays of Elia*, London: Walter Scott, 1890, 297–8.
2. V. J. Cheng, *Shakespeare and Joyce: A Study of Finnegans Wake*, University Park: Pennsylvania State University Press, 1984.
3. The Shakespearean genealogy of psychoanalytic thought is brilliantly explored in Joel Fineman's work; cf. J. Fineman, *The Subjectivity Effect in Western Literary Tradition: Essays Toward the Release of Shakespeare's Will*, Cambridge, MA: MIT Press, 1991.
4. S. André, 'Clinique et noeud borroméen', *Actes de l'Ecole de la Cause freudienne*, 1982, no. 2, 89.

5. J. Joyce, 'A Portrait of the Artist' (1904), in *Poems and Shorter Writings*, London: Faber, 1991, 218.

6. B. Fink, *The Lacanian Subject*, Princeton: Princeton University Press, 1995, 110, emphasis original.

7. Cf. J. Lacan, *The Psychoses* (S3), London: Routledge, 1993, 75–88; and *E:S* 189–204.

8. J. Atherton, *The Books at the Wake*, London: Faber, 1959, 31.

9. Cf. Frank Kermode's discussion of the carnivalesque sexual impersonation in his *Twelfth Night*: *Shakespeare's Language*, London: Penguin, 2000, 66–9.

10. M. Blanchot, *The Space of Literature*, Lincoln, NB: University of Nebraska Press, 1982, 103.

11. J.-D. Nasio, *Cinq Leçons sur la théorie de Jacques Lacan*, Paris: Rivages, 1992, 186 (my translation).

12. S. Žižek, *Enjoy your Symptom!* London: Routledge, 1992, 46.

13. The *Oxford English Dictionary* notes the occurrence of 'prick' as vulgar slang for 'penis' as early as 1592, in the *Hypnerotomachia*, and again in 1598 in a text by Florio. Shakespeare's audience was certainly familiar with that sense when *Macbeth* was staged around 1605.

14. Cf. C. Belsey, 'Shakespeare's "Vaulting Ambition"', *English Language Notes* 10, 1972, 198–201; R. N. Watson, 'Horsemanship in Shakespeare's Second Tetralogy', *English Literary Renaissance* 13.1, 1983, 274–300.

15. Cheng, *Shakespeare and Joyce*, 45; F. Senn, '"Notes" on Dublin Theatres', *A Wake Newslitter*, Old Series 2, April 1962, 5–8.

16. S. Fitzpatrick, *Dublin: A Historical and Topographical Account of the City*, 249, quoted in Senn, '"Notes"', 5.

17. S. Freud, *Jokes and their Relation to the Unconscious*, SE 8:228.

18. Stephen Greenblatt reads *Othello* as a Shakespearean exploration of 'the improvisation of power' in the theatre as well as in politics, and notes a sense of the dramatist's 'affinity with the malicious improvisor' Iago. Cf. his *Renaissance Self-Fashioning*, Chicago: University of Chicago Press, 1980, 252.

19. A. Symons, 'The Symbolist Movement', in A. E. Dyson, ed., *Poetry Criticism and Practice: Developments since the Symbolists*, London: Macmillan, 1986, 33.

20. T. Gautier, *Portraits et souvenirs littéraires* (1875), Paris: Vert-Logis, 1938.

21. See Harold Jenkins's note in the Arden edition, referring to the use of 'equivocation' in R. Scot, *The Discovery of Witchcraft*, 1584. *Hamlet*, ed. H. Jenkins, 384 n.

22. P. Skriabine, 'Clinique et topologie', *La cause freudienne*, 1989, 131. The diagram on the left indicates the 'fault' in the knot, which causes the imaginary to drop out; its restoration through the agency of the *sinthome* (marked as 'ego') corresponds to the reopening of the unconscious in the subject (as Skriabine indicates in the bottom right-hand corner).

23. J. Copjec, 'Introduction: Evil in the Time of the Finite World', in J. Copjec, ed., *Radical Evil*, London: Verso, 1986, xi.

24. Žižek, *Enjoy your Symptom!*, 136–7.

25. J. Lacan, *The Ethics of Psychoanalysis* (S7), London: Routledge, 1992, 322.

26. *Hamlet*, IV.v.25; and cf. editor's note, Arden edition, 349.
27. A 'cockle hat' might also be, in Joyce's protean 'wavespeech' (*U* 3.457), a *cuckold* hat: precisely the kind of grotesque headgear given to the bard in the 'Circe' episode.

5 EGOMEN AND WOMEN

1. R. L. Stevenson, 'Books Which Have Influenced Me', in *Essays Literary and Critical*, London: Heinemann, 1904.
2. G. Agamben, 'The Thing Itself', in *Potentialities: Collected Essays in Philosophy*, Stanford: Stanford University Press, 1999, 33.
3. L. Trilling, 'Freud and Literature', in *The Liberal Imagination*, London: Secker & Warburg, 1955, 34.
4. J. Lacan, *Le sinthome*, 13 January 1976, (S23) Texte de i'Association freudienne internationale, Paris, 1991, 62.
5. J. Atherton, *The Books at the Wake*, London: Faber, 1959, 41.
6. S. Kofman, 'The Double is/and the Devil', in *Freud and Fiction*, Cambridge: Polity, 1991, 160.
7. See J. Derrida, 'Ulysses Gramophone: Hear Say Yes in Joyce', in *Acts of Literature*, London: Routledge, 1992, for a meditation on the Joycean problematic of repetition, signature and affirmation.
8. J. Lacan, 'The Signification of the Phallus', *E:S* 271–80.
9. S. André, 'Clinique et noeud borroméen', *Actes de l'Ecole de la Cause freudienne*, 1982, no. 2, 89.
10. S. Freud, 'The Uncanny', *SE* 17: 224.
11. J. Hogg, *The Private Memoirs and Confessions of a Justified Sinner* (1824), London: Penguin, 1983, 181.
12. F. Senn, *Joyce's Dislocutions: Essays on Reading as Translation*, Baltimore: Johns Hopkins University Press, 1984, 96.
13. When Max Eastman asked Joyce why he did not supply more help to the reader of *Finnegans Wake*, the reply is worth noting: 'You know people never value anything unless they have to steal it. Even an alley cat would rather snake an old bone out of the garbage than come up and eat a nicely prepared chop from your saucer': *JJ* 495 n.
14. Note that the letter 'r' has a special status in *Finnegans Wake*, as it is the basic unit of various key puns on *ars* (Latin for 'art'), *arse*, *erse* (Irish for earth): 'those ars, rrrr!' (*FW* 122.6).
15. O. Wilde, 'The Critic as Artist', in *Intentions* (1891), reprinted in R. Ellmann, ed., *The Artist as Critic: The Critical Writings of Oscar Wilde*, Chicago: University of Chicago Press, 1982, 383.
16. Idem, *The Picture of Dorian Gray* (1891), London: Penguin, 1985, 246.
17. Idem, 'The Critic as Artist', 382.
18. R. L. Stevenson, *The Strange Case of Dr Jekyll and Mr Hyde* (1886) (hereafter *JH*), London: Penguin, 1979, 82.

19. J. Lacan, *Encore* (S20), New York: Norton, 2000, 32. Here Lacan is referring back to his work in Seminar 17 (1969–70), *L'Envers de la psychanalyse* (Paris: Seuil, 1991), on the 'four discourses'. For a lucid exploration of Freud's concept of *Bindung*, see M. Borch-Jakobsen, *The Freudian Subject*, Stanford: Stanford University Press, 1988, 127–239.

20. Wilde, *The Picture of Dorian Gray*, 246.

21. J. Lacan, *The Four Fundamental Concepts of Psychoanalysis* (S11), London: Hogarth, and the Institute of Psychoanalysis, 1977, 129.

22. *Joyce's Ulysses Notesheets in the British Museum*, 420, cited in S. Brivic, *Joyce the Creator*, Madison: University of Wisconsin Press, 1985, 125.

23. S. Benstock, 'The Genuine Christine: Psychodynamics of Issy', in S. Henke and E. Unkeless, eds., *Women in Joyce*, Brighton: Harvester, 1982; A. Glashine, '*Finnegans Wake* and the Girls from Boston, Mass.', *Hudson Review* 7, Spring 1954.

24. M. Prince, *Psychotherapy and Multiple Personality: Selected Essays*, Cambridge, MA: Harvard University Press, 1975, 201.

25. Brivic, *Joyce the Creator*, 124.

26. M. Prince, *The Dissociation of a Personality: A Biographical Study in Abnormal Psychology*, London: Longmans, Green & Co., 1906, 316.

27. Brivic, *Joyce the Creator*, 126.

28. R. Leys, 'The Real Miss Beauchamp: Gender and the Subject of Imitation', in J. Butler and J. W. Scott, eds., *Feminists Theorize the Political*, New York and London: Routledge, 1992, 169.

29. Ibid., 196.

30. Atherton, *Books at the Wake*, 41.

31. J. Lacan, 'Joyce le symptôme 1', in J. Aubert, ed., *Joyce avec Lacan*, Paris: Navarin, 1987, 23–4.

32. During his time in Trieste, Joyce purchased a pamphlet by Jung entitled *Die Bedeutung des Vaters für das Shicksal des Einzelnen* ('The Significance of the Father in the Destiny of the Individual', 1909). Written while Jung was still an orthodox Freudian, the article used case histories to build an argument about the predominance of the father in the aetiology of neurosis. As we shall see below, the question of paternity in Joyce is crucially inflected by psychoanalytic thinking.

33. P. Hutchins, *James Joyce's World*, 184–5, quoted in *JJ* 679.

34. Ibid.

35. '*Ulysses*: A Monologue' (henceforth *UM*), in *The Collected Works of C. G. Jung*, xv, 134. Ellmann recognises the equivalence here: 'A man who had so misconstrued *Ulysses* could scarcely be expected by Joyce to construe Lucia correctly': *JJ* 680.

36. Cf. *UM* 132.

37. See the Introduction to Jung's lecture 'Psychology and Literature', which appeared, translated by Eugene Jolas, in *transition* in 1930; *The Collected Works of C. G. Jung*, xv, 84–5.

38. Appendix, *UM* 134.
39. E. Curtius, *James Joyce und sein Ulysses*, Zurich, 1929, 30.
40. *UM* 117. Note that for Yeats, writing in *A Vision*, Joyce entailed above all a 'hatred of the abstract': *JJ* 596 n.
41. Cf. R. Barthes, *S/Z*, 4–5.
42. Freud's 'Der Moses des Michelangelo' was published *anonymously* in 1914 (in the journal *Imago*). 'It was only much later that I legitimized this non-analytical child,' wrote Freud to a correspondent in 1933; the article was translated into English only in 1925. The question therefore arises of whether Joyce is likely to have known this text, in particular while he was writing *Ulysses*. It could be another of the pure coincidences of which Joyce was fond, but in the context of Freud's anonymous Moses, we cannot overlook the appearance of 'Anonymoses!' (*FW* 47.19) in a self-styled 'new book of Morses' (*FW* 123.35).
43. Atherton, *Books at the Wake*, 86.
44. J. Lacan, *The Ethics of Psychoanalysis* (S7), London: Routledge, 1992, 173–4.
45. Cf. U. Eco, *The Open Work*, London: Hutchinson, 1989.
46. Cf. Jeri Johnson's notes to her edition of the original 1922 text of *Ulysses*, Oxford: Oxford University Press, 1993, 933.
47. *UM* 113, 110. Note how Jung echoes Iago here!
48. Lacan, *Ethics of Psychoanalysis* (S7), 83.
49. Derrida, 'Ulysses Gramophone: Hear Say Yes in Joyce', 129.
50. Johnson, notes to 1922 edition of *Ulysses*, 815.
51. H. Kenner, *'Ulysses'*, Baltimore: John Hopkins University Press, 1980, 61–5.
52. F. Budgen, 'James Joyce', in S. Givens, ed., *James Joyce: Two Decades of Criticism*, New York: Vanguard, 24.
53. Atherton, *Books at the Wake*, 48–51.

6 GOD'S REAL NAME

1. Thomas Aquinas, *Summa Theologica* I-II, q. 31.
2. J. Lacan, Seminar of 31 March 1954 (S1), in *The Seminar of Jacques Lacan: Book I: Freud's Papers on Technique 1953–4*, Cambridge: Cambridge University Press, 1987, 142.
3. S. Žižek, *Enjoy Your Symptom!* London: Routledge, 1992, 46.
4. G. Bruno, 'On Magic', in *Cause, Principle and Unity*, Cambridge: Cambridge University Press, 1998, 114–15.
5. See Véronique Voruz's discussion of the proper/common-noun duality in L. Thurston, ed., *Reinventing the Symptom: Essays on the Final Lacan*, New York: The Other Press, 127–8.
6. G. Agamben, 'Tradition of the Immemorial', in *Potentialities: Collected Essays in Philosophy*, Stanford: Stanford University Press, 1999, 107 (emphasis original).
7. 'The soul makes new compositions, but it must not make any new thing.' III *Sent.* 37.1.1. Quoted in U. Eco, *The Aesthetics of Thomas Aquinas*, London: Radius, 1988, 173.

8. L. Carroll, *Through the Looking-Glass and What Alice Found There* (1871), Rutland: Tuttle, 1968, 143.

9. H. Cixous, 'Joyce: The (R)Use of Writing', in D. Attridge and D. Ferrer, eds., *Post-Structuralist Joyce*, Cambridge: Cambridge University Press, 1984, 20.

10. D. Gifford, *Ulysses Annotated*, Berkeley: University of California Press, 1988, 33.

11. Thomas Aquinas, *Summa Theologica* I, q. 84, a. 7, corp. Quoted in W. T. Noon, *Joyce and Aquinas*, New Haven: Yale University Press, 1957, 69.

12. J. Joyce, *Stephen Hero*, London: Cape, 1969, 216.

13. J. Derrida, 'Ulysses Gramophone: Hear Say Yes in Joyce', in *Acts of Literature*, London: Routledge, 1992, 70.

14. C. Millot, 'Epiphanies', in J. Aubert, ed., *Joyce avec Lacan*, Paris: Navarin, 1987, 91.

15. J. Joyce, Epiphany 19, March 1902, in *Poems and Epiphanies*, New York: Viking, 1990, 179.

16. What Ellmann terms Joyce's 'disavowal' of interest in psychoanalysis takes the form of the celebrated rhetorical question: 'Why all this fuss and bother about the mystery of the unconscious? . . . What about the mystery of the conscious?' (*JJ* 436).

17. 'O God, I could be bounded in a nutshell and count myself a king of infinite space – were it not that I have bad dreams.' *Hamlet*, II.ii.254–6.

18. Joyce, 'A Portrait of the Artist', in *Poems and Epiphanies*, 211.

19. J. Atherton, *The Books at the Wake*, London: Faber, 1959, 51.

20. 1 *Sent.* 8.1.1. Quoted in G. Agamben, *Language and Death: The Place of Negativity*, Minneapolis: University of Minnesota Press, 1991, 29.

21. Agamben, *Language and Death*, 30.

22. Ibid.

23. Cf. for example S. Gilbert, *James Joyce's Ulysses: A Study*, London: Faber, 1930, 66–72, 289–90.

24. Note how the other actress mentioned here, Kate Bateman, also has a name with implications of castrating 'nomanclatter'; 'bate' being an apheric form of 'abate', lessen, diminish, etc.

25. Gifford, *Ulysses Annotated*, 89.

26. Ibid., 452.

27. J. Lacan, *Les non-dupes errent* (S21), quoted in *Feminine Sexuality*, London: Palgrave Macmillan, 1982, 46.

28. Letter of February 1921, *Letters of James Joyce*, vol. 1, New York: Viking, 1957, 190.

29. Note that Joyce's *der Fleisch* echoes the Freudian notion that libido may be inherently 'masculine'. See S. Freud, *Three Essays on the Theory of Sexuality* (1915), *SE* 7:219.

30. K. Lawrence, 'Joyce and Feminism', in D. Attridge, ed., *The Cambridge Companion to James Joyce*, Cambridge: Cambridge University Press, 253 (emphasis original).

31. J. Lacan, *Anxiety* (S10), unpublished. Cf. R. Harari, *Lacan's Seminar on Anxiety: An Introduction*, New York: The Other Press, 2001.

32. Cf. J. Laplanche, 'Psychoanalysis as Anti-Hermeneutics', *Radical Philosophy*, September–October 1996.

33. C. G. Jung, Appendix, *UM* 134.

34. R. McHugh, *Annotations to Finnegans Wake*, Baltimore: Johns Hopkins University Press, 1991, 293.

35. D. Rose and J. O'Hanlon, *Understanding 'Finnegans Wake': A Guide to the Narrative of James Joyce's Masterpiece*, New York: Garland, 1982, 156.

36. Genesis 21:1–6.

37. Cf. B. Fink, 'The Master Signifier and the Four Discourses', in D. Nobus, ed., *Key Concepts of Lacanian Psychoanalysis*, London: Rebus, 1997, 29–36.

38. Note how the fracture of 'paperspace' into text and footnote offers another version of the textual 'Zweispaltung' that Joyce purloins from Prince's 'Laughing Sally' – and of the multiplication of feminine identity that Atherton reads throughout the *Wake*.

39. J. Lacan, *The Psychoses* (S3) (1955–6), London: Routledge, 1993, 175 (emphasis added).

40. J. Lacan, *RSI* (S22), 17 December 1974, *Ornicar?* 2, 100.

41. Cf. J. Derrida, 'Le facteur de vérité', in *The Postcard: From Freud to Socrates and Beyond*, Chicago: University of Chicago Press, 1987.

42. J. Lacan, *Le sinthome* (S23), 18 November 1975, Texte de l'Association freudienne internationale, Paris, 1997, 21.

43. Ibid., 9 December 1975, 41.

CONCLUSION: MEMEMORMEE

1. J. Lacan, *Le sinthome* (S23), 10 February 1976, Texte de l'Association freudienne internationale, Paris, 1997, 107.

2. Jean-Michel Rabaté has linked atonement to Joycean paternity and identification, in a discussion that bears on many of our themes here. 'The Father and the Son idea' is clearly at stake in my own relation to Rabaté as a critical predecessor. My attempt to defy St Bonaventure and introduce something *new* is best shown in my reading of 'Ecce Puer', which differs from Rabaté's in stressing the uncanny or apparitional aspect of the poem (an aspect that incidentally reveals its trivial, comic underside in my own predicament as a belated critic, given that I had not in fact read *James Joyce: Authorized Reader* before completing all but the final notes of the present study). See J.-M. Rabaté, *James Joyce: Authorized Reader*, Baltimore: Johns Hopkins University Press, 1991, 50–75.

3. S. Gilbert, *James Joyce's Ulysses: A Study*, London: Faber, 1930, 92.

4. J. Joyce, 'Ecce Puer', in *Poems and Shorter Writings*, London: Faber, 1991, 67.

5. Cf. *JJ* 591–2.

6. F. Nietzsche, *Ecce Homo*, London: Penguin, 1979, 134.

7. Lacan, *Le sinthome* (S23), 10 February 1976, 98–9.

8. J. Joyce, 'A Portrait of the Artist', in *Poems and Shorter Writings*, 212.

9. J. Kimball, *Odyssey of the Psyche: Jungian Patterns in Joyce's Ulysses*, Carbondale: S. Illinois University Press, 1997, 133.

10. B. Schlossman, *Joyce's Catholic Comedy of Language*, Madison: University of Wisconsin Press, 1985, 41–53.

11. S. Freud, 'Creative Writers and Day-dreaming' (1907), *SE* 9:152.

12. S. Žižek, *Enjoy Your Symptom!* London: Routledge, 1992, 46.

Bibliography

Agamben, Giorgio, *Language and Death: The Place of Negativity*, trans. K. E. Pinkus, Minneapolis: University of Minnesota Press, 1991

    Potentialities: Collected Essays in Philosophy, ed. and trans. D. Heller-Roazen, Stanford: Stanford University Press, 1999

André, Serge, 'Clinique et noeud borroméen', *Actes de l'École de la Cause freudienne*, 1982, no. 2

Atherton, James S., *The Books at the Wake*, London: Faber, 1959

Attridge, Derek, *The Cambridge Companion to James Joyce*, Cambridge: Cambridge University Press, 1990

    Joyce Effects: On Language, Theory and History, Cambridge: Cambridge University Press, 2000

Aubert, Jacques, ed., *Joyce avec Lacan*, Paris: Navarin, 1987

Austin, J. L., *How to Do Things with Words* (1962), Oxford: Clarendon, 1975

Barthes, Roland, *Le plaisir du texte*, Paris: Seuil, 1972

    The Pleasure of the Text, trans. R. Miller, New York: Farrar, Straus & Giroux, 1975

    S/Z, trans. R. Miller, London: Cape, 1975

Baudelaire, Charles, 'Mon coeur mis à nu', in *Œuvres complètes*, ed. C. Pichois, Paris: Gallimard, 1961

Beckett, Samuel, 'Dante . . . Bruno . . . Vico . . . Joyce', in *Our Exagmination Round his Factification for Incamination of Work in Progress*, Paris: Shakespeare & Co., 1929; reprinted in *Disjecta*, London: John Calder, 1983

Beja, Maurice, ed., *James Joyce: Dubliners and A Portrait of the Artist as a Young Man: Casebook*, London: Macmillan, 1973

Benstock, Shari, 'The Genuine Christine: Psychodynamics of Issy', in S. Henke and E. Unkeless, eds., *Women in Joyce*, Brighton: Harvester, 1982

Blanchot, Maurice, *The Infinite Conversation* (1969), trans. S. Hanson, Minneapolis: University of Minnesota Press, 1993

    The Space of Literature (1955), trans. A. Smock, Lincoln, NB: University of Nebraska Press, 1982

Borch-Jakobsen, Mikkel, *The Freudian Subject*, trans. C. Porter, Stanford: Stanford University Press, 1988

Bowie, Malcolm, *Lacan*, London: Harvard University Press, 1991

Bradley, A. C., *Shakespearean Tragedy*, London: Macmillan, 1904

Brivic, Sheldon, *Joyce Between Freud and Jung*, Fort Washington: Kennikat, 1980
  Joyce the Creator, Madison: University of Wisconsin Press, 1985

Bruni, Leonardo, *The Humanism of Leonardo Bruni*, trans. G. Griffiths, J. Hankins
  and D. Thompson, New York: SUNY Press, 1987

Bruno, Giordano, 'On Magic' (1588), in *Cause, Principle and Unity*, trans. and ed.
  R. J. Blackwell and R. de Lucca, Cambridge: Cambridge University Press,
  1998

Carroll, Lewis, *Through the Looking-Glass and What Alice Found There* (1871),
  Rutland: Tuttle, 1968

Cheng, Vincent J., *Shakespeare and Joyce: A Study of Finnegans Wake*, University
  Park: Pennsylvania State University Press, 1984

Childs, B. S., *Exodus: A Commentary*, London: SCM, 1974

Cixous, Hélène, 'Joyce: The (R)Use of Writing', in D. Attridge and D. Ferrer, eds.,
  Post-Structuralist Joyce, Cambridge: Cambridge University Press, 1984

Copjec, Joan, ed., *Radical Evil*, London: Verso, 1996

Critchley, Simon, *Very Little . . . Almost Nothing: Death, Philosophy, Literature*,
  London: Routledge, 1997

Curtius, E., *James Joyce und sein Ulysses*, Zurich, 1929

David-Ménard, Monique, *Hysteria from Freud to Lacan: Body and Language in
  Psychoanalysis*, trans. C. Porter, Ithaca: Cornell University Press, 1989

Derrida, Jacques, *The Postcard: From Socrates to Freud and Beyond*, trans. A. Bass,
  Chicago: University of Chicago Press, 1987
  'Ulysses Gramophone: Hear Say Yes in Joyce', in *Acts of Literature*, ed. D.
  Attridge, London: Routledge, 1992

Eco, Umberto, *The Aesthetics of Thomas Aquinas*, trans. H. Bredin, London: Radius,
  1988
  The Open Work (1962), Cambridge, MA: Harvard University Press, 1989

Eliot, T. S., *Selected Prose of T. S. Eliot*, ed. F. Kermode, London: Faber, 1975

Ellmann, Richard, *The Consciousness of Joyce*, Oxford: Oxford University Press,
  1977
  James Joyce (1959), Revised edition, Oxford and New York: Oxford University
  Press, 1982

Felman, Shoshana, *The Literary Speech Act*, trans. C. Porter, Ithaca: Cornell Uni-
  versity Press, 1983
  *Le Scandale du corps parlant: Don Juan avec Austin, ou, la séduction en deux
  langues*, Paris: Seuil, 1980
  Writing and Madness (1978), trans. M. N. Evans, Ithaca: Cornell University
  Press, 1985
  ed., *Literature and Psychoanalysis, The Question of Reading: Otherwise*, Baltimore:
  Johns Hopkins University Press, 1982

Fineman, Joel, *Shakespeare's Perjured Eye: The Invention of Poetic Subjectivity in the
  Sonnets*, Berkeley: University of California Press, 1986
  *The Subjectivity Effect in Western Literary Tradition: Essays Toward the Release of
  Shakespeare's Will*, Cambridge, MA: MIT Press, 1991

Fink, Bruce, *The Lacanian Subject*, Princeton: Princeton University Press, 1995
Foucault, Michel, 'What is an Author?', in *Language, Counter-Memory, Practice*, ed. D. Bouchard, Ithaca: Cornell University Press, 1977
Freud, Sigmund, *The Complete Letters of Sigmund Freud to Wilhelm Fliess*, trans. and ed. J. M. Masson, Cambridge, MA: Bellknap, 1985
   The Diary of Sigmund Freud 1929–39, trans. M. Molnar, London: Hogarth Press, 1992
   Sigmund Freud as a Consultant: Recollections of a Pioneer in Psychoanalysis (letters from Freud to Edoardo Weiss), New York: Intercontinental Medical Book Corporation, 1970
   The Standard Edition of the Complete Psychological Works of Sigmund Freud, trans. J. Strachey et al., London: Hogarth, and the Institute of Psychoanalysis, 1953–74
Frye, R. M., *The Renaissance Hamlet: Issues and Responses in 1600*, Princeton: Princeton University Press, 1984
Garber, Marjorie, *Shakespeare's Ghost Writers: Literature as Uncanny Causality*, New York: Methuen, 1987
Gatti, Hilary, *The Renaissance Drama of Knowledge: Giordano Bruno in England*, London: Routledge, 1989
Gautier, Théophile, *Portraits et souvenirs littéraires* (1875), Paris: Vert-Logis, 1938
Gay, Peter, *Freud: A Life for our Times*, London: Macmillan, 1988
Gifford, Don, *Ulysses Annotated*, Berkeley: University of California Press, 1988
Gilbert, Stuart, *James Joyce's Ulysses: A Study*, London: Faber, 1930
Givens, Seon, ed., *James Joyce: Two Decades of Criticism*, New York: Vanguard, 1963
Glashine, Adaline, '*Finnegans Wake* and the Girls from Boston, Mass.', *Hudson Review* 7, Spring 1954
Gorman, Herbert, *James Joyce*, New York: Farrar & Rinehart, 1939
Greenblatt, Stephen, *Hamlet in Purgatory*, Princeton: Princeton University Press, 2001
   Renaissance Self-Fashioning, Chicago: University of Chicago Press, 1980
Harari, Roberto, *How James Joyce Made His Name: A Reading of the Final Lacan*, New York: The Other Press, 2002
   Lacan's Seminar on Anxiety: An Introduction, New York, The Other Press, 2001
Hayman, David, *The 'Wake' in Transit*, Ithaca: Cornell University Press, 1990
Henry, Michel, *The Genealogy of Psychoanalysis* (1985), trans. D. Brick, Stanford: Stanford University Press, 1993
Herring, P. F., ed., *Joyce's Ulysses Notesheets in the British Museum*, Charlottesville: University Press of Virginia, 1972
Hogg, James, *The Private Memoirs and Confessions of a Justified Sinner* (1824), London: Penguin, 1983
Jones, Ernest, *Sigmund Freud: Life and Work*, 3 volumes, London: Hogarth, 1953–7
Joyce, James, *The Critical Writings of James Joyce*, ed. E. Mason and R. Ellmann, London: Faber, 1959
   Dubliners (1914), ed. R. Scholes, London: Cape, 1967
   Finnegans Wake (1939), London: Faber, 1939

Letters of James Joyce, vol. I., ed. S. Gilbert, New York: Viking, 1957

Poems and Epiphanies, ed. R. Ellman and A. W. Litz, New York: Viking, 1990

'A Portrait of the Artist' (1904), in *Poems and Shorter Writings*, ed. R. Ellmann, A. W. Litz and J. Whittier-Ferguson, London: Faber, 1991

A Portrait of the Artist as a Young Man (1916), ed. C. Anderson, London: Cape, 1968

The Selected Letters of James Joyce, ed. R. Ellmann, London: Faber, 1975

Stephen Hero (1944), ed. T. Spencer, J. J. Slocum and H. Cahoon, London: Cape, 1969

Ulysses (1922), ed. W. Gabler, London: The Bodley Head, 1986

Ulysses (1922), ed. Jeri Johnson, Oxford: Oxford University Press, 1993

Jung, Carl Gustav, '*Ulysses*: A Monologue', in *The Collected Works of C. G. Jung*, vol. xv, London: Routledge, 1966

Kenner, Hugh, '*Ulysses*', Baltimore: Johns Hopkins University Press, 1980

Kermode, Frank, *Twelfth Night: Shakespeare's Language*, London: Penguin, 2000

Kimball, Jean, *Joyce and the Early Freudians: A Synchronic Dialogue of Texts*, Gainesville: University Press of Florida, 2003

    Odyssey of the Psyche: Jungian Patterns in Joyce's Ulysses, Carbondale: S. Illinois University Press, 1997

Klossowski, Pierre, *Nietzsche and the Vicious Circle* (1969), trans. D. W. Smith, London: Athlone, 1997

Kofman, Sarah, *Freud and Fiction*, trans. S. Wykes, Cambridge: Polity, 1991

Lacan, Jacques, *Ecrits*, Paris: Seuil, 1966

    Ecrits: A Selection, trans. B. Fink, New York: Norton, 2002

    Le Séminaire de Jacques Lacan, Livre XI: *Les Quatres concepts fondamentaux de la psychoanalyse*, Paris: Seuil, 1975

    Le Séminaire de Jacques Lacan: Livre XVII: *L'Envers de la psychanalyse*, Paris: Seuil, 1991

    Le Séminaire de Jacques Lacan: Livre XXIII: *Le sinthome*, Texte de l'Association freudienne internationale, Paris, 1997

    The Seminar of Jacques Lacan: Book I: *Freud's Papers on Technique, 1953–4*, trans. with notes by J. Forrester, Cambridge: Cambridge University Press, 1987

    The Seminar of Jacques Lacan: Book VII: *The Psychoses*, 1955–6, trans. with notes by R. Grigg, London: Routledge, 1993

    The Seminar of Jacques Lacan: Book: *The Ethics of Psychoanalysis*, ed. J.-A. Miller, trans. D. Porter, London: Routledge, 1992

    The Seminar of Jacques Lacan: Book XI: *The Four Fundamental Concepts of Psychoanalysis*, London: Hogarth, and the Institute of Psychoanalysis, 1977

    The Seminar of Jacques Lacan: Book XX: *Encore 1972–1973*, trans B. Fink, New York: Norton, 2000

    Yale University, Kanzer Seminar, 24 November 1975, *Scilicet 6/7*, Paris: Seuil, 1976, 7–31

Lamb, Charles, 'Sanity of True Genius' (*New Monthly Magazine*, May 1826), in *Essays of Elia*, London: Walter Scott, 1890

Lawrence, Karen, ed., *Transcultural Joyce*, Cambridge: Cambridge University Press, 1998

Lecercle, Jean-Jacques, *Philosophy of Nonsense: The Intuitions of Victorian Nonsense Literature*, London: Routledge, 1994

Leys, R., 'The Real Miss Beauchamp: Gender and the Subject of Imitation', in J. Butler and J. W. Scott, eds., *Feminists Theorize the Political*, New York and London: Routledge, 1992

MacCabe, Colin, *James Joyce and the Revolution of the Word*, London: Macmillan, 1979

McHugh, Roland, *Annotations to Finnegans Wake*, Baltimore: Johns Hopkins University Press, 1991

Millot, Cathérine, 'Epiphanies', in J. Aubert, ed., *Joyce avec Lacan*, Paris: Navarin, 1987

Nasio, J.-D., *Cinq Leçons sur la théorie de Jacques Lacan*, Paris: Rivages, 1992

Nietzsche, Friedrich, *Ecce Homo* (1888), trans. R. J. Hollingdale, London: Penguin, 1979

    The Gay Science (1882), trans. W. Kaufmann, New York: Random House, 1974

    Thus Spake Zarathustra (1885), trans. R. J. Hollingdale, London: Penguin, 1961

Nobus, Dany, ed., *Key Concepts of Lacanian Psychoanalysis*, London: Rebus, 1997

Noon, William T., *Joyce and Aquinas*, New Haven: Yale University Press, 1957

Prince, Morton, *The Dissociation of a Personality: A Biographical Study in Abnormal Psychology*, London: Longmans, Green & Co., 1906

    Psychotherapy and Multiple Personality: Selected Essays, ed. N. G. Hale, Cambridge, MA: Harvard University Press, 1975

Rabaté, Jean-Michel, *James Joyce: Authorized Reader*, Baltimore: Johns Hopkins University Press, 1991

Roberts, Julian, *German Philosophy: An Introduction*, Cambridge: Polity, 1988

Rose, D., and O'Hanlon, J., *Understanding 'Finnegans Wake': A Guide to the Narrative of James Joyce's Masterpiece*, New York: Garland, 1982

Royle, Nicholas, *After Derrida*, Manchester: Manchester University Press, 1995

Schlossman, Beryl, *Joyce's Catholic Comedy of Language*, Madison: University of Wisconsin Press, 1985

Senn, Fritz, *Joyce's Dislocutions: Essays on Reading as Translation*, ed. J. P. Riquelme, Baltimore: Johns Hopkins University Press, 1984

    '"Notes" on Dublin Theatres', *A Wake Newslitter*, Old Series 2, April 1962

Skriabine, Pierre, 'Clinique et Topologie', in *La cause freudienne*, Paris: Navarin, 1989

Steiner, George, *After Babel*, 1975, 3rd edition, Oxford: Oxford University Press, 1998

Stevenson, Robert Louis, 'Books Which Have Influenced Me', in *Essays Literary and Critical*, London: Heinemann, 1904

    The Strange Case of Dr Jekyll and Mr Hyde (1886), ed. J. Calder, London: Penguin, 1979

Symons, Arthur, 'The Symbolist Movement', in A. E. Dyson, ed., *Poetry Criticism and Practice: Developments since the Symbolists*, London: Macmillan, 1986

Thurston, Luke, ed., *Re-inventing the Symptom: Essays on the Final Lacan*, New York: The Other Press, 2002

Trilling, Lionel, 'Freud and Literature', in *The Liberal Imagination*, London: Secker & Warburg, 1955

Trotter, David, *The English Novel in History*, London: Routledge, 1993

Wilde, Oscar, 'The Critic As Artist', in *Intentions* (1891), reprinted in *The Artist As Critic: The Critical Writings of Oscar Wilde*, ed. R. Ellmann, Chicago: University of Chicago Press, 1982

The Picture of Dorian Gray (1891), London: Penguin, 1985

Wilder, Thornton, 'Giordano Bruno's Last Meal in *Finnegans Wake*', *A Wake Newslitter*, Old Series 6, October 1962

Žižek, Slavoj, *Enjoy your Symptom!* London: Routledge, 1992

Index

Prince, Morton, 110, 126–9, 191; *see also* multiple
  personality
Puttenham, George, 26, 27

quadrivium, medieval category of, 149; *see also*
  trivium

Rabaté, Jean-Michel, 20, 40
real, Lacanian register of the, 10, 28, 50
repetition, 2, 4, 5, 26
Richards, Grant, 20
Ritvo, Lucille, 19
rivalry, literary, 79–80, 84, 115
Rose, D. and O'Hanlon, 185

Schelling, F. W. J., 114, 117
Schlossman, Beryl, 205
Schopenhauer, Arthur, 5
Senn, Fritz, 65, 70, 90, 115
sexual difference, Joyce's writing of, 111, 167–8,
  182
Shakespeare, 7, 10, 75, 91, 149, 156, 183
  and Joyce, 77, 78, 79, 80, 82, 84, 85–92, 100
  *see also Hamlet; Macbeth; Othello; Troilus and
  Cressida*
Skriabine, Pierre, 95
Sophocles, 31, 61
Steiner, George, 65, 70
Stephen Hero, 164, 204
Stephens, James, 203
Stevenson, Robert Louis, 12, 110, 119–24
subject, Lacan's theory of the, 96
suicide, 6, 53, 87–8, 159, 178, 179, 208
symbolic, Lacanian register of the, 84, 89, 90,
  122, 125, 138
Symbolism, literary, 92, 147
Symons, Arthur, 92, 147

theology and literary criticism, 40–1
Thing, Lacan's concept of the, 61
thing, literary, 6, 7, 21, 80, 149, 155, 171
Thomas Aquinas, St, 163–4, 170–1, 174
traduction, 27, 28, 37, 39, 42, 45–6, 47, 48–9, 51,
  55, 62, 64–5, 70–1, 76, 100–1, 149, 155, 184,
  197, 209
transference, psychoanalytic, 120, 124–5, 127,
  129, 130, 135, 136, 141, 147
translation, 12, 27, 45, 60, 64, 66, 67–8, 70
Trilling, Lionel, 104
trivium, medieval category of, 146; *see also*
  quadrivium
Troilus and Cressida, 81–2

Ulysses, 13, 17, 18, 22, 53, 105, 126, 139
  'Aeolus', 136–7, 143, 144, 147, 152, 153
  'Circe', 98, 105, 140–1, 146, 150, 151, 173, 180,
    181, 182, 186
  'Cyclops', 79, 165
  'Eumaeus', 172
  'Ithaca', 111, 179, 181, 182, 188
  'Lotus Eaters', 176–7
  'Nestor', 100, 108, 160, 162–3, 164, 169, 172
  'Oxen of the Sun' , 207
  'Penelope', 139, 182, 184, 186
  'Proteus', 98, 99, 151, 206
  'Scylla and Charybdis', 82, 108, 146
  'Telemachus', 181, 201, 206–7, 208–9

Vico, Giambattista, 84, 105

Weiss, Edoardo, 43
Wilde, Oscar, 12, 110, 118–9, 124
Wilder, Thornton, 69

Žižek, Slavoj, 10, 209